AFTER IRAQ

AFTER IRAQ

The Imperiled American Imperium

CHARLES W. KEGLEY, JR.

Carnegie Council for Ethics in International Affairs

GREGORY A. RAYMOND

Boise State University

New York   Oxford

OXFORD UNIVERSITY PRESS

2007

Oxford University Press, Inc., publishes works that further Oxford University's objective of excellence in research, scholarship, and education.

Oxford New York
Auckland Cape Town Dar es Salaam Hong Kong Karachi
Kuala Lumpur Madrid Melbourne Mexico City Nairobi
New Delhi Shanghai Taipei Toronto

With offices in
Argentina Austria Brazil Chile Czech Republic France Greece
Guatemala Hungary Italy Japan Poland Portugal Singapore
South Korea Switzerland Thailand Turkey Ukraine Vietnam

Published by Oxford University Press, Inc.
198 Madison Avenue, New York, New York 10016
http://www.oup.com

Library of Congress Cataloging-in-Publication Data
Kegley, Charles W.
After Iraq: the imperiled American imperium / by Charles W. Kegley, Jr. and Gregory A. Raymond.
p. cm.
Includes bibliographical references and index.
ISBN-13: 978-0-19-517703-9
ISBN-10: 0-19-517703-7
ISBN-13: 978-0-19-517702-2 (pbk. : alk. paper)
ISBN-10: 0-19-517702-9 (pbk. : alk. paper)
1. United States—Foreign relations. 2. War on Terrorism, 2001– 3. Hegemony—United States. 4. International relations. 5. United States—Politics and government—2001– I. Raymond, Gregory A. II. Title.

JZ1480.K44 2006
327.73—dc22

2006040064

9 8 7 6 5 4 3 2 1

Printed in the United States of America
on acid-free paper

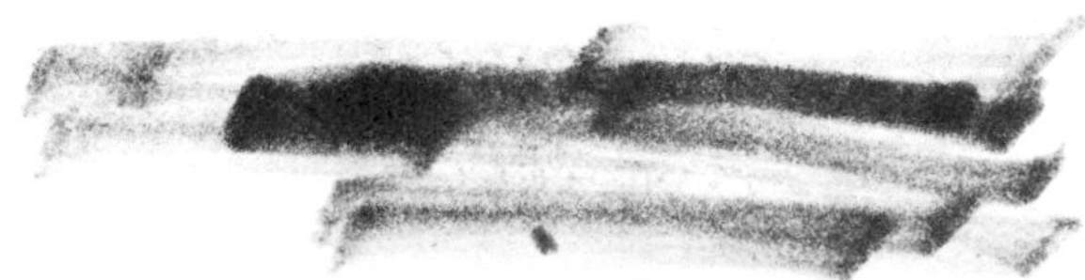

To the Carnegie Council for Ethics in International Affairs, whose educational mission serves the global future,

–CWK

and in memory of Senator Frank Church, who understood the perils of drinking too deeply from the cup of foreign intervention,

–GAR

with the hope that our work will encourage critical thinking and lead to a more secure and just world.

O fortuna, velut luna statu variabilis,
semper crescis aut decrescis.

[Oh fortune, like the moon ever-changing,
rising first then declining.]

—Carmina Burana
Scene 1

CONTENTS

PREFACE

Speaking about the war in Iraq at the National Endowment for Democracy on October 6, 2005, U.S. President George W. Bush declared that "our time in history will be remembered for new challenges and unprecedented dangers." No one "should underestimate the difficulties ahead," he warned, since we are dealing with "as brutal an enemy as we've ever faced." In the president's opinion, America had to stay the course because terrorists with global reach had made Iraq "the central front in their war against humanity." While acknowledging that he did not know the sacrifices that might be required to win in Iraq, Bush insisted that the United States would "never back down, never give in, and never accept anything less than complete victory."

Although the conduct of the war in Iraq currently preoccupies policymakers and pundits alike, at some point in the future that war, like all others, will eventually end. This book is not about the alternative paths to its conclusion. Rather, it looks forward to the conditions likely to prevail in the war's aftermath. At a time when the United States possesses unparalleled military might and thus is unlikely to be challenged by another nation-state in a conventional war, have its political leaders developed a viable strategy for dealing with the unconventional threats emanating from terrorist networks and enemies bent on acquiring weapons of mass destruction? Or have U.S. leaders implemented counterproductive policies that will exacerbate these threats, sow distrust among America's allies, and undermine U.S. security? Will today's decisions steer the ship of state into a safe harbor, or turn it toward rough seas?

We take as our point of departure the long-term ramifications of America's experiment with a new security strategy that centers on preventive uses of military force. Our purpose is to project the probable consequences of that strategy, which we fear will leave the United States less safe in the years ahead. In the chapters that follow, we discuss the reasons we believe that President Bush's muscular, unilateralist foreign policy will erode America's reputation and squander the influence so critical for it to exercise the leadership needed to address many pressing global issues. By attempting to solve today's security problems with a strategy that asserts the right to use force in a preventive, unilateral manner, we argue that the United States will create more difficult challenges for itself tomorrow. Meanwhile, driven by a misunderstanding of where modern power lies and how it can be preserved and exercised, the United States will likely pursue a misguided foreign policy that distracts it from serious ongoing problems, such as the growing national debt, energy shortages, global climate change, and the rise of China and other peer competitors.

The idea for this book arose from the spirited debates over military ethics that occurred during a March 2003 conference on "Democracies and Dirty Wars," sponsored by the McCormick Tribune Foundation at the Cantigny First Division Museum Conference Center in Wheaton, Illinois. Despite days of wrestling with how liberal democracies ought to respond to shadowy transnational networks like Al Qaeda that rely on terrorist tactics to achieve their goals, neither of us felt satisfied that all of the relevant questions surrounding America's post-9/11 security strategy had been fully explored. How should the United States deal with cunning, ruthless adversaries who flout the prevailing rules of war? When fighting them, does military necessity absolve Washington from observing the United Nations Charter's limitations on the use of force? Do grave threats from irregular combatants excuse behavior toward prisoners that otherwise would be prohibited under the Geneva Conventions? What will happen if the standards of behavior America sets for itself in the war on terrorism eventually become the code of conduct for others? Will the world be a safer place?

Despite the intervention into Afghanistan and the hostilities within Iraq, serious public discussions of these questions have been rare. The shock of what happened to the World Trade Center and the Pentagon in 2001 has muted criticism of the new Bush strategy. Given the lack of attention being given to the strategy's long-term effects, we have chosen to focus on the future: How will America's foreign policy since 9/11 affect the international norms, or general rules of conduct, that promote orderly behavior in world politics?

Every multistate system in recorded history has operated within a normative climate of opinion that delineated the obligations of its members. However, these norms were never immutable; without consistent reinforcement, they tended to be challenged by those seeking to replace them with other rules of conduct. Sometimes the new rules of the game fostered peace and stability, though not always. With its emphasis on preventive warfare, the Bush administration's post-9/11 strategy represents a significant challenge to prevailing global norms restricting the use of military force. As the globe's sole reigning superpower at the moment, how the United States behaves sets standards that others will emulate, and if America's security strategy countenances preventive warfare, this transformation of the current normative order is certain to undermine both American and international security. The United States will be imperiled, whether in the best scenario as a new era of rivalry among self-interested states takes root, or more pessimistically, another epoch of warfare unfolds in a world that condones preemptive wars for preventive purposes, and in which America's advantages recede relative to rising competitors.

Although we have closely collaborated on numerous publications in the fields of American foreign policy and world politics over the past three decades, no book can be written without the support and advice of others, and we are indebted to many for their generous assistance. At its inception, Peter Labella, our senior editor at Oxford University Press, expressed great enthusiasm for the project. We also wish to thank Diane Lange, our copy editor, and John Carey and Chelsea Gilmore, our production team at Oxford University Press.

In addition, the development of this book was greatly assisted by the advice provided by anonymous referees, as well as by various scholars who read drafts or listened to presentations and offered suggestions on how to refine our arguments. We are especially grateful to Les Alm, Flore-Anne Bourgeois, Alan Brinton, Dan Caldwell, Klaus-Gerd Giesen, Howard Hensel, Loch Johnson, Urs Luterbacher, Richard Moore, April Morgan, Ana Perisic, Don Puchala, Ignacio de la Rasilla del Moral, Neil Richardson, Joel Rosenthal, Alpo Rusi, Dragan Simić, and David Sylvan.

We have also benefited from comments and questions raised by our students at the University of South Carolina, the Graduate Institute of International Studies–Geneva, and Boise State University, on whom we tested our ideas in graduate seminars and undergraduate honors courses. Likewise, we learned much about the range of reactions to America's post-9/11 foreign policy from the academic participants in the 2003–2005 Fulbright American Studies Institutes on U.S. Foreign Policy, which were funded by the U.S. Department of State and held at the University of South Carolina.

At the University of South Carolina, we wish to express our gratitude for the manuscript preparation assistance provided by Gordon Smith, the director of the Richard L. Walker Institute of International and Area Studies, and his predecessor Roger Coate. Both were also instrumental in providing opportunities for us to work together. Harvey Starr, chair of the Department of Political Science, deserves special recognition for offering Kegley the chance to teach specialized courses on the subject of this book, as well as for facilitating his appointment as a senior visiting scholar at the Graduate Institute of International Studies in Geneva, where he taught and conducted research on American foreign policy.

At Boise State University, President Bob Kustra, Associate Academic Vice President Stephanie Witt, and the Board of Directors of the Frank Church Institute helped create a nurturing intellectual environment. In addition, Raymond owes a special debt to Bethine Church for her unflagging encouragement, as well as to Martha and Rick Ripple for their friendship and support. He also is grateful to the staff at the library of the International Court of Justice in The Hague for assisting his research on the laws of war.

To sharpen our thinking about the complex moral, legal, and strategic issues surrounding preventive warfare, we presented papers at scholarly conferences in Aix-en-Provance, Belgrade, Budapest, Geneva, The Hague, Las Vegas, New York, Oxford, Portland, and Salzburg, where we received valuable feedback from discussants and those in attendance. Equally important was the reception our preliminary thoughts on these topics received in essays published in the *Fletcher Forum of World Affairs, International Studies Perspectives, International Politics* (London), and *USA Today*. Although we have built upon these early efforts, the analysis offered here is a substantial revision and extension of our previous work.

Finally, our biggest debts are to our wives, Debbie and Christine, who remain our greatest sources of comfort and inspiration.

C.W.K.
G.A.R.

Sun Valley,
Idaho

ABOUT THE AUTHORS

Charles W. Kegley, Jr. is Corporate Secretary of the Carnegie Council for Ethics in International Affairs. The Distinguished Pearce Professor of International Relations Emeritus at the University of South Carolina, he also serves as the Moynihan Faculty Research Associate in the Moynihan Institute of Global Affairs at Syracuse University. A graduate of American University and Syracuse University, and a Pew Faculty Fellow at Harvard University, Kegley is a past president of the International Studies Association (1993–1994). Kegley has held faculty appointments at Georgetown University, the University of Texas, Rutgers University, the People's University of China, and the Graduate Institute of International Studies-Geneva. Recently published among his four dozen books are *World Politics: Trend and Transformation*, 11th edition (2007), *The New Global Terrorism* (2003), and *American Foreign Policy: Pattern and Process*, 6th edition (2002).

Gregory A. Raymond is the Frank Church Professor of International Relations at Boise State University, where he is also director of the Honors College. A graduate of Park College and the University of South Carolina, and a Pew Faculty Fellow at Harvard University, Raymond was selected in 1994 as the Idaho Professor of the Year by the Carnegie Foundation for the Advancement of Teaching. Raymond has published extensively in scholarly journals and is the author of *Conflict Resolution and the Structure of the State System* (1980), coauthor of *The Other Western Europe: A Comparative Analysis of the Smaller Democracies*, 2nd edition (1983), and coeditor of *Third World Policies of Industrialized Nations* (1982), which received an Outstanding Academic Book Award from the American Library Association.

Together Kegley and Raymond have coauthored *The Global Future* (2005), *From War to Peace: Fateful Decisions in International Politics* (2002), *Exorcising the Ghost of Westphalia: Building International Peace in the New Millennium* (2002), *How Nations Make Peace* (1999), *A Multipolar Peace? Great-Power Politics in the Twenty-first Century* (1994), and *When Trust Breaks Down: Alliance Norms and World Politics* (1990). They have also coedited *International Events and the Comparative Analysis of Foreign Policy* (1975) and coauthored over three dozen articles in such periodicals as the *International Studies Quarterly*, the *Journal of Conflict Resolution*, the *Journal of Politics*, the *Journal of Peace Research*, *International Interactions*, and the *Harvard International Review*. They have also spoken on international issues at universities and research institutes in 24 countries.

1

America and the Global Future

> I sometimes wonder whether . . . [the American] democracy is uncomfortably similar to one of those prehistoric monsters with a body as long as this room and a brain the size of a pin. He lies there in his comfortable primeval mud and pays little attention to his environment; he is slow to wrath—in fact, you practically have to whack his tail off to make him aware that his interests are being disturbed; but once he grasps this, he lays about him with such blind determination that he not only destroys his adversary but largely wrecks his native habitat.
>
> —George F. Kennan

The United States is in a paradoxical position. On the one hand, it stands at the pinnacle of global power, with the military might and economic resources to dominate world affairs at levels unprecedented in history. On the other hand, it is haunted by a pervasive sense of insecurity, despite being the preeminent actor on the international stage. Awesome military and economic capabilities have not eliminated serious threats. On the contrary, America is vulnerable at precisely the moment its strength is overwhelming.

Americans began the new millennium with hopes of peace and prosperity. Many believed that globalization—a set of processes interconnecting markets for capital, commodities, information, and services—was uniting humanity and generating immense wealth. From their perspective, a safe, prosperous world was emerging as people across the planet were becoming linked tighter and tighter into a single, integrated global community. Few could have imagined that serious threats were looming on the international horizon.

Globalization has been called "the greatest historic transformation since the Industrial Revolution."[1] Until the fifteenth century, most civilizations remained relatively isolated from one another. Circumscribed by slow, costly, and often dangerous transportation routes, international exchanges tended to occur within self-contained regions of the world. Except for intermittent trade, occasional waves of migrants, and periodic clashes with invaders, contact with distant peoples was rare. Over the next four centuries, however, advances in communication and transportation technology gradually widened and deepened global interconnectedness. By the end of the 1990s, money, goods, and information were moving across national boundaries at an accelerating pace, joining societies in ways that seemed to promise an age of political stability and economic growth.

The horrific events of September 11, 2001, destroyed this air of confidence. When Al Qaeda operatives crashed hijacked airliners into the World Trade Center and the Pentagon, they shattered widespread optimism about the prospects for the twenty-first century. Progress no longer seemed inevitable, a matter of steady, predictable advances toward a bright, promising future. Americans now braced themselves for a protracted struggle against a welter of elusive adversaries. Humanity, as United Nations Secretary-General Kofi Annan observed, had "entered the third millennium through a gate of fire."[2]

America's Foreign Policy Challenge

The United States stands at a critical juncture. Although no country appears capable of rivaling U.S. military power in the immediate future, the National Intelligence Council warns that Americans and their interests abroad "will remain prime terrorist targets." Although Al Qaeda's core membership will probably dwindle, it is likely to be "superseded by similarly inspired but more diffuse Islamic extremist groups" who "might acquire biological agents or less likely, a nuclear device, either of which could cause mass casualties."[3] Twenty-first–century warfare may pit the United States against decentralized networks of violent extremists rather than traditional nation-states, but these new adversaries will not pose any less of a threat. War "in its elemental Hobbesian sense," predicts one prominent military historian, will remain "as deadly as ever."[4]

How Washington responds to dangerous, unconventional threats will shape the world for decades to come. Selecting a strategy for defending the country's vital interests is never easy, however. Honest differences of opinion can exist over whether perceived threats are exaggerated, or conversely whether they are underestimated. Even when a consensus emerges, vigorous debates frequently continue over how to counter grave dangers. What goals should national leaders seek? What are the costs, benefits, and risks associated with using different instruments of statecraft for attaining these goals? What human and material resources are needed to support the instruments that have been selected? While these are critically important questions to ask, their answers are not self-evident.

Our aim in this book is to contribute to this important discussion by evaluating the current foreign policy of the United States and by encouraging our readers to assess the long-term global consequences that are likely to result from the path the United States has charted in its global "war on terror."[5] We look beyond the wars in Afghanistan and Iraq to an indeterminate future, when the effects of the choices made in these wars will exert their influence on the security of the United States and the world at large. Of course, any analysis of the future is a hazardous undertaking; even the most thoughtful scholarship may be overtaken by events. But it is precisely this condition of ferment and uncertainty that compels our close attention to the future of American foreign policy and the global environment in which it must evolve. This is a tough age for would-be prophets, and in our fast-paced era there is great risk in making predictions by extrapolating from present trends. Although our analysis of conditions extant at the time this book went to press may be affected by unforseen developments, we are convinced that a policy review that sheds new light on dark corners can reduce errors in foreign-policy judgment and minimize the damage of those that are made.

National Security and the International Environment

Following the terrorist attacks on New York and Washington, the Bush administration forged a new national security strategy to deal with terrorist networks and the states that harbored them. Bold and visionary, it has been described as the most sweeping reformulation of U.S. strategic thinking in more than half a century.[6] The strategy hinges on being proactive: preventive military action would henceforth be used to eliminate future threats, even if the United States was forced to act unilaterally. "This nation will not wait to be attacked again," President Bush asserted in defense of his decision to topple Saddam Hussein in 2003. "We will take the fight to the enemy," because "if evil is not confronted, it gains strength and audacity, and returns to strike us again." Arguing that the United States must defeat terrorists "abroad before they attack us at home," the president repeatedly voiced his conviction that Iraq was the "central front in the war on terror."[7]

Shortly after the fall of Saddam Hussein's government, Iraq experienced an upswing in civil strife, which the Bush administration initially dismissed as the sporadic acts of looters, criminals, and remnants of the old Baathist regime. In fact, Iraq was being swept up in a growing tide of *organized* resistance. The August 2003 truck bombing of the United Nations headquarters in Baghdad was one of many events that underscored Iraq's slide into chaos, not the stability and liberty that had been promised by Washington when it launched "Operation Iraqi Freedom."[8] Moreover, the expanding number of insurgents had both the means and numerous opportunities to frustrate American efforts at building a democratic Iraq.[9] Not only had U.S. forces failed to secure ammunition dumps while advancing on the Iraqi capital, but a series of additional mistakes revealed that the president lacked a coherent plan for coping with a tenacious enemy, who now had access to an ample supply of weaponry. In brief, the administration erred several ways: it ignored the requests of military leaders for sufficient troops and equipment to pacify and democratize a country of 25 million people composed of three contending groups; it diverted resources from the critical tasks of destroying Al Qaeda and rebuilding Afghanistan; it redirected precious intelligence assets to the futile search for weapons of mass destruction; and it disbanded the Iraqi army and civil service, which provided numerous recruits for the fledging insurgency.[10] Although the president later claimed that the unrest was caused by foreign jihadists, most of those participating in the insurrection turned out to be Iraqis seeking to drive out U.S. occupation forces while forming regional militias to protect rival ethnic and religious sects from each other. Despite massive assaults over the next three years on insurgent strongholds from Fallujah to Tall 'Afar, the United States had difficulty recovering from its early miscalculations (see Map 1.1). As one veteran observer of Middle Eastern affairs summarized the situation: "I think the significance of what's been set off in Iraq will play out for decades."[11]

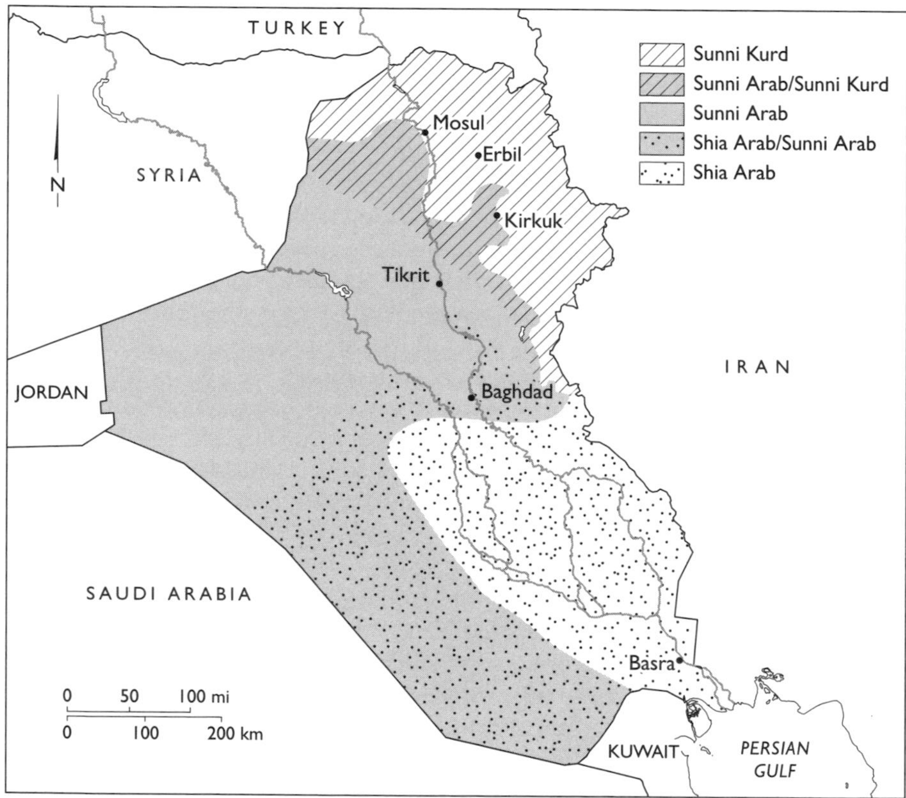

Map 1.1 Costs of War in a Divided Land By June 2006, three years after the onset of war in Iraq, more than 2,500 U.S. troops had been killed in action and over 18,400 wounded. Non-U.S. coalition military fatalities exceeded 200, and estimates of the number of Iraqi civilians killed vary between 17,000 and 31,000. According to polls, in June only 29% of the American public approved of the way that the Bush administration was handling the war, and 60% felt that the war had not been worth its costs. *Sources: http://www.brookings.edu/iraqindex and http://pollingreport.com/iraq2.htm.*

The U.S. intervention in Iraq threatens to be longer than any previous American military engagement (U.S. involvement in World War I lasted 1 year, 7 months; World War II, 3 years, 8 months; the Korean conflict, 3 years, 1 month; Vietnam, 8 years, 7 months). Most anticipate an end no sooner than 2015, although, with no exit strategy in sight, President Bush announced in April 2006 that the timing for U.S. withdrawal would be left to the next administration after the 2008 elections. With casualties climbing and costs escalating, criticism that Iraq was the wrong war at the wrong time against the wrong foe has grown exponentially, fueled by increasing concern that the United States has created economic chaos and sparked a communal civil war. Reflective of this mood was the opinion of Francis Fukuyama, who argued that the "occupation of Iraq has served as a tremendous stimulus for Arab and Muslim anti-Americanism and thus has made radical Islamist terrorism significantly worse than it would otherwise be." Agreeing with Fukuyama's fear that the central government "will remain weak for years to come" and may become "an Iranian-style rule by clerics" rather than a liberal democracy once the Shiite parties have established their rule, public opinion polls taken between the fall of 2005 and the spring of 2006 revealed growing disenchantment with the administration's clumsy, ill-prepared occupation of Iraq. Only 3 in 10 Americans approved of President Bush's handling of the war, and just 38 percent approved of his management of U.S. foreign policy.[12] Although the president asserted that the war against Saddam Hussein would make the United States safer from terrorism, only 30 percent of Americans agreed. A total of 48 percent of those surveyed admitted that the fighting has been harder than they thought it would be, with 83 percent expressing concern that the war was expending resources needed elsewhere and 75 percent doubting that Bush had a viable plan for getting U.S. troops out of Iraq.[13] Three fourths of Americans also feared that the nation was unprepared for a nuclear, biological, or chemical attack,[14] 72 percent indicated that events in Iraq led them to question the possibility of using military force to bring about regime change in other countries,[15] and only 28 percent believed that the country was headed in the right direction.[16] American public opinion, concluded pollster Daniel Yankelovich, was approaching a "tipping point" on the war in Iraq: the moment at which a significant majority of the population feels strongly that the government can and should make changes in U.S. foreign policy.[17]

The problems surrounding the beleaguered U.S. mission in Iraq raise anew the concerns that George F. Kennan expressed more than a half-century ago, when he asked whether democracies like the United States were prone to lurch in world affairs from "undiscriminating indifference to a holy wrath equally undiscriminating."[18] By initially overlooking the unconventional security threats posed by global terrorism but then responding to the September 11 attacks with a unilateralist doctrine of preventive warfare, the Bush administration has dramatically illustrated the relevance of Kennan's concerns. Indeed, some chroniclers of U.S. foreign policy argue that American's undiscriminating, blind determination to destroy its adversaries is currently despoiling more than the environment external to the United States; unlike previous periods of U.S. global involvement, the current one appears to have reached proportions that threaten to damage severely the nation within as well as the world without.[19]

The Bush administration's post-9/11 foreign policy is certain to have long-lasting consequences for the United States and the world at large. The way the president has tried to address the nation's current security threats has created new perils for the next generation of Americans, primarily because little attention was devoted to considering how solving one problem often formulates the next. With seemingly the best intentions, Bush produced the worst effects. His policies are destined to cast a shadow on the range of choice available to future American policymakers. Therefore, it is important to look at the conditions and thinking that prevailed when these strategic choices were made in order to anticipate the probable circumstances that will shape the options available in the wake of the Iraq War.

Among other things, Bush's brusque rhetoric and heavy-handed behavior since 9/11 will make it difficult for subsequent presidents to rebuild America's image abroad and garner support for future U.S. policies. The toll will be heavy. Laments Richard Haass, a former aide to President George H. W. Bush, "The war has absorbed a tremendous amount of U.S. military capacity, the result being that the U.S. has far less spare or available capacity to use in the active sense. It has weakened [America's] position against both North Korea and Iran. It has exacerbated U.S. fiscal problems. The war has also contributed to the world's alienation from the U.S. and made it more difficult to galvanize international support for U.S. policy toward other challenges."[20] Although multilateral support will be crucial in the years ahead, according to one European political analyst, "Washington has shown an extraordinary capacity for losing partners as fast as they had been won to the U.S. cause."[21] Going it alone did not seem to trouble President Bush, however. "At some point," he told former Secretary of State Colin Powell, "we may be the only ones left [in the war on global terror]. That's okay with me. We are America."[22]

Our Approach and Argument

The tragic events of September 11, 2001, changed the way America's political leaders think about national security in ways that are largely counterproductive. We contend that the current course of American foreign policy will harm the long-term interests of the United States by undermining the moral and legal restraints, built painstakingly over the past century, on when and how states may use military force.

How can we best gain insight into the dilemmas that the United States will face in the future as a result of the choices that led to the March 2003 invasion of Iraq? The principle underlying our approach is that the safest basis for evaluating the consequences of the thinking that underpins contemporary American foreign policy is to extract insights from the past that speak to the linkage between strategic choice and security consequence. For that analytic goal, this book will look for historical parallels and parables that sensitize us to the foreign-policy dilemmas that faced previous preponderant powers and to the pitfalls and payoffs of alternative strategic choices that those historical precedents illustrate. As the reader will soon discover, many of our examples are from the distant past, although others are relatively recent. Some may believe that America's current situation is historically unique. We disagree. However novel America's standing in the world may appear at this moment, its precedents are multiple and deeply rooted. Our method of analysis will be to open a lens on the position of primacy that presently describes America's relations with the rest of the world and to examine it against the backdrop of history to illuminate the opportunities and risks the United States will face when the war in Iraq someday no longer dominates the headlines.

The reader should also note that our focus will be on how the strategic choices made after 9/11 will most likely affect the evolution of the international normative order—the general standards of behavior and specific "rules of the game" that delineate when and how states can legitimately use military force. We make no pretense of providing an in-depth analysis of how these decisions may affect U.S. defense spending, the federal deficit, or American civil liberties. Nor do we provide a comprehensive survey of the vast body of theories that seek to describe, explain, predict, and offer policy prescriptions about the coming world. This book does not purport to be a summary of the disparate visions scholars and journalists have about the future. Its goal is to cut into the thicket of real-world problems and offer an analysis backed by empirical evidence of the most probable security circumstances that the United States is likely to find itself in after the Iraq War and to offer our interpretation of the alternative paths open to Washington about how, given the choices that have already been made, America might accommodate itself to the probable challenges ahead.

To make our case, we begin in Chapter 2 by drawing parallels between the United States and other imperial powers that dominated the international relations of their day. One of the problems that plagued these powers was their confusion of military primacy with omnipotence. Even preeminent actors on the world stage are not immune to the dangers that can arise from brash actions. Like the leaders of many previous states at the summit of international power, members of the inner circle of the Bush administration failed to calibrate the nation's military instruments with its long-run interests. Overconfident in America's ability to win a short, decisive war against Saddam Hussein as an avenue for combating global terrorism and dismissive of the need for a coherent plan for democratic nation-building, they ignored America's traditional ideals and bulldozed their way into a political morass.

The history of powerful empires becoming mired in inconclusive wars may date back to antiquity, but the United States, at least since the end of the Cold War, has been depicted as being more resilient than most of these earlier leviathans. In Chapter 3 we examine the sources of American military, economic, and cultural influence and why the United States cannot be adequately understood as a traditional empire. We argue that the most accurate description of the United States today is one that speaks to the imperious attitude that now animates the American quest to preserve its position of primacy and assert its will unilaterally. Rather than governing a hierarchical empire, the United States oversees a loose, consensual "imperium," relying on a mixture of carrots and sticks to advance its interests.

Chapter 4 describes how recent changes in the geostrategic landscape have raised formidable problems for the American Imperium. In view of America's unparalleled strength in ground, naval, and air forces, the threat of being attacked by the conventional military of another nation-state has greatly receded. However, a new form of warfare has emerged in which nation-states are pitted against the irregular forces of militant transnational actors in asymmetrical wars that lack front lines and clear distinctions between soldiers and civilians. Unable to defeat U.S. troops on the field of battle, the country's adversaries focus instead on America's political will, using patience, ingenuity, and gruesome acts of terror in an effort to compel Washington to weigh the mounting costs of continuing a long, drawn-out struggle with tactics that alienate allies and reduce America's moral standing in the world.

In Chapter 5 we profile the American response to this new type of threat by analyzing the Bush Doctrine, which we depict as a radical and relentless effort to permanently shift American security policy. Though expressed in the language of preemption, this strategy actually calls for the preventive use of military force. Whereas the grounds for preemption lies in evidence of a credible, imminent threat, the basis for prevention rests on the suspicion of an incipient, contingent threat. By asserting that the risks posed by biological, chemical, and nuclear terrorism make it reckless for the United States to hold off on military action until an attack is impending, the Bush administration has expanded the legal concept of self-defense to include preventive wars against potential future dangers.

Our examination of the Bush Doctrine leads us in Chapter 6 to evaluate the costs and consequences of this new strategy, with the balance sheet pointing to the perils that lie ahead. Once the dominant state in the world system claims that anticipatory self-defense justifies a first strike against suspected threats, there will remain few barriers to restrain others from doing the same. A security strategy anchored in preventive uses of military force will not only undermine restraints on when states may legitimately use military force, but will also erode longstanding restrictions on how force should be used.

Finally, in Chapter 7 we discuss why it is important to be attentive to how the security strategies of the world's preponderant state powerfully condition the international norms that shape global interactions. Although some people believe that the absence of a central arbiter in world politics condemns nations to an existence of ruthless competition and unlimited discord, there is a growing body of evidence that suggests the web of expectations created by international norms can provide a modicum of order and predictability in world politics, even without centralized mechanisms to enforce compliance with their injunctions (providing that arbitrary unilateral expressions of the philosophy "might makes right" are rejected). International norms are mutable. Unless deliberate steps are taken to reinforce those norms that mitigate the most pernicious aspects of international anarchy, they can decay and be replaced by norms that countenance the ruthless pursuit of advantage. Because the actions of the globe's leading power exert an extraordinary force on the evolution of these norms, how the United States acts today will have significant ramifications for the normative climate of tomorrow.

When the dominant state promotes a new code of conduct, it alters the normative frame of reference for virtually everyone else. Because the United States currently holds a position of global primacy, we submit that the test of American statecraft will be whether Washington can use its preeminence to forge a normative order that ushers in a period of peace and justice. Yet, as former U.S. Secretary of State Henry Kissinger points out, "No nation, no matter how powerful, can organize the international system by itself."[23] Washington must work with others to craft the rules and cultivate the sense of shared responsibility necessary for achieving these goals. "The United States today has a chance to set a pattern of fair, universal, and enforceable rules that could last for years to come and make the entire world more secure and prosperous," observes Javier Solana, secretary-general of the Council of the European Union. "If the United States leads, others will follow. If the United States does not, they will go their own way, and the world will be the poorer for it."[24]

Unfortunately, the Bush administration has not provided the leadership Mr. Solana hoped to see. On the contrary, the thrust of its foreign policy has been either to act independently or to rely on improvised "coalitions of the willing" while ridiculing the "illusory international community"[25] and scorning multilateral accords such as those treaties reached on climate change, biodiversity, antipersonnel landmines, the Prisoners of War Convention, and the Comprehensive Test Ban Treaty. By holding one normative standard for itself and a different standard for others, the Bush administration has changed the way other countries respond to American primacy. The United States may be a genuinely benevolent force in today's world, writes political scientist Stephen Walt, but unless others accept its preponderant position as legitimate and regard U.S. behavior as generally beneficial and consistent with established moral standards, political leaders in Washington will find themselves in a resentful world that is constantly searching for opportunities to restrain and undermine American power and policies.[26]

In summary, we worry that the United States has strayed from its highest ideals. Just as people tend to take on the attributes of those with whom they interact, so, too, victims can take on the characteristics of their oppressors. If a threatened America lowers itself to the standards of those who have attacked it, the United States will risk losing its most valuable possession—its reputation for virtue. The pursuit of parochial self-interest is a temptation for all powers, but especially for great powers intoxicated with their military and economic strength. If the United States careens from one ambitious, ill-conceived foreign intervention to another under the banner of anticipatory self-defense or to forcefully spread its institutions to all corners of the globe, it could erode everything in which its citizens take pride. Worse still, the normative foundations of the international community that have been meticulously built up to control the unilateral exercise of military force may also dissolve. Should this happen, an exceptional opportunity to safeguard peace and security will have been lost, and with it the opportunity to ground America's policies on the ideals that animated the country at its birth. As U.S. Secretary of State John Quincy Adams warned not long after the founding of the Republic, an America that "goes abroad in search of monsters to destroy might become the dictatress of the world," but "would no longer be the ruler of her own spirit."[27]

The Past as Prologue

Not since the Vietnam War have Americans been so uncertain about the role their country should play in world affairs. At the same time that the Bush administration proclaims "we will keep our nerve" and "not tire, or rest, until the war on terror is won,"[28] critics declare that the "wheels have fallen off the cart in Iraq, and only those in the farthest reaches of denial are hanging on to the illusion of an American triumph."[29] One of the reasons why the rift over Iraq has cast a pall of uncertainty over U.S. foreign policy is an inability to understand America's situation within a larger historic context. As economic historian Robert Heilbroner argues, "If current events strike us as all surprise it is because we cannot see these events in a meaningful framework."[30]

In the next chapter we shall begin our analysis of U.S. foreign policy by placing America's current situation in a larger, more meaningful framework. For most observers the defining feature of that situation is the country's paramount position. The United States stands supreme; it is the only state "with the military, diplomatic, political and economic assets to be a decisive player in any conflict in whatever part of the world it chooses to involve itself."[31] While America's position is unique in the modern era, other states have held dominion over their contemporaries in the more distant past. For example, the Persian empire from the mid-sixth to the early fifth century B.C.E. was a realm unto itself, a proto-superpower without peer competitors. Although different in countless ways from the United States, its history nonetheless highlights some of the trials dominant states face when they ignore the limits of their military and economic might. To borrow the late historian Barbara Tuchman's phrase, ancient Persia offers us a "distant mirror" for reflecting on America's moment at the pinnacle of world power.[32]

Notes

1. Joel Krieger, *Globalization and State Power* (New York: Pearson Longman, 2005), p. 9.
2. Cited in Philip Gourevitch, "The Optimist," *The New Yorker* (March 3, 2003): 52.
3. National Intelligence Council, *Mapping the Global Future* (Washington, DC: Government Printing Office, 2004), pp. 93–95. Also see Paul R. Pillar, *Terrorism and U.S. Foreign Policy* (Washington, DC: Brookings, 2001), p. 72. By 2006, many of Al Qaeda's top operatives had been captured, including Abu Zubaydah, Ramzi Binalshibh, Kalid Sheikh Mohammed, Riduan Isamuddin, and Abu Faraj al-Libbi. In addition, Mohammed Atef and, most importantly, Abu Mousab al-Zarqawi have been killed, and the following are believed dead: Hamza Rabia, Abdul Rahman al-Maghrebi, Abu Ubayda al-Masri, and Abu Khabab al-Masri.
4. Martin Van Creveld, *The Art of War: War and Military Thought* (New York: Collins/Smithsonian, 2005), p. 217.
5. Although President Bush has continued to portray the war on terror as "the first war of the 21st century," other members of the administration have moved away from talking about war against a concept. Secretary of Defense Donald Rumsfeld, for example, now speaks of a "global struggle against violent extremists." Similarly, the March 2005 *National Military Strategic Plan for the War on Terrorism* defined the threat as "extremist Sunni and Shia movements that exploit Islam for political ends" and belong to a "global web of enemy networks." See the speech by President George W. Bush in Nampa, Idaho on August 24, 2005, retrieved at http://whitehouse.gov/news/releases/2005/08/print/20050824.html. Also see *U.S. News & World Report* 139 (August 1, 2005): 28.
6. John Lewis Gaddis, "A Grand Strategy," *Foreign Policy* 133 (November/December 2002): 55–56.
7. Speech delivered at Fort Bragg, North Carolina, on June 28, 2005, retrieved at http://www.whitehouse.gov/news/releases/2005/06/print/20050628-7.html.
8. For a first-hand account of the turmoil, see L. Paul Bremer III, with Malcolm McConnell, *My Year in Iraq* (New York: Simon & Schuster, 2006). Whereas Secretary of State Condoleezza Rice suggested that America's problems in Iraq were the result of thousands of "tactical errors," Marine Lieutenant General (Ret.) Greg Newbold countered that they emanated from the administration's "gross errors in strategy." Greg Newbold, "Why Iraq Was a Mistake," *Time* (April 27, 2006): 43.
9. Equally disturbing, Taliban forces in Afghanistan have emulated the tactics of the Iraqi resistance, using shaped-charge IEDs (improvised explosive devices) and suicide attacks. According to Afghan Defense Minister Abdur Rahim Wardak, by the fall of 2005 the Taliban had "more men, equipment, money, better explosives and remote-controlled detonators" than at any time since they were ousted from power in late 2001. Cited in *Newsweek* (September 26, 2005): 40. Lieutenant General Michael Maples, head of the U.S. Defense Intelligence Agency, testified on Capitol Hill that Taliban attacks grew 20 percent in 2005 and "now represent a greater threat to the expansion of Afghan government authority" than at any point since 2001. *Newsweek* (September 26, 2005): 40; *U.S. News & World Report* (March 13, 2006): 22.

10. Michael R. Gordon and Bernard E. Trainer, *Cobra II: The Inside Story of the Invasion and Occupation of Iraq* (New York: Pantheon, 2006), pp. 497–507; Joe Klein, "Saddam's Revenge," *Time* (September 26, 2005): 45–52.
11. Adnan Abu Odeh (former advisor to Jordan's King Hussein), as cited in *The Wall Street Journal Europe* (October 10, 2005): A9. Some observers worry that the historical division between Sunnis and Shiites has intensified under the U.S. occupation of Iraq and threatens to ignite wider sectarian hostilities elsewhere in the Islamic world. Others add that the occupation has reinvigorated Al Qaeda, spawning numerous battle-hardened militants, who will infiltrate and eventually destabilize other countries in the region. Fawaz A. Gerges, *The Far Enemy: Why Jihad Went Global* (New York: Cambridge University Press, 2005); Amin Saikal, "Iraq's Conflict Fuels a Bitter Mideast Split," *International Herald Tribune* (October 10, 2005): 6; Stephen Biddle, "Seeing Baghdad, Thinking Saigon," *Foreign Affairs* 85 (March/April 2006): 2–14.
12. CNN/*USA Today*/Gallup poll of 818 adults, interviewed by telephone on September 16–18, 2005. The poll has a sampling error of plus or minus 4 percentage points. CBS News poll of 1,018 adults, interviewed by telephone on Febrauary 22–26, 2006. The poll had a sampling error of plus or minus 3 percentage points. Fukuyama cited in *Time* (March 27, 2006): 28. Whereas Secretary of Defense Rumsfeld predicted that the cost of the war and occupation would not exceed $60 billion, and his former deputy Paul Wolfowitz asserted that this would be covered by Iraq's oil revenues, current estimates of the long-term costs range from $540 billion to $2.24 trillion. Meanwhile, Iraqi oil production averaged just over 2 million barrels per day in March 2006, short of the prewar U.S. projection of 2.5 million and far below the country's peak production of 3.7 million during the 1970s. *The Economist* (April 8, 2006): 33.
13. CBS News poll of 1,167 adults, interviewed by telephone on September 9–13, 2005. The poll has a sampling error of plus or minus 3 percentage points. Public opinion surveys taken at roughly the same time in other countries that have sent troops to Iraq also show frustration with the apparent lack of an exit strategy. A majority of the public in Italy (60%), Poland (59%), the United Kingdom (57%), Japan (56%), and Australia (53%) advocates withdrawing their troops from Iraq. A plurality of Danes (48%) support removing their forces, and two thirds of South Koreans call for withdrawing (42%) or reducing (24%) their contingent in Iraq. Data reported by the University of Maryland's Program on International Policy Attitudes, retrieved at http://www.pipa.org/analyses/10_13_2005/IraqCoalition_Oct05_art.pdf.
14. NBC/*Wall Street Journal* poll of 1,013 adults, interviewed by telephone on September 9–12, 2005. The poll has a sampling error of plus or minus 3.1 percentage points.
15. Chicago Council of Foreign Affairs and University of Maryland Program on International Policy Attitudes poll of 808 adults, interviewed by telephone on September 15–21, 2005. The poll has a sampling error of plus or minus 4 percentage points.
16. NBC/*Wall Street Journal* poll of 807 adults, interviewed by telephone on October 8–10, 2005. The poll has a sampling error of plus or minus 3.4 percentage points.
17. Daniel Yankelovich, "Poll Positions: What Americans Really Think About U.S. Foreign Policy," *Foreign Affairs* 84 (September/October 2005): 3, 13–14.
18. George F. Kennan, *American Diplomacy, 1900–1950* (New York: New American Library, 1951), p. 59.

19. See Andrew J. Bacevich, *The New American Militarism* (New York: Oxford University Press, 2005). Efforts by Attorney General John Ashcroft following the September 11 attacks to restrict civil liberties in the name of state security exemplify this concern. In Ashcroft's opinion, criticism of the USA Patriot Act was unhealthy; it would "aid terrorists" and "give ammunition to America's enemies." Cited in Richard Falk, *The Great Terror War* (New York: Olive Branch Press, 2003), p. 133. In certain respects, civic discourse in the United States regarding the global war on terror resembled public discussions of the Peloponnesian War in ancient Athens after the collapse of the Peace of Nicias (421–414 B.C.E.). Whereas Athenians had once prided themselves on seeing vigorous debate as "an indispensable preliminary" to wise foreign policy, the ancient Greek historian Thucydides reports that reckless ambition ultimately led the Athenians into "projects unjust to both themselves and to their allies—projects whose success would only conduce to the honor and advantage of private persons, and whose failure entailed certain disaster on the country in the war." Having abandoned their tradition of critical appraisal through free and open discussion, the Athenians committed numerous errors. The ill-fated Sicilian expedition, for instance, was formulated without adequate information on the island's geography and inhabitants and approved in a climate where "the few that did not like it feared to appear unpatriotic by holding up their hands against it, and so kept quiet." Robert B. Strassler, ed., *The Landmark Thucydides* (New York: Free Press, 1996), pp. 113, 127, 375.
20. *Time* (March 27, 2006): 31. For an elaboration of this thesis, see Robert Jervis, "Why the Bush Doctrine Cannot Be Sustained," *Political Science Quarterly* 120 (Fall 2005): 377.
21. Bruno Tertrais, *War Without End: The View From Abroad*, translated by Franklin Philip (New York: New Press, 2004), pp. 73–74.
22. Cited in Bob Woodward, *Bush at War* (New York: Simon & Schuster, 2002), p. 81.
23. Henry A. Kissinger, "America's Assignment," *Newsweek* (November 8, 2004): 35.
24. Javier Solana, "Rules with Teeth," *Foreign Policy* 144 (September/October 2004): 75.
25. Condoleezza Rice, "Promoting the National Interest," *Foreign Affairs* 79 (January/February 2000): 62.
26. Stephen M. Walt, *Taming American Power: The Global Response to U.S. Primacy* (New York. Norton, 2005), pp. 160–161, 179.
27. Speech on July 4, 1821, to the U.S. House of Representatives.
28. Speech by President George W. Bush at the National Endowment for Democracy in Washington, DC, on October 6, 2005, retrieved at http://www.whitehouse.gov/news/releases/2005/10/print/20051006-3.html. For an equally optimistic appraisal, see Richard Miniter, *Shadow War: The Untold Story of How Bush is Winning the War on Terror* (Washington, DC: Regnery, 2004).
29. Bob Herbert, "An Unwinnable War, for No Good Reason," *International Herald Tribune* (October 4, 2005): 8.
30. Robert L. Heilbroner, *The Future as History* (New York: Grove Press, 1960), p. 15.
31. Charles Krauthammer, "The Unipolar Moment," *Foreign Affairs* 70 (Winter 1990–1991): 24.
32. Barbara W. Tuchman, *A Distant Mirror: The Calamitous 14th Century* (New York: Ballantine, 1978).

2

Imperial Temptations

When waves of trouble burst on us,
each new event fills us with terror;
but when Fortune's wind blows soft
We think to enjoy the same fair weather all our lives.

—Atossa, from Aeschylus' *The Persians*
(translated by Philip Vellacott)

Herodotus, the ancient Greek historian and ethnographer, begins his famous account of the Persian Wars of 490 and 480–79 B.C.E. by describing an encounter between the Athenian sage Solon and Croesus, king of Lydia.[1] The two men shared little in common. Celebrated for his wisdom and political acumen, Solon had authored a series of sweeping reforms that laid the foundation for Athenian democracy. Renowned for his wealth and military power, Croesus had conquered most of what today is western Turkey. Herodotus uses their meeting in the Lydian capital of Sardis to introduce the underlying theme of his history: the vagaries of human fortune.

Solon's first days in Sardis were spent touring the city, where he was shown the royal treasury and the king's magnificent court. Feeling smug, Croesus asked Solon who was the most fortunate (*olbios*) person he had ever met. "Tellus," responded Solon. "He was blessed with fine sons and grandchildren, had the means to live comfortably, and died bravely protecting his home."

Annoyed by Solon's answer, Croesus demanded to know the next most fortunate person. "Cleobis and Biton," replied Solon. "So devout were these young men that once when the oxen did not return from the fields in time to transport their elderly mother to a festival honoring the goddess Hera, they yoked themselves to her ox-cart and pulled it six miles to the temple, where they died at the height of their fame."

By now, the Lydian king was utterly frustrated. Recognizing Croesus' indignation at being compared unfavorably with such common folk, Solon tried to explain the importance of looking to the end of all things. "No matter how well off someone may seem at a given moment," counseled Solon, "it is imprudent to count on good fortune continuing indefinitely. The future bears down upon us with all the hazards of the unknown. Tellus, Cleobis, and Biton can be called fortunate because we can assess the totality of their lives. In contrast, our contemporaries who appear to be doing well may yet behave in ways that bring disaster down upon themselves. Until the end is known, someone who seems *olbios* may only be *eutuches* (lucky)."[2]

A few years after Solon's departure, Croesus launched a preventive war against neighboring Persia, believing that a surprise first strike by the Lydians would check the growth of Persian power before it became a serious threat. Told by the Delphic Oracle that if he attacked the Persians, he would destroy a mighty empire, Croesus marched east across the Halys River into Cappadocia. Everything pointed to victory: the Lydians were superb cavalrymen and courageous fighters, and the omens seemed to favor their advance. However, Croesus' expectations were shattered when his forces failed to defeat the Persians at Pteria. After suffering heavy losses in an indecisive battle, Croesus withdrew to Sardis, with the Persians in hot pursuit. His troops bravely defended their capital, but it fell to the Persian leader Cyrus the Great after a two-week siege. Croesus had indeed destroyed a mighty empire—his own.

The Fate of Nations

For Herodotus, the vicissitudes of human fortune were paralleled by radical and often unanticipated shifts in the fortunes of states. "Most of those [states] which were great once are small today; and those which used to be small were great in my time," he remarked at the beginning of his narrative.[3] Like other entities within the social and physical worlds he observed, states underwent a dynamic process of growth and decline, which made their rank-order mutable. Implicit in his history, then, is a conceptualization of international relations that highlights the thrust and parry of states on the horizontal axis of geopolitical competition, as well as their upward and downward movement on the vertical axis of relative strength.[4]

The dominant power at the time of Herodotus' birth was the Persian Empire. Stretching from the Aegean Sea to the Indus River, and from the Libyan desert to the Hindu Kush, it was the largest, most wealthy political entity prior to the rise of Imperial Rome and Han China. Welded together by an elaborate system of roads, administered by an immense, cosmopolitan bureaucracy, and governed by a spirit of tolerance toward foreign customs and religions, the Persians under Cyrus (reign 559–530 B.C.E.) are said by one historian to have succeeded "in establishing the political center of the world."[5]

Preeminence and the Illusion of Omnipotence

The political entity founded by Cyrus has been described as "an imperially regulated confederacy" that "exercised a radial rather than a territorially delimited authority."[6] At its zenith, it contained 20 satrapies, each ruled by a

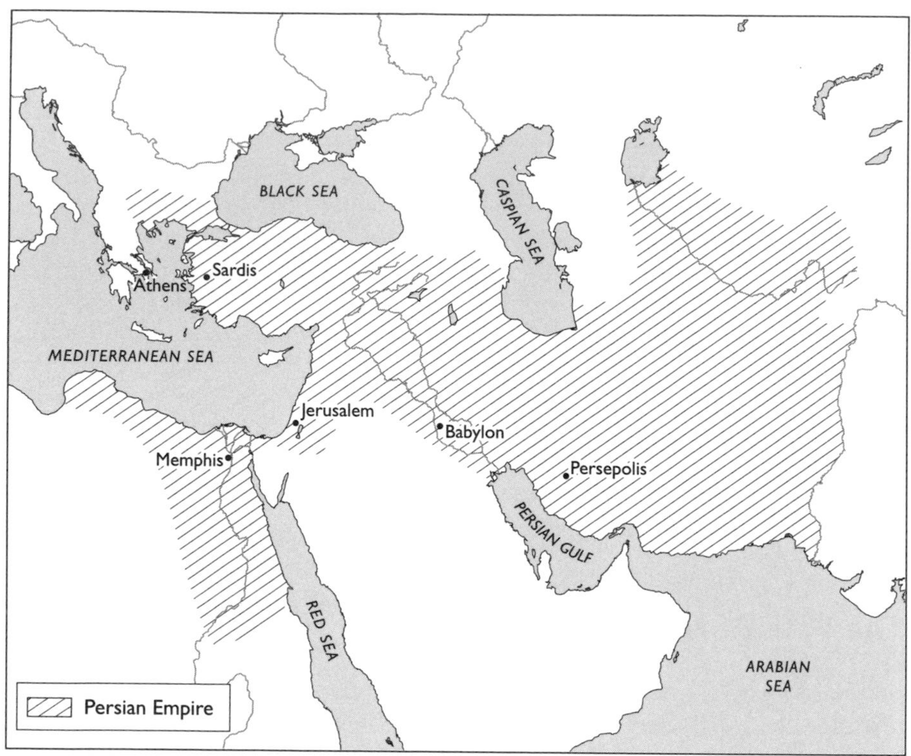

Map 2.1 The Persian Empire At its greatest extent, Achaemenid Persia included territories in Africa, Asia, and Europe.

provincial governor (*satrap*) who was responsible to the Persian king (see Map 2.1). Although the Persians established garrisons at strategic locations throughout these vast, heterogeneous lands, outlying regions functioned like quasi-autonomous client states, with native elites often wielding considerable power. To supervise them, traveling inspectors (known as the "king's eyes and ears") made annual reports on each province.

Cyrus died during a campaign against the Massagetae, a tribe threatening the empire's frontier near the Caspian Sea. He bequeathed what contemporary international relations theorists would call a "unipolar moment."[7] Persia under the three Achaemenid monarchs that succeeded him—Cambyses, Darius, and Xerxes—was the preeminent actor on the world stage. Like the United States following the Cold War, Persia's unequaled military and economic capabilities allowed its rulers to advance their national interests across a wide range of issues. But also like political leaders in Washington today, the Achaemenids faced difficult questions about how to preserve their state's dominant international position.[8]

In their quest to solidify and perpetuate Persian preeminence, each of Cyrus's immediate successors undertook military expeditions along the flanks of the empire. Despite Persia's might, some of these expeditions proved disastrous for reasons that would be familiar to students of early twenty-first–century American foreign policy. Cambyses, the eldest son of Cyrus, marched against Egypt, defeating the pharaoh Psammenitus III at Pelusium in 525 B.C.E. and later seizing the capital city of Memphis. Having captured lower Egypt, he sent an expeditionary force of some 50,000 troops against Siwa in the west and led his remaining forces southward, presumably with the objective of annexing the Kush kingdom in Nubia, and possibly pre-Axumite Ethiopia as well. Unprepared for the conditions they faced, the first contingent of soldiers perished in a sandstorm; lacking adequate provisions, the second was eventually reduced to cannibalism. Irate that his ambitions were thwarted, Herodotus reports that Cambyses committed numerous outrages, violating longstanding moral norms and making many enemies as a result.[9]

Darius, a member of a collateral branch of the Achaemenids who ascended to the throne following Cambyses' death, also experienced military setbacks that stemmed from overconfidence, flawed intelligence, and inadequate preparation. Interested in controlling the lucrative grain trade of the eastern Mediterranean, in 513 B.C.E. he led an army into Scythia, located in what today is the Ukranian region of the Black Sea. As a nomadic people with no cities to defend, the Scythians responded by luring Darius deeper into their territory, ravaging the sources of food and water that Darius's troops might use, and harassing the Persians with continuous hit-and-run raids. Running perilously low on supplies and frustrated with his inability to engage the enemy in a fixed-point battle, Darius ultimately was compelled to withdraw, barely escaping across the Danube before the Scythians delivered their counterattack.

Heartened by the poor performance of Darius's forces in Scythia, Miletus, a Greek city-state on the eastern shore of the Aegean Sea, revolted from Persian rule in 499 B.C.E. and sought help from the mainland Greeks. Although Athens sent 20 warships, Darius's forces were eventually able to reimpose control. To punish the Athenians for meddling in Persian affairs, Darius ordered an invasion of Greece. Three years later his troops landed on the coastal plane of Marathon, 26 miles northeast of Athens. Fighting with verve and using topography as an ally, the vastly outnumbered Athenians enveloped the Persians between the sea and a swampy marsh. Stunned by the ferocious and well-designed attack, the Persian infantry fled in disarray. Darius took the defeat as a personal insult and vowed revenge; however, he died before he could assemble another invasion force. His son, Xerxes, who assumed the Persian throne in 486 B.C.E., pledged to vindicate his father by vanquishing the Greeks.

The instrument of Xerxes' vengeance was an immense army, an equally massive fleet of merchant ships to transport the army's rations, and still another fleet of warships to protect the merchant marine.[10] Although warned by his uncle Artabanus of the risks, Xerxes set out to subjugate Greece in the spring of 480 B.C.E. Buoyed by the optimism of confidants such as Maedonius and Achaemenes, who scoffed at Greek military capabilities, and primed by Greek expatriates, some of whom hoped to be rewarded with key positions in their homeland following a Persian victory, the young king moved his forces inexorably forward.

Initial Greek efforts to stop the Persian juggernaut on land at Thermopylae and at sea near Artemisium failed. With public morale ebbing, Themistocles, one of Athens' generals, devised a bold plan. He persuaded the Athenians to evacuate their homeland for refuge on the nearby island of Salamis, while also convincing the jittery commanders of the allied Greek navy to deploy their ships in the narrow straits separating the mainland from Salamis. Meanwhile, Themistocles sent a servant to tell Xerxes that he had accepted the inevitable. If the great king would hurl his mighty warships against the smaller Greek flotilla at Salamis, the Athenian ships under his command would betray their allies and Persia would be able to destroy the remainder of the Greek navy before it escaped the confines of the straits.

Themistocles' plan rested on three assumptions: First, the Greeks could not win in open water; only fighting within cramped straits could offset Persia's numerical superiority. Second, Persian warships were difficult to maneuver in heavy swells; by enticing the Persians into a morning attack, the Greeks could use the wind to their advantage. Third, the nervous commanders of allied Greek units were in awe of the Persian military; encouraging Xerxes to attack would force the Greeks to fight when they might otherwise have fled southward to the Peloponnese.

When Persia's vast fleet began its dreaded attack one early September morning, just as Themistocles had anticipated, a strong wind kicked up heavy swells. Sitting lower in the water than their Persian counterparts, the Greek ships were unaffected; on the other hand, the taller Persian vessels were swung broadside and suddenly found themselves open to ramming. Cornered in a tight channel, Xerxes' fleet could not evade its pursuers, nor could it bring its numerical advantage into play. The bulky, less maneuverable Persian warships obstructed one another while the smaller Greek vessels darted among them with impunity. By the end of the day, the Greeks had routed the Persian navy. Without a fleet to supply it, the Persian army became vulnerable and was crushed the following year at Plataea by Greek hoplites under the Spartan king Pausanias. With Xerxes reeling in defeat, Greek city-states throughout Asia Minor and the eastern Aegean revolted against their Persian overlords. Athens promptly organized these states into a defensive alliance called the Delian League and drove what was left of the Persian military from the region.

Like Cambyses and Darius, Xerxes confused Persian military preeminence with omnipotence. He discounted warnings, underestimated his opponent, believed he was immune to dangers that might arise from brash action, and failed to calibrate his military instruments with clearly articulated political goals. According to one assessment, Xerxes was "a pawn of his own preconceptions."[11] Much like Croesus, he imagined that his nation's preponderance would continue unabated. Yet for Persia, fortune's wind did not blow soft after the losses at Salamis and Plataea. The empire's phenomenal wealth and military power could not guarantee mastery over its fate.

The Roots of Folly

What accounts for the failure of political leaders such Cambyses, Darius, and Xerxes to anticipate foreseeable military fiascoes? Why were the leaders of such a powerful state unable to adapt to new and unexpected circumstances? How can we explain the pursuit of policies that were contrary to their own interests?

Herodotus focused his attention on the Persian Wars because he believed that by commemorating great human achievements he would allow his audience to learn valuable lessons from the past. A product of the Ionian Enlightenment, with intellectual debts to the geographer Hecataeus and the Milesian School of pre-Socratic philosophy, Herodotus sought to explain the reasons why Persia's leaders behaved as they did. Although occasionally criticized for being a rambling, garrulous storyteller,[12] we submit that he was a profound, pioneering scholar, whose commentary on the misuse of preeminent power speaks eloquently to the perils of all unipolar moments.[13]

"People court failure in predictable ways," observes psychologist Dietrich Dörner. Rather than striking like a bolt from the blue, failure develops gradually from habits of thought that cause political leaders to misperceive the problems they are attempting to solve, while overlooking the side effects and long-term repercussions of the solutions they implement.[14] Cambyses in Africa, Darius in Scythia, and Xerxes in Greece exemplified these counterproductive habits of thought. Believing themselves to be divinely favored, overconfident in the instruments of state power, and dismissive of information that raised questions about their policies, they showed symptoms of what the ancient Greeks called *hybris*—insolence or unbridled arrogance, which generally involves wanton violence and a disregard of the rights of others.[15] Those afflicted by *hybris* lack wisdom and self-control; consequently, they easily succumb to *atē*, the commission of an outrageous, morally blind act that leads to their destruction, or *nemesis*.[16]

Thus, for Herodotus, even the preeminent actor on the world stage stands on precarious footing. Good fortune can abruptly dissipate when the powerful overreach and transgress the boundaries that separate right from wrong, prudence from temerity. Just as Cambyses, Daius, and Xerxes impetuously crossed the desert, the Danube, and the Hellespont in their ill-fated efforts to expand the Persian empire, those basking in future unipolar moments will be tempted to act in a bold, unilateral manner by inflated images of their interests and capabilities. Dominant states, Herodotus suggests, often see their foreign policy challenges as military in nature, and frequently conclude that armed force offers the best solution to what actually may be complex political problems. To quote an old adage, when you have a hammer, every problem looks like a nail.

The Future as History

Croesus, Solon, and the Achaemenids are removed from us by two and a half millennia. Their stories are fascinating, but what insights can we glean from their experiences that might apply to contemporary American foreign policy? After all, much about international relations has changed since these former leaders occupied the center stage of world affairs.

Change is riveting; it captures our attention. Still, we must be mindful of the continuities that exist between the present and the distant past. Certain features of interstate interactions have remained the same over the centuries. For example, although new technologies have profoundly altered the way twenty-first–century armed forces wield violence, international relations continues to unfold in an anarchical environment where war remains the final arbiter of serious disputes. Moreover, those responsible for the ultimate decisions on war and peace today continue to commit many of the same errors that political leaders made in antiquity. All too often, they are woefully uninformed about the cultures of their adversaries, treat assumptions about them as if they were facts, rush to judgment without an adequate appreciation of the underlying problem, and make scant effort to weigh tradeoffs and prepare contingency plans in case their policies are derailed.[17] Folly, historian Barbara Tuchman reminds us, "is independent of era or locality; it is timeless and universal."[18]

Of course, studying history is no guarantee that we can avoid the kinds of decision-making traps that led to Persia's debacles in Africa, Scythia, and Greece. "The future can never look exactly like the past," note Richard Neustadt and Ernest May, "but past conditions can offer clues to future possibilities."[19] Reflecting on previous unipolar moments can help us frame sharper questions about the best policies to pursue in the current era of American primacy. Furthermore, it can alert us to the pitfalls that have ensnared states that once held similar positions of military and economic preponderance. When used carefully, history can provide a source of ideas, suggest alternatives that might otherwise have been overlooked, and sensitize us to the probable consequences of our choices. If, as Robert Jervis argues, contemporary American foreign policy "tracks in important ways with what very powerful states have done in the past,"[20] then drawing upon history in a critical, discriminating manner can give us a deeper, more nuanced perspective on the challenges and opportunities inherent in today's unipolar moment.

Foreign Policy in an Era of Convulsive Change

Not long ago it was fashionable for commentators on world affairs to write about the end of history. Many of them saw the collapse of the Soviet Union as the completion of humanity's political evolution, with Western liberal democracy triumphing as the final form of government.[21] Intoxicated by victory in the Cold War, a self-congratulatory mood spread across the United States. With Soviet communism vanquished, America seemed invulnerable to attack.[22] Furthermore, with enormous resources at its disposal, active American involvement appeared essential for solving the world's problems. "We stand tall and therefore we can see further [than other countries]," boasted Madeline Albright,

President Bill Clinton's secretary of state.[23] Comforted by the belief that the United States was an "indispensable nation," many officials in Washington expected their country's good fortune to continue indefinitely.

Rather than witnessing an end to history, however, Americans have experienced a period of convulsive change. Since the September 11, 2001, terrorist attacks on the World Trade Center and the Pentagon, government officials in Washington have defined threats and measured risks differently than most of their counterparts elsewhere, leading the United States to uproot the Taliban regime in Afghanistan by the end of 2001 and to a full-scale invasion of Iraq in March 2003.

The war in Iraq has been an epochal event in the history of American national security policy, encouraging many people to reassess both the conceptual foundations of that policy and of Washington's understanding of the world in which that policy has been based. Although the invasion of Iraq began in March 2003 with substantial public support, 19 months later more than half of the Americans surveyed by the Gallup organization had decided that the war was not worth it. By June 2005, a majority of Americans added that they would be upset if the United States expanded military operations.[24] On the eve of the president's 2006 State of the Union address, 60 percent of Americans disapproved of the way President Bush was handling the war,[25] and only 25 percent said that they wanted him to take the lead in setting policy for the country.[26] At every critical juncture since Hussein's ouster, notes a participant in the U.S. Department of State's "Future of Iraq" project, the administration has claimed that the war in Iraq was turning the corner. Yet, he complains, "not much has changed."[27] The country's occupation, adds Stanley Hoffmann, "has been marked by an overestimation of Iraq's capacity for fast reconstruction . . . and an underestimation of the funds needed and the strength of internal antagonisms."[28] In the words of a former senior advisor to the Coalition Provisional Authority in Baghdad, America's quest to democraticize Iraq has been "one of the major overseas blunders in U.S. history."[29]

Solon's advice to Croesus on recognizing one's limits, which foreshadowed the blunders suffered by Cambyses, Darius, and Xerxes, deserves our attention today because it provides a sobering frame of reference for the discussion of a very difficult but compelling question: When the ongoing strife in Iraq finally ends, what principles should guide American security policy? If there are limits to what the preeminent military and economic power in the world can accomplish, what should be the parameters of America's global involvement? How can the United States avoid *hybris*, which begets foreign policy follies (*atē*) that can prove to be its *nemesis*?

Although the war in Iraq serves as a point of departure for the analysis that follows, our concern here is not with the Iraq war per se, its origins, its conduct, or when or how it will be concluded. These are all critically important subjects of inquiry and have properly received attention elsewhere.[30] The questions we pose are not whether the United States should be castigated for its involvement in the Middle East, or whether American policy will be vindicated.

Nor do they concern whether the withdrawal of the United States will be accomplished quickly or in years hence, or whether such a withdrawal should be regarded as a triumph or sellout. Rather, our aim is to explore, in the midst of an increasingly divisive conflict whose end cannot be clearly seen, the basic tenets that should underpin U.S. security policy in the years ahead.

Focusing on the principles that should guide American foreign policy in the future is a risky undertaking. Surprising events can always alter the course of history and make even the most sober recommendations obsolete. However, the difficulties of seeing over the horizon should not dissuade us from the effort. It is worthwhile to ask whether Washington should get involved elsewhere in the world, such as in the international dispute over Iran's efforts to acquire nuclear weapons. Moreover, it is imperative to assess how potential new military interventions overseas could be undertaken and, if so, on what scale. Consensus as to what ought to be done may be elusive, but a thoughtful, searching review of priorities is essential. It would be tragic if the legacy of Iraq was for the nation to view foreign policy as a Hobson's choice between muscular interventionism and languid indifference to problems beyond America's shores.

Challenge and Opportunity

After losing his empire to the Persians, Croesus offered Solon-like advice to the Cyrus the Great. Reflecting on his fate, he avowed that "human life was like a revolving wheel."[31] Neither people nor states that had attained great stature could count on the durability of their status. Persia had risen from obscurity to achieve the preeminent position in world affairs, but remaining at the apex of international power would be a challenge. Persia's future depended on its leaders. Cyrus and his successors might, through their wisdom or folly, either preserve or erode Persia's unipolar moment.

By calling for a serious reconsideration of the precepts that will guide the future direction of American security policy, we are raising an issue foreshadowed by Croesus' advice to Cyrus. A world dominated by a single preponderant state is rare in modern history. Since the Peace of Westphalia (1648), which gave rise to the current state system, unipolar periods have been fleeting.[32] Expanding commitments abroad have often strained the preeminent power's resources at the very time that its closest potential rivals were enjoying rapid economic development. Over the past three and a half centuries, this combination of imperial overstretch and uneven growth has tended to transform the international pecking order by enabling peer competitors to challenge the dominant state's primacy.[33]

Given the fleeting duration of unipolar moments in modern history, the primary political challenge in the years ahead is likely to be dealing with wrenching structural shifts in the geopolitical landscape that erode American primacy. Meeting this challenge will be difficult. Washington is normally reluctant to make radical changes in foreign affairs. Governed by inertia and momentum, U.S. security policies are resistant to adaptive change except under the most intense pressure. The reasons are not difficult to identify. Rethinking national purpose and building a consensus in support of revising an established policy are not tasks most political leaders welcome, largely because a domestic price is paid by anyone bold enough to try redirecting policy. Such changes inevitably threaten entrenched domestic constituencies who have a stake in preserving existing policies. Incentives for continuity usually far outweigh the rewards for reorienting America's foreign policy posture.

Yet the United States has occasionally altered its foreign policy course, sometimes dramatically. The shock of being insufficiently prepared for a serious threat, argues John Lewis Gaddis, has historically triggered shifts in the country's national security strategy. The responses to the August 24, 1814, British burning of the Capitol and White House, as well as the December 7, 1941, Japanese attack on Pearl Harbor, exemplify for Gaddis the American propensity to face dangers head-on, rather than flee from them as most nations do.[34]

If it has done anything, the growing debate over the U.S. role in Iraq has ignited renewed interest in the goals that America must achieve to produce international security, the military and nonmilitary actions that must be taken to attain those goals, and how scarce human and material resources should be coordinated to support those actions. As Richard Haass has argued, the United States now has a unique opportunity to confront global dangers head-on and shape the course of the twenty-first century for the better. Not only does it possess unrivaled capabilities, but compared to other times, the number of territorial disputes among the great powers is relatively low, as is the perceived utility of war as an instrument for great powers to use against one another.[35]

The time is ripe for the United States to forge a grand strategy aimed at mitigating the turmoil that would likely accompany any waning of America's primacy. The central question for the United States, concludes Charles Kupchan, "is not how much longer the unipolar moment will last, but whether the multipolar world that lies ahead emerges by default or design."[36]

The United States is depicted nowadays as balanced on a razor's edge,[37] with little margin for error if it is to seize this opportunity to design a solid foundation for the global future. In the chapters ahead we will examine the strengths and limitations of America's current security strategy. To place our analysis in its proper context, we must first evaluate the international position that the United States will likely hold in the wake of its war in Iraq. It is to that task we turn in the next chapter.

Notes

1. Herodotus, *The Histories*, translated by Aubrey de Sélincourt and revised by John M. Marincola (London: Penguin, 1996), pp. 12–15. Many classicists doubt that this meeting took place, largely because Solon's travels are thought to have occurred during the decade after his archonship ended in 593 B.C.E., while Croesus did not

assume the throne until 560 B.C.E. Herodotus, they contend, used the meeting as a literary device, juxtaposing the sagacious Athenian with the headstrong Lydian for the reader's moral instruction. The dialogue in this section is based on two versions of the meeting, one presented by Herodotus and the other by Plutarch, in *The Rise and Fall of Athens: Nine Greek Lives*, translated by Ian Scott-Kilvert (London: Penguin, 1960), pp. 69–71. Unfortunately, the histories of Persia written by Charon of Lampsacus, Dionysius of Miletus, Scylax of Caryanda, and Hellanicus of Lesbos, which might shed more light on this alleged meeting, have been either been lost or survive only in fragments.

2. A similar point is made by the chorus of elders at the conclusion of Sophocles' *Oedipus the King* (translation by Dudley Fitts and Robert Fitzgerald):

   Men of Thebes: look upon Oedipus.
   This is the king who solved the famous riddle
   And towered up, the most powerful of men.
   No mortal eyes but looked on him with envy.
   Yet in the end ruin swept over him.
   Let every man in mankind's frailty
   Consider his last day; and none
   Presume on his good fortune until he find
   Life, at his death, a memory without pain.

   Like Croesus, Oedipus is a mulish, arrogant leader whose character (*ēthos*) ultimately leads to a reversal of fortune. According to Herodotus, political leaders have freedom of choice, but their character foreshadows how things will turn out in the long run. As Heracleitus bluntly put it: "A man's character is his fate." Cited in Bernard Williams, *Shame and Necessity* (Berkeley: University of California Press, 1993), p. 136.

3. Herodotus, *The Histories*, p. 5.

4. Herodotus' *Histories* contain a tacit, rudimentary precursor to what today is known as power-cycle theory, according to which the trajectory of a state's power follows a cycle of growth, maturation, and decline, based on the ratio of its strength relative to others. For a summary of the literature on power-cycle theory, see the following works by Charles F. Doran: "Confronting the Principles of the Power Cycle: Changing Systems Structure, Expectations, and War," in Manus I. Midlarsky, ed., *Handbook of War Studies II* (Ann Arbor: University of Michigan Press, 2000), pp. 332–368; and "Power Cycle Theory of Systems Structure and Stability: Commonalities and Complementarities," in Manus I. Midlarsky, ed., *Handbook of War Studies* (New York: Unwin Hyman), pp. 83–110.

5. Adda B. Bozeman, *Politics and Culture in International History* (Princeton, NJ: Princeton University Press, 1960), p. 43.

6. Adam Watson, *The Evolution of International Society* (London: Routledge, 1992), pp. 40, 42.

7. Scholars use the term "polarity" to describe the distribution of military, economic, and other war-making capabilities among the members of the state system. In a unipolar distribution of power, more than 50 percent of the world's total of available capabilities are concentrated in the hands of a single preponderant state, which is strong enough to forestall any combination of states from amassing superior strength. See George Modelski, *World Power Concentrations: Typology, Data,*

Explanatory Framework (Morristown, NJ: General Learning Press, 1974), p. 2. In contrast, bipolar distributions of power contain two approximately equal states with significantly greater material capabilities than the remaing members of the state system, while multipolar distributions have three or more roughly equal states with significantly greater capabilities than anyone else. Some international relations theorists consider differences in the polarity of the interstate system important because they define how states are positioned, which, in turn, affects their decision latitude. Preponderant states in unipolar systems, such as Persia during the reign of the early Achaemenids, have more latitude to use armed force and intervene in the affairs of others than even the strongest states in multipolar systems, largely because there are no peer rivals to impede their actions. For a discussion of systemic theories that focus on how states are positioned relative to one another, see Robert Jervis, *System Effects: Complexity in Political and Social Life* (Princeton, NJ: Princeton University Press, 1997), pp. 92–118; and Kenneth N. Waltz, *Theory of International Relations* (Reading, MA: Addison-Wesley, 1979), pp. 81–82, 97–101.

8. See Michael Mastanduno, "Preserving the Unipolar Moment: Realist Theories and U.S. Grand Strategy After the Cold War," in Ethan B. Kapstein and Michael Mastanduno, eds., *Unipolar Politics: Realism and State Strategies After the Cold War* (New York: Columbia University Press, 1999), pp. 138–181.

9. According to Herodotus, Cambyses "was completely out of his mind," mocking and assaulting "everything which ancient law and custom have made sacred." Herodotus, *The Histories*, p. 169. Despite the contention that Cambyses behaved like a madman, some historians draw upon other ancient sources to rebut this charge. See, for example, A. T. Olmstead, *History of the Persian Empire* (Chicago: University of Chicago Press, 1948), pp. 89–92. Also see J. M. Cook, *The Persian Empire* (New York: Schocken, 1983).

10. In addition to mobilizing a colossal military force, Xerxes forged an alliance with the Carthaginians to prevent Greeks in Sicily from reinforcing their mainland brethren. While the Persians dealt with the eastern Mediterranean, the Carthaginians would neutralize Gelon of Syracuse, the most powerful Greek ruler in the west. Gelon, however, won a decisive victory over the Carthaginians at Himera in 480 B.C.E. Peter Green, *The Greco-Persian Wars* (Berkeley: University of California Press, 1996), pp. 83, 120–122, 148–149.

11. Barry S. Strauss and Josiah Ober, *The Anatomy of Error: Ancient Military Disasters and Their Lessons for Modern Strategists* (New York: St. Martin's Press, 1990), p. 42.

12. Although widely acclaimed as the "father of history," Herodotus is both esteemed for his erudition and criticized for his credulity. Cf. Kendrick W. Pritchett, *The Liar School of Herodotus* (Amsterdam: J. C. Gieben, 1993), and Detlev Fehling, *Herodotus and His "Sources": Citation, Invention, and Narrative Art*, translated by J. G. Howie (Leeds: Francis Cairns, 1989). Also see T. J. Luce, *The Greek Historians* (London: Routledge, 1997), pp. 17–18, 27–28, 36; Michael Grant, *The Ancient Historians* (New York: Barnes and Noble, 1970), p. 52; and J. B. Bury, *The Ancient Greek Historians* (New York: Dover, 1958), p. 57.

13. One of the most important types of individuals in the *Histories* is the "tragic warner," a person who appears in the narrative at critical junctures to alert someone of an impending danger. More often than not, the warnings are ignored and a disaster occurs. Writing decades after the Persian Wars, Herodotus witnessed the

dramatic rise of Athenian power. Through his *Histories*, he became a tragic warner, cautioning the Athenians against repeating the Achaemenid's mistake of assuming their strength was immutable. His concerns about rashly expanding Athenian imperial domination were echoed by Pericles at the beginning of the Peloponnesian War (431–404 B.C.E.). In a speech to the Athenians, Pericles admitted: "I am more afraid of our own blunders than of the enemy's devices." His fears may have been kindled by a recognition that Persian errors contributed to their failure in the wars against Greece. As the Corinthians remined the delegates to an assembly held in Sparta during 432 B.C.E., "the rock on which the barbarian was wrecked was himself." Thucydides, *The Peloponnesian War*, translated by Richard Crawley (New York: Modern Library, 1951), pp. 38, 82.

14. Dietrich Dörner, *The Logic of Failure: Recognizing and Avoiding Error in Complex Situations*, translated by Rita and Robert Kimber (New York: Perseus, 1996), p. 10.

15. Walter Kaufmann, *Tragedy and Philosophy* (Garden City, NY: Doubleday Anchor, 1969), pp. 74–79. One of the earliest examples of *hybris* can be found in the myth of Niobe, the wealthy, powerful queen of Thebes who was punished by the gods for boasting that she was more worthy of veneration than Leto, mother of Apollo and Artemis. Seduced by Croesus-like prosperity, she lost sight of her human limitations and mistakenly believed anything she desired was possible. The fullest surviving account of this ancient Greek myth comes from the Roman poet Ovid. See *Tales From Ovid*, translated by Ted Hughes (New York: Farrar, Straus and Giroux, 1997), pp. 198–208.

16. A similar position is voiced by Jocasta in Euripides' *Phoenician Women* (translated by Elizabeth Wyckoff). Overweening ambition, the distraught queen bemoans, "is an unjust goddess. She comes into prosperous homes and cities, and when she goes out, she leaves destruction for those who entertained her." In Jocasta's lament, Euripides echoes the tragedian Aeschylus' contention that "All arrogance will reap a harvest rich in tears." Cited in Edith Hamilton, *The Greek Way to Western Civilization* (New York: Mentor-Norton, 1942), p. 127.

17. Herodotus mentions numerous instances where fiascoes occurred because political leaders misunderstood the cultural practices of their adversaries. For instance, the presents Cambyses offered to the Ethiopians only served to irritate them; the gifts sent to Darius by the Scythian king Idanthyrsos were misconstrued by the Persians; and the behavior of the Spartans prior to the battle of Thermopylae simply baffled Xerxes. For an analysis of these kinds of cross-cultural confusions, see David Braund, "Herodotus on the Problematics of Reciprocity," in Christopher Gill, Norman Postlethwaite, and Richard Seaford, eds., *Reciprocity in Ancient Greece* (Oxford: Clarendon, 1998), pp. 159–180.

18. Barbara W. Tuchman, *The March of Folly: From Troy to Vietnam* (New York: Ballantine–Random House, 1984), p. 6.

19. Richard E. Neustadt and Ernest R. May, *Thinking in Time: The Uses of History for Decision Makers* (New York: Free Press, 1986), pp. 91–92. Similarly, Robert Conquest asserts that "any understanding of the future is only possible if it includes a reasonable understanding of the past." Robert Conquest, *The Dragons of Expectation: Reality and Delusion in the Course of History* (New York: Norton, 2005), p. 5.

20. Robert Jervis, *American Foreign Policy in a New Era* (New York: Routledge, 2005), p. 2.

21. Francis Fukuyama, "The End of History?" *The National Interest* 16 (Summer 1989): 3–16. Also see his *The End of History and the Last Man* (New York: Free Press, 1992), and "Second Thoughts: The Last Man in a Bottle," *The National Interest* 56 (Summer 1999): 16-33.
22. Eric A. Nordlinger, *Isolationism Reconfigured: American Foreign Policy for a New Century* (Princeton, NJ: Princeton University Press, 1995), pp. 63–91.
23. Interview of Secretary of State Madeleine Albright on ABC-TV's "Nightline" with Ted Koppel, February 20, 1998. For a similar argument, see William C. Wohlforth, "The Stability of a Unipolar World," *International Security* 24 (Summer 1999): 40. Albright's bravado is reminiscent of the claim by French king Louis XIV that by virtue of holding a rank "superior to all other men, he sees things more perfectly than they do." Cited in Christian Reus-Smit, *American Power and World Order* (Cambridge, U.K.: Polity, 2004), p. 29.
24. Gallup poll data on trends in U.S. public opinion on the war in Iraq, retrieved at http://www.gallup.com/poll/content/?ci=16771.
25. ABC News/*Washington Post* poll of 1,002 adults, interviewed on January 23–26, 2006. The poll has a sampling error of plus or minus 3 percentage points.
26. NBC News/*Wall Street Journal* poll of 1,011 adults interviewed on January 26–29, 2006. The poll has a sampling error of plus or minus 3.1 percentage points.
27. David L. Phillips, *Losing Iraq: Inside the Postwar Reconstruction Fiasco* (Boulder, CO: Westview, 2005), p. 222.
28. Stanley Hoffmann, with Frédéric Bozo, *Gulliver Unbound: America's Imperial Temptation and the War in Iraq* (Lanham, MD: Rowman & Littlefield, 2004), p. 106. By the spring of 2006, 32 percent of Iraqis had access to clean drinking water and 19 percent had functioning sewer connections, compared with roughly 50 and 24 percent before the war. Whereas over $20 billion has been allocated for Iraq's reconstruction, current estimates place the cost of repairing the country's infrastructure at more than $70 billion. *Idaho Statesman* (April 9, 2006): 5.
29. Larry Diamond, *Squandered Victory: The American Occupation and the Bungled Effort to Bring Democracy to Iraq* (New York: Times Books–Henry Holt, 2005), p. 279. Also see Michael Hirsh, *At War with Ourselves: Why America Is Squandering Its Chance to Build a Better World* (Oxford: Oxford University Press, 2003).
30. For example, see John Keegan, *The Iraq War* (New York: Vintage, 2005); Noah Feldman, *What We Owe Iraq: War and the Ethics of Nation Building* (Princeton, NJ: Princeton University Press, 2004); Ron Suskind, *The One Percent Doctrine: Deep Inside America's Pursuit of its Enemies Since 9/11* (New York: Simon & Schuster, 2006); Williamson Murray and Robert H. Scales, Jr., *The Iraq War: A Military History* (Cambridge, MA: Belknap Press, 2003); and Michael Gordon and Bernard Trainor, *Cobra II: The Inside Story of the Invasion and Occupation of Iraq* (New York: Pantheon, 2006).
31. Herodotus, *The Histories*, p. 81. There are several legends about what happened to Croesus after the fall of Sardis. Although Herodotus claims that he became an advisor to Cyrus, others believe that he was either killed by the Persians or committed suicide by self-immolation, as was the custom of defeated monarchs in his day. Regardless of what actually happened, Herodotus uses him to convey a cyclical conception of history. In contrast to those who saw historical events following an inexorable linear path (whether ascending toward a more desirable state of affairs

or descending toward some apocalyptic end), Herodotus envisioned a repetitive circular pattern, oscillating between growth and decline.

32. Because of differences in the measurement of national power, social scientists disagree about the precise dates when the structure of the modern state system was unipolar. They generally agree, however, that unipolar periods after 1648 were relatively brief. Cf. David Wilkinson, "Unipolarity Without Hegemony," *International Studies Review* 1 (Summer 1999): 141–172; William R. Thompson, *On Global War: Historical-Structural Approaches to World Politics* (Columbia: University of South Carolina Press, 1988), pp. 211–214; and Jack S. Levy, "The Polarity of the System and International Stability: An Empirical Analysis," pp. 41–66 in Alan Ned Sabrosky, ed., *Polarity and War: The Changing Structure of International Conflict* (Boulder, CO: Westview, 1985).

33. Paul Kennedy, *The Rise and Fall of Great Powers: Economic Change and Military Conflict From 1500–2000* (New York: Random House, 1987), p. xvi. Also see Christopher Layne, "The Unipolar Illusion: Why New Great Powers Will Rise," *International Security* 17 (Spring 1993): 8–16, 31–32; and Robert Gilpin, *War and Change in World Politics* (Cambridge, U.K.: Cambridge University Press, 1981), p. 13.

34. John Lewis Gaddis, *Surprise, Security, and the American Experience* (Cambridge, MA: Harvard University Press, 2004), p. 13.

35. Richard N. Haass, *The Opportunity: America's Moment to Alter History's Course* (New York: PublicAffairs, 2005), pp. 4–8.

36. Charles A. Kupchan, *The End of the American Era: U.S. Foreign Policy and the Geopolitics of the Twenty-First Century* (New York: Alfred A. Knopf, 2002), p. 263. Several types of multipolar systems have existed since the birth of the modern state system. For evidence on the war-proneness of different types of multipolarity and policy recommendations on how to avoid those that have proven so destructive in the past, see Charles W. Kegley, Jr., and Gregory A. Raymond, *A Multipolar Peace? Great-Power Politics in the Twenty-first Century* (New York: St. Martin's Press, 1994).

37. James Kitfield, *War and Destiny: How the Bush Revolution in Foreign and Military Affairs Redefined American Power* (Washington, DC: Potomac Books, 2005), p. 325.

3

An American Imperium

> America is no mere international citizen. It is the dominant power in the world, more dominant than any since Rome. Accordingly, America is in a position to re-shape norms, alter expectations and create new realities.
>
> —Charles Krauthammer

On February 5, 2003, U.S. Secretary of State Colin L. Powell delivered a lengthy address to the United Nations Security Council, charging Iraq with a material breach of its disarmament obligations under UN Security Council Resolution 1441. American intelligence agencies, Powell asserted, had evidence that Saddam Hussein's regime possessed weapons of mass destruction (WMDs). "This is true. This is well-documented," he was instructed to insist. After emphasizing the gravity of the threat these weapons posed, Powell reminded his audience of the Iraqi leader's ruthlessness and warned that he would "stop at nothing until something stops him."[1]

Over the next few weeks, U.S. President George W. Bush and other members of his administration reiterated these accusations. On March 17, Bush claimed that Iraq possessed "some of the most lethal weapons ever devised" and threatened military action if Saddam Hussein did not leave the country within 48 hours. When Hussein failed to comply, the United States and its allies launched a series of precision air strikes and powerful ground attacks that quickly overwhelmed Iraqi defenses. Speaking to the nation from the flight deck of the *USS Abraham Lincoln* on May 1, Bush announced that "major combat operations in Iraq have ended."

Yet a year after declaring victory, American and allied troops were locked in fierce fighting with Sunni insurgents in the central Iraqi city of Falluja and with Shiite militia loyal to the firebrand cleric Muqtada al-Sadr in various southern cities. Meanwhile, militants linked to Abu Mousab al-Zarqawi were brazenly kidnaping and beheading foreigners, turning sections of the country into "no-go" zones for those involved in Iraq's reconstruction. Although expecting to be welcomed with rice and rose petals, American forces were seen as occupiers rather than liberators.[2]

Prior to the war, Central Intelligence Agency Director George Tenet had called the evidence on Iraq's illicit weapons "a slam dunk case."[3] However, a government investigation headed by Charles Duelfer later discovered that Iraq's WMD capability "was essentially destroyed" during the 1991 Persian Gulf War, and that UN sanctions limited its "ability to import weapons, technology, and expertise."[4] Acknowledging criticism that the United States had gone to war against a country whose arsenal of chemical, biological, and nuclear weapons was virtually nonexistent, Secretary Powell conceded that some of the intelligence sources that he had relied upon for his UN Security Council speech were weak.[5] Despite the evaporation of the primary justification for the war, as well as the escalating costs of securing Iraq after the fall of the Hussein regime, President Bush still insisted he would do it all over again. "Absolutely," he replied, when asked by Fox Network's Bill O'Reilly whether he would give the same positive appraisal of America's Iraqi policy as the one he delivered on the *Abraham Lincoln*, when he stood under a banner declaring "Mission Accomplished."[6]

Watching the United States on the world stage is frustrating. As the miscalculations about Iraq illustrate, it is often hard to fathom what political leaders in Washington have in mind when they make national security decisions. Confusion has permeated the U.S. foreign policy–making process since the September 11, 2001, attacks on the World Trade Center and the Pentagon.[7] Unprepared for what happened and uncertain about how to respond, American leaders desperately searched for a strategy to deal with frightening new realities. Even a month after the attacks, Bush's war cabinet had not regained its footing. At an October 16 National Security Council meeting on anti-Taliban operations in Afghanistan, Deputy Secretary of State Richard L. Armitage complained, "I think what I'm hearing is FUBAR" (a military expression, meaning F----d Up Beyond All Recognition).[8] The fitful, frenetic efforts to cope with the security challenges posed by Al Qaeda led Treasury Secretary Paul O'Neill to compare the administration's policymaking process to "June bugs hopping around on a lake."[9]

Why would intelligent, conscientious people experience such difficulties? Having seen international affairs through the prism of the Cold War for so long, are American leaders bewildered by nontraditional security threats?[10] Does a reliance on outdated images of world politics and inappropriate historical analogies hinder efforts to craft a coherent strategy for addressing these threats? According to Hans Blix, the former chief UN weapons inspector in Iraq, the members of the Bush administration exercised little critical judgment in their threat assessments. "Like the former days of the witch hunt," he quipped, the administration was convinced that certain dangers existed, "and if you see a black cat, well, that's evidence of the witch."[11]

Perhaps raw emotions emanating from a post-9/11 siege mentality exacerbated these cognitive errors, leading Bush's war cabinet to oversimplify the problems they faced and frame policy deliberations in ways that engendered counterproductive responses. Amid fears over what might happen next, did anger sparked by Osama bin Laden's strikes against New York and Washington ignite concurrence-seeking pressures within the administration, prompting it make hasty, unsubstantiated assumptions about Al Qaeda and Iraq?[12] If so, why were these assumptions subsequently treated as if they were facts, guiding a war that the president declared would "not end until every terrorist group of global reach has been found, stopped, and defeated?[13]

Although there are many reasons to be frustrated by the current direction of U.S. foreign policy, we remain optimistic about the possibility of charting a different course. The world may have looked different to the Bush administration after the terrorist attacks of September 11, 2001, but the tragic events of that day did not lock the country on an unalterable strategic heading. Other paths are possible; other approaches, viable. But regardless of the direction taken in the future, America's posture in international affairs will be affected by the awesome power it possesses relative to that of all other potential rivals for global leadership. By any measure, the United States is the world's dominant state, a condition that widens the range of its foreign policy choices.

America's Deep Footprint

Power can be distributed in many ways within the international system. It may be concentrated in the hands of one preponderant state (unipolarity), spread between two roughly equivalent rivals (bipolarity), or diffused among several great-power competitors occupying positions of relative parity (multipolarity). At the dawn of the twenty-first century, the United States stands at the apex of a unipolar system. It is the only country with the assets to be decisive "in any conflict in whatever part of the world it chooses to involve itself."[14]

American primacy has many sources. To begin with, the country possesses unprecedented military might. The U.S. military is not just stronger than anybody—it is stronger than everybody. As shown in Figure 3.1, American military expenditures at the onset of the war with Iraq far exceeded those of other major powers. Beyond supporting a formidable strategic nuclear arsenal,[15] these funds have allowed Washington to build a conventional military capability without peer: on the ground, U.S. forces possess awesome speed, agility, and firepower; in the skies, they combine innovative stealth technology with precision-guided munitions; and at sea, they face no serious blue water challenge. With the American military operating eight operational Nimitz-class aircraft carriers (with two more under construction) and 725 foreign bases, nowhere on Earth lies beyond its striking range. When the strategic airlift capabilities of C-5As and C-17s are added to SL-7-type fast sealift ships, the United States has the singular capacity to project its power rapidly over vast distances. And that military-capability supremacy is likely to increase.[16]

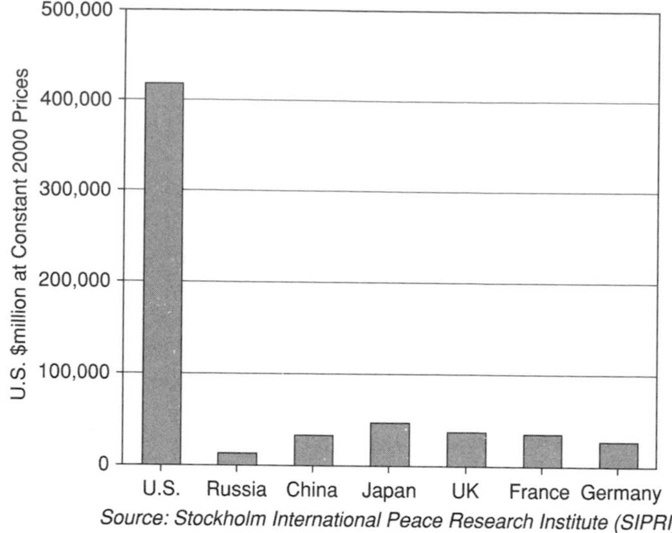

Figure 3.1 Major Power Military Spending, 2003 American military spending has climbed since 2003, with the proposed FY 2007 budget allocating $513 billion to national defense, not including another $420 billion of emergency appropriations by June 15, 2006 for the wars in Afghanistan and Iraq. *Source: The Defense Monitor 35 (March/April 2006): 4.*

Complementing America's military muscle is its economic strength, which accounts for 43 percent of the world's production and 50 percent of its research and development. In 2004 the United States ranked first in global competitiveness, was the home of 29 of the 50 largest companies in the world, served as the source of 62 of the top 100 international brands, and comprised roughly 33 percent of the global gross domestic product (GDP).[17] As illustrated in Figure 3.2, the large, dynamic U.S. economy provides a sturdy foundation for the country's defense establishment. Remarkably, America's military prowess has been maintained by spending only 4.0 percent of its $12 trillion GDP, less than a third of that spent during the Second World War. "Nothing has ever existed like this disparity of power; nothing. Being Number One at great cost is one thing; being the world's single superpower on the cheap is astonishing."[18] As one student of U.S. national security policy has put it, America has the capacity to keep its "edge without even breathing hard."[19]

The United States also leads the world in technological connectivity, ranking first in the number of computers, Internet website hosts, secure servers, and mobile cellular telephones. In addition, it ranks first globally in the number of Nobel laureates in physics, first in government funding for science research, first in patent grants, first in the production of Ph.D.s in science, second in the amount of high-technology goods as a share of manufactured exports, and third in the percentage of the population using the Internet.[20] In short, the United States enjoys a commanding lead over its competitors in those technologies that

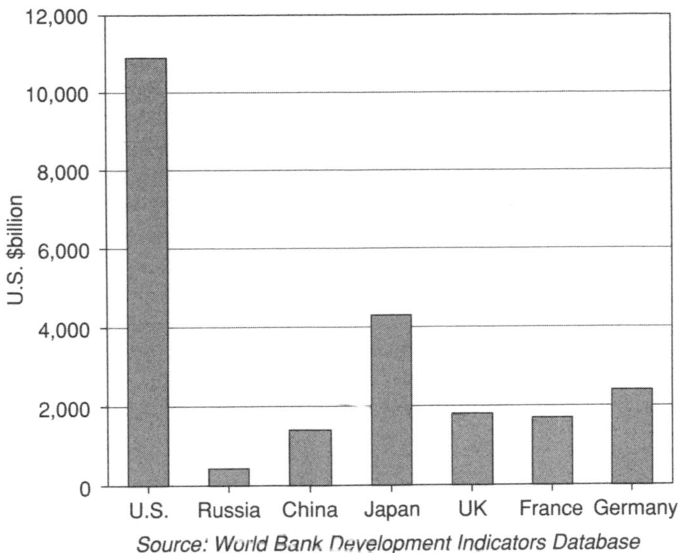

Figure 3.2 Gross Domestic Product, Major Powers, 2003 When gross domestic product is expressed in purchasing-power parity, Russia's total rises from $432.9 to $1,323.8, and China's from $1,417.0 to $6,445.9. Japan's total drops from $4,300.9 to $3,567.8. The figures for the other states do not change significantly. However, *The Economist's* Intelligence Unit forecasts that by the year 2020 China will narrowly outstrip the U.S. economy. *Sources: United Nations Development Programme,* Human Development Report 2005 *(New York: Oxford University Press, 2005), pp. 266–267;* Economist *(April 1, 2006): 84.*

have national security applications. It alone has the capability to conduct digital warfare, using networked communications to merge multiple streams of data from satellites, reconnaissance drones, Airborne Warning and Control System (AWACS) planes, and special operations units inserted behind enemy lines. Instead of facing the chaos that cloaked yesterday's battlefields, U.S. commanders can monitor developments as they happen and orchestrate a combined arms response, overwhelming opponents with well-trained ground maneuver forces supported by a blizzard of interdiction and close air support sorties.

Finally, beyond the military, economic, and technological sources of its power, the United States wields unparalleled influence as an open, alluring society located at the hub of global telecommunications. American music, films, television programs, and popular culture command wide attention throughout the world. Moreover, its institutions of higher education attract many of them to study in the United States.[21] America may be seen abroad as parochial and self-centered, writes journalist Mark Hertsgaard, but it is also admired as "an exciting, inspiring place that combines personal freedom and economic abundance with invigorating energy and inventiveness."[22] These images of a land of opportunity contribute to the country's "soft" power; that is, the ability to entice others to do what the United States wants through the attractiveness of its culture and ideals rather than by threatening coercion or inducing them with payments.[23]

To sum up, the magnitude and scope of American power at the onset of the twenty-first century are extraordinary: "militarily, it has an unmatched global reach; economically, it remains the main locomotive of global growth, even if challenged in some aspects by Japan and Germany (neither of which enjoys the other attributes of global might); technologically, it retains the overall lead in cutting-edge areas of innovation; and culturally, despite some crassness, it enjoys an appeal that is unrivaled, especially among the world's youth."[24] In the words of former French foreign minister Hubert Védrine, the United States is not simply a superpower; it is a "hyperpower" (*hyperpuissance*).

The Meaning of American Primacy

Scholars and journalists disagree over the best word for communicating the significance of America's global power. To many, the United States is an empire.[25] Unfortunately, the term has been employed in so many different ways that one historian has complained that most discussions of its "denotations and connotations inevitably become an exercise in splitting ever more hairs until the central issue is lost in the mangy debris."[26] The term "empire" has been used to describe states that exceed all others "in size, scope, salience, and sense of task,"[27] "multi-ethnic conglomerates held together by transnational organizational and cultural ties,"[28] and political systems with "hublike"structures, whose dominion radiates outward from a strong central core to weaker peripheral regions.[29]

Although there are various contending definitions of the term, the most widely accepted refers to a relationship of formal or informal control imposed by a foreign state over the effective sovereignty of other territories.[30] Empires, in other words, are hierarchical and heterogeneous—powerful states that dominate the foreign *and* domestic policies of weaker nations, who are either incorporated into the imperial state or left with just token independence.

When viewed from this perspective, is the United States an empire? Some observers have doubts. Geir Lundestad, for instance, suggests that the American empire is actually an "empire by invitation."[31] Following the Second World War, he argues, many countries sought military and economic ties with the United States (see Map 3.1), which then forged an organizational structure to set an overall direction for their common policies. Rarely, Lundestad adds, did Washington compel these countries to adopt policies that they would not have otherwise chosen.

Other people have expressed similar qualifications when applying the concept of empire to the United States. For Niall Ferguson, the United States is a "liberal empire,"[32] one that enhances its own well-being by providing the rest of the world with beneficial public goods, such as military security and an

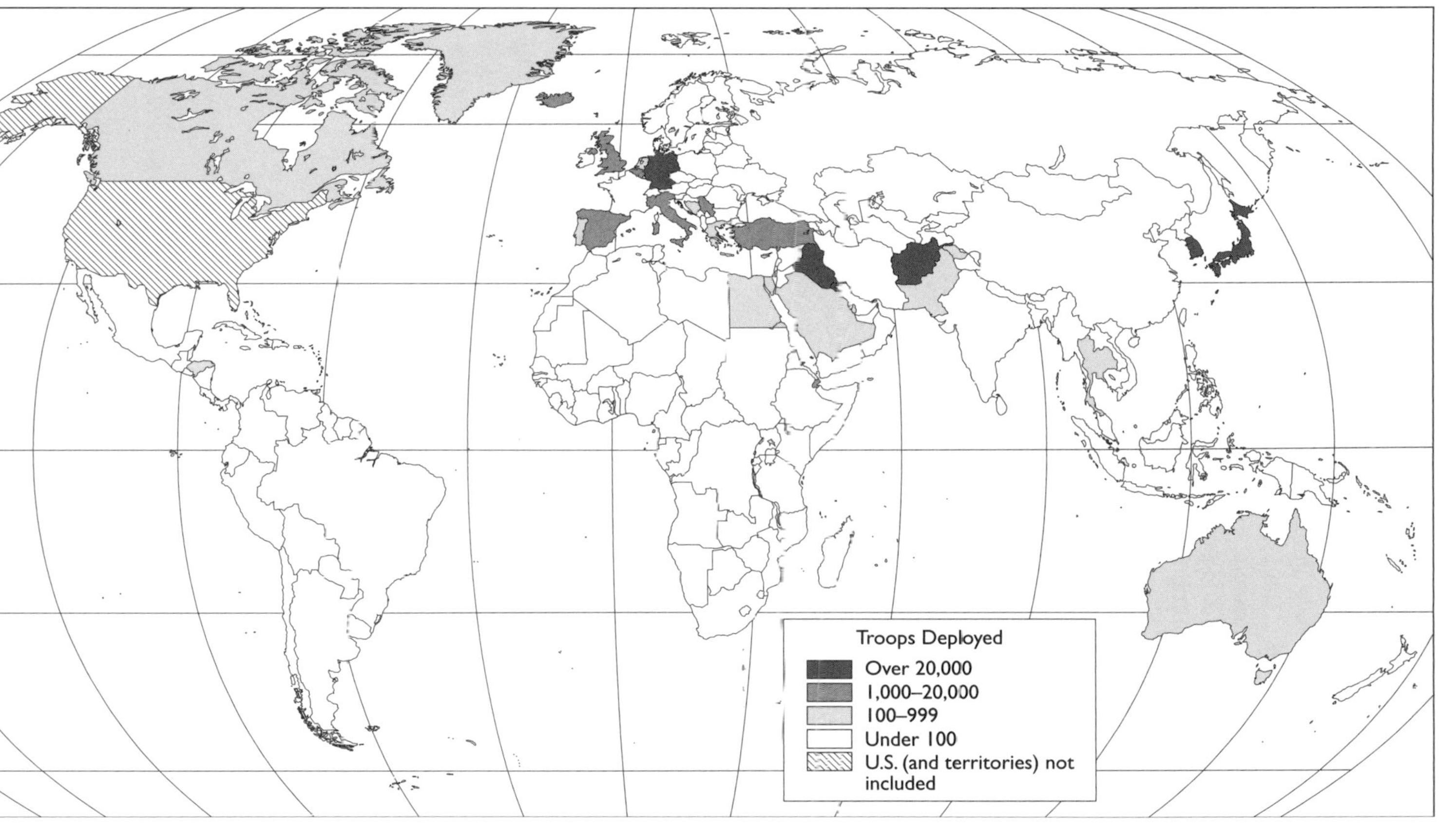

Map 3.1 American Military Deployment outside of the United States and Territories. In 2005, approximately 20% of America's 1.4 million troops were deployed outside of the United States and its territories. An estimated 207,000 were part of Operation Iraqi Freedom, and an estimated 20,400 were part of Operation Enduring Freedom in Afghanistan. *Source: Statistical Information Analysis Division, Defense Manpower Data Center.*

open trading regime. Charles Maier describes a "consensual empire,"[33] where subordinate states have a voice in America's policymaking process. Finally, Victor Davis Hanson writes about "a funny sort of empire,"[34] Wesley Clark about a "virtual empire,"[35] and Michael Ignatieff about "empire lite,"[36] pointing to how Washington's exercise of influence through international institutions binds its allies as well as itself. Rather than being an empire in the classical sense, these analysts recommend that we view the United States as the core of a distinctive kind of empire. It is "a sui generis regime-type," conclude William Odom and Robert Dujarric. Unlike in previous empires, membership in the American empire is voluntary and economically advantageous to all who belong.[37]

If the United States is at the center of an empire like no other, to what extent is the concept of empire useful in examining American foreign policy? Does the so-called "American empire" share significant commonalities with previous empires? Or, as G. John Ikenberry argues,[38] is the international political order constructed by the United States without historical antecedent? While we acknowledge that U.S. leaders have acted in an imperial manner toward various countries (especially within the Western Hemisphere), it seems misleading to describe the United States as the core of a global empire. Not only does this exaggerate the degree of control Washington exerts throughout the world, but it minimizes the extent to which other international actors constrain the United States.

If the United States is not an empire in the classical meaning of the term, what concept provides a better description? Some observers propose the term "hegemony."[39] But it, too, suffers from ambiguity. As one commentator has quipped, there seems to be "something intrinsic to the topic of hegemony that mysteriously inhibits its analysts from engaging in specificity about what the concept means."[40] Some writers never define the term, apparently assuming its meaning is self-evident. Others offer definitions, but disagree over whether hegemony means a "single powerful state [that] controls or dominates the lesser states in the system,"[41] a country that achieves productive, commercial, and financial superiority over its rivals,[42] or "a complex of international social relationships" sustained by ideas that connect classes in different countries."[43] Whereas most scholars focus on the exercise of power by a single state, a few argue that two or more great powers can comprise a hegemony, which only adds to the confusion plaguing the term by blurring the distinctions among hegemonies, concerts, and condominia.[44] Finally, still other scholars regard hegemony as a form of legitimate (rather than naked) domination, therein conflating the term with the international legal concept of suzerainty.[45]

In summary, hegemony is a contested concept, one that is open to divergent interpretations. Rather than sifting through its multiple meanings in the hope of finding one that fits the United States better than calling it a unique form of empire, we shall employ the concept of imperium (from the Latin *imperare*, meaning to rule or command), and thus avoid suggesting any connotations of hegemony that we do not intend. In our view, the most accurate adjective to capture America's foreign policy is one that speaks to the imperious *attitude* that now animates the U.S. quest to preserve its position of primacy and to assert its will unilaterally. An imperium is an imposed order that arises when the preponderant state in a unipolar distribution of international power functions as the supreme normative agent, establishing and maintaining rules of conduct by making pronouncements and applying sanctions, rather than by engaging in multilateral negotiation and working through consensual institutions.[46]

To speak of an American Imperium is not to rule out a transition to true empire. An imperium becomes an imperial power when it projects its unrivaled military might without apology, claiming to be pursuing a moral mission.[47] An imperium becomes an imperial power when it tries to remake the world in its own image, occupying conquered lands and planting its political culture and institutions on foreign soil.[48] Members of the Bush administration insist it is hyperbole to ascribe imperial ambitions to contemporary American foreign policy. "America is not an imperial power," protested President George W. Bush at a press conference on April 3, 2004, it is "a liberating power."[49] Indeed, prior to the 9/11 attacks, only critics associated the United States with empire. Since then, observes Robert Hunter Wade, "many neoconservative commentators have talked with pride and promise of the 'new American empire,' 'the new Rome,' referring to the unipolar structure of the interstate system and America's dominant position of military and political power."[50] Niall Ferguson sees a parallel with the British Empire, noting that "Like the United States today, Britain did not set out to rule a quarter of the world's land surface. . . . Its empire began as a network of coastal bases and informal spheres of influence. . . . But real and perceived threats to their commercial interests tempted the British to progress from informal to formal imperialism."[51] As history unfolds, will the American Imperium succumb to the same temptations that Ferguson attributes to the British? "The United States does not have a choice as to whether it will or will not play a great part in the world, mused President Theodore Roosevelt at the end of the nineteenth century. "Fate has made that choice for us. The only question is whether we will play that part well or badly."

The Roots of America's Imperious Attitude

The characterization of American attitudes toward the rest of the world as imperious is not new. Ever since John Winthrop declared in 1630 that the immigrants to the New World would establish a "city on the hill," many Americans have believed that they were fated to become a moral beacon for humanity. Following the birth of the Republic, they assumed that the United States was different from other countries; it was the "First Universal Nation," animated by a unique set of ideals and institutions that others could emulate.[52] When Benjamin Franklin wrote in 1777 that "our Cause is the Cause of Mankind," he foreshadowed Woodrow Wilson's 1919 proclamation that "the idea of

America is to serve humanity" and John F. Kennedy's assertion four decades later that "We in this country . . . are by destiny rather than choice, the watchmen on the walls of world freedom."[53] It was this same messianic spirit that led George W. Bush to declare in his 2003 State of the Union address that "Our calling as a blessed country is to make the world better" and a month later to tell the American Enterprise Institute that while part of the history of the civilized world was written by others, "the rest will be written by us."[54]

American exceptionalism—the belief that the United States is not an ordinary country—embodies the conviction that Americans have a higher purpose to serve in the world than others. Theirs is a special charge to champion freedom and promote democracy. However, following the American Revolution, most of the country's political leaders thought that purpose was served best by isolating the fledgling republic from the rest of world and serving as a "monument and example" as to how a free society could run its affairs.[55] But as the country evolved, its foreign policy embraced acting unilaterally, not in concert with others. Thus, the United States alone fostered the creation of Liberia in the 1820s, forcibly opened Japan to commercial relations in the 1850s, and scrambled to control Samoa in the 1880s. For a nation with a beneficent self-image and a crusading ideology, unilateralism reflected a preference for autonomy, which would allow an elect, chosen people to pursue their manifest destiny without interference.

Over time, Americans have modified the definition of their mission in the world in response to changing social, economic, and military circumstances. Before the Revolution, many of the early settlers from Puritan England saw the mission as creating the Kingdom of God on Earth. During the two centuries after the Revolution, Americans talked first of spreading individual liberty, then of spreading civilization to so-called "savage" lands, and most recently of spreading democracy abroad.[56] Although some Americans maintain that the United States should rely on the force of example to promote democracy, others advocate more active measures, including military intervention. The desire to bring about what is today called "regime change" springs from this longstanding missionary impulse to remake the world in America's image, exporting representational government and converting others to liberal values.[57] As historian Niall Ferguson has quipped, "when Americans speak of nation building, they actually mean state replicating."[58]

Although a foreign policy of isolationism held sway during several periods of U.S. diplomatic history, World War II provoked an internationalist turn in America's mood, leading the United States to pursue a truly global policy. The editor of *Time* in 1941, Henry R. Luce, predicted the advent of an "American century," in which he hoped the United States would become the powerhouse of freedom and justice. Shortly after the war, President Harry S Truman unabashedly proclaimed that "the United States should take the lead in running the world the way the world ought to be run."[59] For some scholars this way of thinking culminated in the April 1950 top-secret national security memorandum, NSC-68, which set in motion the militarization of American foreign policy and the containment strategy that would persist throughout the Cold War. In addition to recommending the development of superior military strength to deter aggression by the Soviet Union, NSC-68 called for a nonmilitary counteroffensive against the Soviets, which included covert economic, political, and psychological warfare designed to foment unrest and revolt in Soviet bloc countries.

With containment, America had made a covenant with power politics. Perhaps no episode in modern American foreign policy highlighted the dilemmas associated with global activism than the war in Vietnam. George Liska's *Imperial America*, Robert Tucker's *Nation or Empire?*, and Raymond Aron's *The Imperial Republic* responded to the extension of containment to Asia by raising questions about America's military power and foreign policy purposes.[60] Were the receding European colonial empires being replaced by a *Pax Americana*? In the name of containing communism, was the United States installing protectorates and imposing its values throughout the Third World?

Recoiling against America's growing imperious attitude, liberal critics of the war argued that the United States would betray its heritage if it continued to equate power with virtue.[61] Even many political realists acknowledged that there were limits to American military power and warned that the nation's foreign policy would fail unless its leaders learned to distinguish among what was desirable, what was essential, and what was possible.[62] Together, these criticisms led various scholars to recommend retrenchment from the global stage[63] and to propose how the United States might behave as an "ordinary" country.[64]

The raging debates over Vietnam eventually gave way to new disagreements over whether the United States was suffering through a decline.[65] However, with the collapse of the Soviet Union in 1991 and the economic growth enjoyed by the United States throughout the remainder of the decade, attention quickly returned to questions about American imperial power. Yet now there was a new twist: illiberal means, many argued, could be used to for liberal ends; military intervention could advance the cause democratization. "Without too much difficulty," noted Stephen Peter Rosen, an interested reader could "find numerous references to contemporary American imperialism in newspapers and journals of opinion. Attacks on American imperialism were, of course, easy to find in the 1960s and 1970s. What is new is that many such references are neither hostile nor apologetic. . . . Moreover, what is being discussed is not simply the reach and influence of American capitalism or culture, but the harder kind of imperialism—the kind exercised by coercive intimidation and actual soldiers on the ground."[66]

Superpower Solitaire

Contemporary America has been called a "new and historically strange" political entity,[67] one that does not fit adequately within the traditional definitions of "empire" or "hegemony." We submit that the key to understanding this unique actor on the world stage is the imperious attitude that now underpins Washington's efforts to preserve U.S. primacy and assert its will unilaterally. Embedded within the American creed of exceptionalism is an element of superiority.[68] Asserting the right of the mighty to rule, and the singular ability of the strong to distinguish good from evil,[69] the Bush administration has taken on an ambitious mission in the wake of the 9/11 terrorist attacks. According to Secretary of Defense Donald Rumsfeld, it has sought to "refashion the world."[70]

What are the potential consequences of such a hubristic policy? Could America become a prisoner of its redeeming mission and in the process corrode at home the values it seeks to advance abroad? If the promotion externally of American democratic values and institutions is Washington's ultimate goal, can it pursue these objectives without undermining freedom and prosperity internally? Might seeking to change regimes overseas engender domestic changes that weaken America's own economy and civil liberties? These concerns bothered the visionaries who founded the American Republic, who were sobered by Socrates' warnings to Athenians about the dangers of reckless ambition. Imperial pursuits increase the power of the state and decrease the power of citizens; Socrates made the argument that "an imperial democracy cannot stay a democracy for long, since the basis of democratic justice—equal shares for all—demands a self-restraint directly at odds with the energies and ambitions of imperialism."[71]

America may at present be a global imperium, but we contend that it is also imperiled as a result of its recent foreign policy choices. The two circumstances are not disconnected or accidental—they are in a symbiotic relationship. The former fosters the latter, and, paradoxically, the latter encourages the former. An imperial approach to global management can generate dangers at home and abroad. True, the world's sole superpower is presently too great to be challenged in conventional war. Yet it remains vulnerable to unconventional threats. In the next chapter we shall survey those threats as a prelude to examining the Bush Doctrine and its long-term consequences for national and international security.

Notes

1. According to Bob Woodward, an assistant managing editor at the *Washington Post*, Powell had previously been skeptical of U.S. intelligence on Saddam Hussein's capabilities and intentions and cautioned against war with Iraq. In contrast, Vice President Richard B. Cheney was a "powerful, steamrolling force" that pushed for removing Hussein by force. Together with his chief aide, Lewis Libby, Deputy Defense Secretary Paul Wolfowitz, and Undersecretary of Defense Douglas Feith, Cheney advocated military action from the onset of the Bush presidency. "There is no doubt that Saddam Hussein now has weapons of mass destruction," Cheney declared on August 26, 2002, at the 103rd national convention of the Veterans of Foreign Wars. "The Iraqi regime has in fact been very busy enhancing its capabilities in the field of chemical and biological agents. And they continue to pursue

the nuclear program they began so many years ago." Questioning the ability of inspectors to assure Iraq's compliance with UN disarmament resolutions, Cheney suggested that the "risks of inaction are far greater than the risk of [military] action." See Bob Woodward, *Plan of Attack* (New York: Simon & Schuster, 2004), p. 4.

2. The American experience in Iraq was preceded almost a century earlier by a British invasion and occupation. Seeking to protect their strategic interests in the region from German encroachment during World War I, British forces entered Basra in late 1914, stormed up the Tigris and Euphrates Rivers, and seized Baghdad in 1917. Although proclaiming they had come as liberators, the British faced growing nationalist and Islamist opposition, which culminated in a widespread revolt during 1920. In London then, as in Washington recently, "different officials made promises, announced policies, and declared war aims that were ambiguous and contradictory." Judith S. Yaphe, "War and Occupation in Iraq: What Went Right? What Could Go Wrong?" *Middle East Journal* 57 (Summer 2003): 394. Although America was not welcomed into Iraq with rose petals, Undersecretary of Defense for Policy Douglas Feith still insists that the Iraqis "had flowers on their minds." Quoted in Jeffrey Goldberg, "A Little Learning," *The New Yorker* (May 9, 2005), p. 40.
3. Quoted in Bob Woodward, *Bush At War* (New York: Simon & Schuster, 2002), p. 244.
4. *Comprehensive Report of the Special Advisor to the DCI on Iraq's WMD* (September 30, 2004), retrieved at http://www.cia.gov/cia/reports/iraq_wmd_2004.
5. September 12, 2004, interview with Tim Russert on NBC News's "Meet the Press," retrieved at http://msnbc.msn.com/id/5981265/. Also Powell's September 9, 2005, interview with Barbara Walters on the ABC News program "20/20," during which he called the incident a "blot" on his record. In a July 2003 interview with Sam Tanenhaus in *Vanity Fair*, Deputy Secretary of Defense Wolfowitz revealed that the administration had stressed WMDs "because it was the one reason [for the war] everyone could agree on." Devon Largio has documented 20 other reasons voiced by officials; see *Foreign Policy* 144 (September/October 2004): 18. Apparently the most persuasive was the allegation of strong ties between Iraq and Al Qaeda. In a *New York Times*/CBS News poll conducted between March 7 and 9, 2003, 45 percent of the respondents expressed the belief that Saddam Hussein was involved in the 9/11 attacks. However, like the WMD claim, this justification ultimately proved groundless. According to the 9/11 Commission, there is no evidence that Al Qaeda and Iraq had a "collaborative operational relationship" or that Saddam Hussein cooperated with Osama bin Laden "in developing or carrying out any attacks against the United States." *Final Report of the National Commission on Terrorist Attacks upon the United States* (New York: Norton, 2004), p. 66. Equally disturbing was the revelation of the person in charge of intelligence in Iraq, Paul Pillar, who reported that the administration selectively "cherry picked" intelligence that would support its prior decision to invade and that President Bush did not request an assessment of the consequences of invading Iraq until a year after the invasion; see Paul Pillar, "Intelligence, Policy, and the War in Iraq," *Foreign Affairs* 85 (March/April 2006): 15–27.
6. Quoted in Elizabeth Kolbert, "Winning," *The New Yorker* (October 11, 2004): 33. As his answer reveals, Bush does not second-guess himself. "I have not looked back on one decision I have made," he once observed, "and wished I had made it a different way." Quoted in Howard Fineman and Martha Brant, "This Is Our Life Now," *Newsweek* (December 3, 2001): 28. Indeed, when asked at an April 13, 2004,

press conference what foreign policy mistakes he might have made after 9/11, Bush replied that he could not think of any at the moment. "I would have gone into Afghanistan the way we went into Afghanistan," he responded. "Even knowing what I know today . . . , I still would have called upon the world to deal with Saddam Hussein." Press Conference of the President, retrieved at http://www.whitehouse.gov/news/releases/2004/04/20040413-20.html.

7. See, for example, the behind-the-scenes account of the administration's foreign policy deliberations in Bob Woodward, *Bush At War* (New York: Simon & Schuster, 2002), pp. 31, 182.

8. Woodward, 2002, p. 244. The policymaking process was in disarray, writes one critic, because Bush's "war cabinet had a loose grasp on the basic facts, did not identify strategic goals, made no attempt to relate means to ends, and acknowledged obvious, massive realities and choices only after having proceeded for weeks as if they didn't exist." Angelo M. Codeville, "Confusion and Power," *Claremont Review of Books* 3 (Spring 2003): 23. Similarly, Richard Clarke, the former counterterrorism advisor to the administration, complained that Bush's inner circle "had no real interest in complicated analyses; on the issues that they cared about, they already knew the answers, it was received wisdom." Richard A. Clarke, *Against All Enemies* (New York: Free Press, 2004), p. 243.

9. Quoted in Ron Suskind, *The Price of Loyalty: George W. Bush, the White House, and the Education of Paul O'Neill* (New York: Simon and Schuster, 2004), p. 306. Critics of Bush's handling of the war, *The Economist* (April 8, 2006): 33, summarizes, complain Bush "Rushed into war, lied about his reasons, failed to plan adequately and botched the execution."

10. Insight into the administration's focus on threats emanating from sovereign, territorial states rather than nonstate actors can be gleaned from positions taken by key officials on the eve of the September 11, 2001, attacks. In a meeting with Republican congressional leaders on August 2, for example, Vice President Cheney described a bold new security plan that would emphasize "missile defenses and modifications to our offensive strategic arms." Similarly, in the text of an undelivered speech by national security advisor Condoleezza Rice, which had been scheduled for September 11, ballistic missile defense was promoted as the cornerstone of a new U.S. security strategy, while no mention was made of potential terrorist attacks by Osama bin Laden, Al Qaeda, or any other Islamic extremist groups, stateless enemies without ballistic missile capabilities against whom such a defensive shield was worthless. Robin Wright, "Rice Speech Focuses on Missile Defense," *The Guardian International* (April 1, 2004), retrieved at http://www.guardian.co.uk/international/story/0,3604,1183735,00.html.

11. Quoted in Warren Hoge, "Former UN Weapons Inspector Has Harsh Words for Bush," *International Herald Tribune Online* (March 16, 2004), p. 1. The central problem, suggests a former national intelligence officer, was that the Bush administration's policy positions drove the intelligence-gathering process. "On any given subject, the intelligence community faces what is in effect a field of rocks, and it lacks the resources to turn over every one to see what threats to national security may lurk underneath. In an unpoliticized environment, intelligence officers decide on which rocks to turn over based on past patterns and their own judgments. But when policymakers repeatedly urge the intelligence community to turn

over only certain rocks, the process becomes biased. The community responds by concentrating its resources on those rocks, eventually producing a body of reporting and analysis that, thanks to quantity and emphasis, leaves the impression that what lies under those same rocks is a bigger part of the problem than it really is." Paul Pillar, "Intelligence, Policy, and the War in Iraq," *Foreign Affairs* 85 (March/April 2006): 23. For an informed account of the sources of intelligence failures and how the problems might be alleviated, see Loch K. Johnson, "A Framework for Strengthening U.S. Intelligence," *Yale Journal of International Affairs I* (Spring 2006): 116–131.

12. Some observers suggest that conformist pressures can be seen in the denigration of economic adviser Lawrence Lindsey's estimate that the cost of the war with Iraq would exceed $100 billion and in Army chief of staff General Erik Shinseki's estimate that controlling the country after the fall of Baghdad would require several hundred thousand troops. Although originally leading the public criticism of these assessments, Deputy Secretary of Defense Paul Wolfowitz later admitted that the administration "turned out to underestimate the problem" (*Milwaukee Journal Sentinal*, July 24, 2004, p. 12A), a position echoed by Paul Bremer after he stepped down as the top U.S. civilian administrator in Iraq. See L. Paul Bremer III with Malcolm McConnell, *My Year in Iraq* (New York: Simon and Schuster, 2006).
13. September 20, 2001, address to a joint session of Congress and the American people, retrieved at http://www.whitehouse.gov/
14. Charles Krauthammer, "The Unipolar Moment," *Foreign Affairs* 70 (Winter 1991): 24; see also his "The Unipolar Moment Revisited," *The National Interest* 70 (Winter 2003): 5–17, which maintains that America's top-dog "moment" in global history persists.
15. In 2006, the United States possessed 5,886 operational strategic nuclear warheads, deployed on an awesome triad of strategic delivery systems, including Minuteman III and MX/Peacekeeper intercontinental ballistic missiles, Trident I C4 and Trident II D5 submarine-launched ballistic missiles, and B-2A and B-52H bombers. It also had more than 1,000 nonstrategic warheads that could be carried on Tomahawk cruise missiles as well as on F-16C/D and F-15E aircraft. Approximately 3,000 more warheads were held in reserve. The following are estimates of the number of strategic weapons possessed by other nuclear powers: Russia (3,503), France (348), United Kingdom (185), China (200–400), Israel (200), India (40–50), Pakistan (30–50), and North Korea (up to 10). "Nuclear Disarmament," *The Economist* (June 10, 2006): 43; see also *Bulletin of Atomic Scientists*, International Institute for Strategic Studies, Stockholm International Peace Research Institute, and the Arms Control Association. Recent trends point to the continuation of U.S. nuclear preeminence, because the U. S. arsenal is expanding while Russia's decays and China's remains small; see Keir A. Lieber and Daryl G. Press, "The Rise of U.S. Nuclear Primacy," *Foreign Affairs* 85 (March/April 2006): 42–54.
16. The actual total may be higher "since some bases exist under leaseholds, informal agreements, or disguises of various kinds." Chalmers Johnson, *The Sorrows of Empire: Militarism, Secrecy, and the End of the Republic* (New York: Metropolitan Books, 2004), p. 154.
17. Economic data taken from the following sources: Fareed Zakaria, "The Arrogant Empire," *Newsweek* (March 24, 2003): 23; International Institute for Management

Development, 2004 World Competitiveness Rankings, retrieved at http://www.finfacts.ie/wcomp.htm; *BusinessWeek* 2004 Global 1000 leaders, retrieved at http://www.businessweek.com/pdfs/2004/global1000_list.pdf; and *BusinessWeek*/Interbrand's top global brands of 2004, retrieved at http://www.finfacts.ie/brands2004.htm. Other rankings support the thesis of America's edge over its global rivals. For example, *Pocket World in Figures, 2006 Edition* (London: Economist, 2005), pp. 34, 45, 54, 58, 60, ranks the United States first in percentage of world exports, manufacturing output, consumption of energy, global competitiveness, and innovation.

18. Paul Kennedy, *Financial Times* (February 2, 2002), op-ed page.
19. Bruce Berkowitz, *The New Face of War: How War Will Be Fought in the 21st Century* (New York: Free Press, 2003), p. 5.
20. Technology data taken from the following sources: "Measuring Globalization," *Foreign Policy* (May/June 2005): 52. Internet Usage and Population Statistics, retrieved at http://www.internetworldstats.com/stats.htm; and Economic and Social Data Rankings, retrieved at http://dataranking.com/English/ed06-3.html; Research indicators from U.S. government agencies as reported in *Time* (February 13, 2006): 34, 36.
21. According to a comparative analysis, American universities comprise 50 of the top 200 institutions of higher education in the world. Fareed Zakaria, "How Long Will America Lead the World?," *Newsweek* (June 12, 2006): 44.
22. Mark Hertsgaard, *The Eagle's Shadow: Why America Fascinates and Infuriates the World* (New York: Picador, 2003), p. 210.
23. Joseph S. Nye, Jr., *Soft Power: The Means to Success in World Politics* (New York: PublicAffairs, 2004), pp. 5–15.
24. Zbigniew Brzezinski, *The Grand Chessboard: American Primacy and Its Geostrategic Imperatives* (New York: Basic Books, 1997), p. 24.
25. For example, Andrew J. Bacevich, *American Empire* (Cambridge, MA: Harvard University Press, 2002); Jim Garrison, *America as Empire* (San Francisco: Berrett-Koehler, 2004); Ivan Eland, *The Empire Has No Clothes: U.S. Foreign Policy Exposed* (Oakland, CA: Independent Institute, 2004); Bruce Cumings, "Is America an Imperial Power?" *Current History* 102 (November, 2003): 355–360; Stephen Peter Rosen, "An Empire, If You Can Keep It," *The National Interest* 71 (Spring 2003): 51–61; and Michael Parenti, *Against Empire* (San Francisco: City Lights Books, 1995). In addition to those who refer to an American empire in a descriptive sense, several commentators have spoken of it in a prescriptive manner. For example, William Kristol, editor of the *Weekly Standard*, Max Boot, a former editor at the *Wall Street Journal*, and Thomas Donnelly, the deputy executive director of the Project for a New American Century, have advocated a muscular, imperial foreign policy. See especially, Max Boot, *The Savage Wars of Peace: Small Wars and the Rise of American Power* (New York: Basic Books, 2002), pp. 348–352.
26. William Appleman Williams, *Empire as a Way of Life* (Oxford: Oxford University Press, 1980), p. 5. From the time of Sargon I (2350 B.C.E.), depicted in Akkadian lore as the "King of Battle" and known today as the founder of the world's first recorded empire, the history of civilization has been shaped by empires. For an overview of how the term has been variously used in modern history, see Dominic Lieven, *Empire* (New Haven, CT: Yale University Press, 2002).

27. George Liska, *Imperial America: The International Politics of Primacy* (Baltimore: The Johns Hopkins Press, 1967), p. 9.

28. P. J. Cain and A. G. Hopkins, *British Imperialism 1688–2000* (London: Longmans, 2002), p. 664.

29. Alexander Motyl, *Imperial Ends: The Decay, Collapse, and Revival of Empires* (New York: Columbia University Press, 2001), p. 4. Often the structure is said to exploitative, where the dominating country appropriates part of the wealth of the dominated country. Albert Szymanski, *The Logic of Imperialism* (New York: Praeger, 1981), pp. 5–6.

30. Michael W. Doyle, *Empires* (Ithaca, NY: Cornell University Press, 1986), pp. 19, 30, 45. Formal control may be direct or indirect. British control over parts of Africa during the nineteenth and early twentieth centuries exemplified indirect rule. Lacking sufficient colonial administrators to govern some regions directly, the British recognized traditional tribal authorities and ruled the local population through these individuals. See Lord Lugard, *The Dual Mandate in British Tropical Africa* (Edinburgh: Blackwood & Sons, 1933); Baron Hailey, *Native Administration in the British African Territories* (London: His Majesty's Stationery Office, 1953); and Robert Huttenback, *The British Imperial Experience* (New York: Harper & Row, 1966).

31. Geir Lundestad, *The American "Empire"* (Oslo: Norwegian University Press, 1990), pp. 37–39, 54–62. Also see John Lewis Gaddis, *We Now Know: Rethinking Cold War History* (New York: Oxford University Press, 1997), p. 52.

32. Niall Ferguson, *Colossus: The Price of America's Empire* (New York: Penguin, 2004), pp. 2, 25. Ferguson predicts that an "apolar" world—a future international system without overwhelming American power—would slide into a new Dark Age of economic stagnation, religious extremism, and the retreat of civilization into fortified enclaves. Also see Michael Mandelbaum, *The Case for Goliath: How America Acts as the World's Government in the 21st Century* (New York: PublicAffairs, 2005), pp. 31–41, 88–94; see also Robert J. Lieber, *The American Era* (New York: Cambridge University Press, 2005), which also contends that U.S. primacy is necessary and beneficial in a world without central authority for global governance.

33. Quoted in G. John Ikenberry, "Illusions of Empire: Defining the American Order," *Foreign Affairs* 83 (March/April 2004): 146. To this, it is often added that the United States is a "reluctant" empire. See Dimitri K. Simes, "America's Imperial Dilemma," *Foreign Affairs* 82 (November/December 2003): 93.

34. Victor Davis Hanson, *Between War and Peace: Lessons from Afghanistan and Iraq* (New York: Random House, 2004), pp. 237–242.

35. Wesley Clark, "America's Virtual Empire," retrieved at http://www.washingtonmonthly.com/features/2003/0311.clark.html.

36. Michael Ignatieff, "American Empire: The Burden," *New York Times Magazine* (January 5, 2003): 22.

37. William E. Odom and Robert Dujarric, *America's Inadvertent Empire* (New Haven, CT: Yale University Press, 2004), p. 36. Also Robert Cooper, *The Breaking of Nations: Order and Chaos in the Twenty-First Century* (New York: Grove Press, 2003), p. 48; Tony Zinni and Tony Koltz, *The Battle for Peace* (New York: Palgrave, 2006), p. 4; and Arthur Schlesinger, Jr., "The American Empire: Not So Fast," *World Policy Journal* 22 (Spring 2005): 45. According to Charles Krauthammer, it is ridiculous to apply

the term "empire" to a country "whose first instinct upon arriving on anyone's soil is to demand an exit strategy." See his *Democratic Realism: An American Foreign Policy for a Unipolar World* (Washington, DC: AEI Press, 2004), p. 2.

38. G. John Ikenberry, "Illusions of Empire: Defining the New American Order," *Foreign Affairs* 83 (March/April 2004): 154. A similar point is made in Jan Nederveen Pieterse, *Globalization or Empire?* (New York: Routledge, 2004), pp. 45–52. "To talk about the United States as an empire," adds another participant in this debate, is "to engage in a useless and potentially dangerous anachronism." Eliot A. Cohen, "History and the Hyperpower," *Foreign Affairs* 83 (July/August 2004): 55.

39. The ancient Greek term "hegemony" (*hēgemonia*, or overlordship) denotes the authority of a paramount state over the external behavior of others and is sometimes contrasted with *archē* (dominance or control based on power). The foremost example in antiquity was the Peloponnesian League, led by Sparta during the fifth century B.C.E. and composed of neighboring states such as Corinth, Elis, and Tega. Each League member swore to have the same friends and enemies as Sparta (unless there were conflicting religious obligations) and to accept Spartan command over any military campaigns undertaken by the League. In contrast, the Athenians, who led the rival Delian League, sought to regulate both the external and internal behavior of their allies. According to Thucydides, Athenian leadership was initially evenhanded, with decisions reached in general congresses where everyone had an equal say in formulating alliance policies. However, following an attempt by Naxos to withdraw from the alliance, the Athenians converted the Delian League into an empire of tribute-paying subjects. When the Mytileneans rebelled in 428 B.C.E., they emphasized their loyalty to Athens during the League's early years, when the Athenians treated them fairly. But when Athens began subjugating one alliance member after another, the Mytileneans confessed that they feared losing their autonomy as well. Thucydides, *The Peloponnesian War*, translated by Richard Crawley (New York: Random House, 1951), pp. 56, 151.

40. William R., Thompson, *On Global War: Historical-Structural Approaches to World Politics* (Columbia: University of South Carolina Press, 1988), p. 113; Elke Krahmann, "American Hegemony or Global Governance? Competing Visions of International Security," *International Studies Review* 7 (December 2005): 533–534; and Felix Ciută, "What Are We Debating? IR Theory Between Empire and the Responsible Hegemon," *International Politics* 43 (April 2006): 173–196.

41. Robert Gilpin, *War and Change in World Politics* (Cambridge: Cambridge University Press, 1981), p. 28. While agreeing with this definition, Mearsheimer differentiates between a global hegemon, which would dominate the world, and regional hegemons, which dominate specific geographical areas. In his opinion, "there has never been a global hegemon, and there is not likely to be one anytime soon." John J. Mearsheimer, *The Tragedy of Great Power Politics* (New York: Norton, 2001), p. 41.

42. Immanuel Wallerstein, *The Politics of the World-Economy* (Cambridge: Cambridge University Press, 1984), pp. 38–39. Also see Robert O. Keohane, *After Hegemony: Cooperation and Discord in the World Political Economy* (Princeton, NJ: Princeton University Press, 1984), p. 32. Prior to the advent of the modern capitalist world system in the sixteenth century, Braudel describes the shifting fortunes hegemonic cities, such as Venice, Antwerp, and Genoa in Europe. Abu-Lughod points to similar power centers beyond Europe. Fernand Braudel, *The Perspective of the World*,

vol. 3 of *Civilization and Capitalism*, translated by Sian Reynolds (New York: Harper & Row, 1984); Janet L. Abu-Lughod, *Before European Hegemony: The World System A.D. 1250–1350* (New York: Oxford University Press, 1989).

43. Robert Cox, "Gramsci, Hegemony and International Relations: An Essay on Method," *Millennium* 12 (No. 2, 1983): 171. Also see David Harvey, *The New Imperialism* (Oxford: Oxford University Press, 2003), p. 36; Alan W. Cafruny, "A Gramscian Concept of Declining Hegemony: Stages of U.S. Power and the Evolution of International Economic Relations," in David P. Rapkin, ed., *World Leadership and Hegemony* (Boulder, CO: Lynn Rienner, 1990), pp. 97–118; and Stephen Gill, *American Hegemony and the Trilateral Commission* (Cambridge: Cambridge University Press, 1989).

44. Adam Watson, *The Evolution of International Society* (London: Routledge, 1992), p. 15. In diplomatic parlance, a concert is a coalition of great powers aimed at managing the international system to prevent conflicts of interest from escalating to war. Concert-based security systems date back to the second millennium B.C.E., when relations among Egypt, the Hittites, Babylonia, Elam, Mitanni, Assyria, and the Cretan Federation displayed many of the characteristics of the nineteenth-century Concert of Europe. Condominial arrangements also date back to antiquity. In contrast to concerts, they involve joint rule over a particular territory, whose ownership often is in dispute. See Adda B. Bozeman, *Politics and Culture in International History* (Princeton, NJ: Princeton University Press, 1960), p. 28; and Charles W. Kegley, Jr., and Gregory A. Raymond, *A Multipolar Peace? Great-Power Politics in the Twenty-first Century* (New York: St. Martin's, 1994), pp. 133–139, 157–158.

45. Mjøset, for example, defines hegemony as "a relationship of *legitimate* domination exercised by one country over the other great powers." Lars Mjøset, "The Turn of Two Centuries: A Comparison of British and U.S. Hegemonies," in David P. Rapkin, ed., *World Leadership and Hegemony* (Boulder, CO: Lynne Rienner, 1990), p. 21, emphasis added. Traditionally, legal authorities have used the term suzerainty to describe situations of legitimate domination. According to Wight, suzerain-state systems, such as Han China, Byzantium, and the Abbasid Caliphate, involve a single, unchallengeable power exercising control over vassals and weak neighbors, who accept the authority of the suzerain power as legitimate. Martin Wight, *Systems of States* (Leicester, U.K.: Leicester University Press, 1977).

46. Christian Reus-Smit, *American Power and World Order* (Cambridge, U.K.: Polity, 2004), p. 87. Even when the United States invested heavily in building international institutions, David Skidmore argues that Washington consistently sought ways to act outside of this organizational framework by demanding special prerogatives, such as exemptions, waivers, weighted voting, and veto powers. See his "Understanding the Unilateralist Turn in U.S. Foreign Policy," *Foreign Policy Analysis* 1 (July 2005): 217.

47. Jedediah Purdy, "Liberal Empire: Assessing the Arguments," *Ethics & International Affairs* 17 (No. 2, 2003): 41, 38. See also Jeanne Morefield, *Covenants Without Swords: Idealist Liberalism and the Spirit of Empire* (Princeton, NJ: Princeton University Press, 2006). The importance of missionary optimism, a belief that one has been chosen by providence to carry out a crusade against enemy infidels, has been stressed by some theories on the origins of empire. According to one school of thought, the primary reason certain states have succeeded in empire-building lies in their possession

of a compelling ideology that links an individual's identity to the state, justifies territorial expansion, and glorifies warfare. Geoffrey W. Conrad and Arthur A. Demarest, *Religion and Empire* (New York: Cambridge University Press, 1984). Also see Henry Kamen, *Empire* (New York: HarperCollins, 2003), pp. 3–47.

48. For an example of this interpretation, see Paul Krugman, "America the Boastful," *Foreign Affairs* 77 (May/June 1998): 32–46.

49. Similarly, in a September 2003 speech, Secretary of State Powell asserted that America did not "seek a territorial empire." "We have never been imperialists," he declared. Speech delivered at George Washington University, retrieved at http://www.state.gov/secretary/rm/2003/23836.htm.

50. Robert Hunter Wade, "The Invisible Hand of the American Empire," *Ethics & International Affairs* 17 (No. 2, 2003): 77. For critiques of those who advocate an imperial role for the United States, see Clyde Prestowitz, *Rogue Nation: American Unilateralism and the Failure of Good Intentions* (New York: Basic Books, 2003); T. D. Allman, *Rogue State: America at War with the World* (New York: Nation Books, 2004); Gore Vidal, *Imperial America* (New York: Nation Books, 2004); John Newhouse, *Imperial America: The Bush Assault on the World Order* (New York: Alfred A. Knopf, 2003); and Josef Joffe, *Überpower: The Imperial Temptation of America* (New York: Norton, 2006).

51. Niall Ferguson, *Empire* (New York: Basic Books, 2003), p. 368.

52. See Ben J. Wattenberg, *The First Universal Nation* (New York: Free Press, 1991), which contends (pp. 367–369) that Alexis de Tocqueville coined the term "American Exceptionalism."

53. From Frank L. Klingberg, *Positive Expectations of America's World Role* (Lanham, MD: University Press of America, 1996), pp. 422, 424, 450. For a penetrating and provocative interpretation of the view that America was ordained by providence to promote American values and democracy worldwide, see Tony Smith, *America's Mission* (Princeton, NJ: Princeton University Press, 1994).

54. Retrieved at http://www.whitehouse.gov/news/releases/2003/01/20030128-19.html; and http://www.whitehouse.gov/news/releases/2003/02/20030226-11.html. Also see William Appleman Williams, *The Tragedy of American Diplomacy*, 2nd ed. (New York: Delta, 1972); and Walter LaFeber, *The American Age*, 2nd ed. (New York: Norton, 1994). On America's impulse toward expansionism, see Albert K. Weinberg, *Manifest Destiny: A Study of Nationalist Expansionism in American History* (Chicago: Quadrangle, 1963).

55. Letter of March 6, 1801, written by Thomas Jefferson to John Dickinson, in Adrienne Koch and William Peden, eds., *The Life and Selected Writings of Thomas Jefferson* (New York: Modern Library, 1944), p. 561.

56. John B. Judis, *The Folly of Empire* (New York: Scribner, 2004), pp. 14–17.

57. See Jonathan Monten, "The Roots of the Bush Doctrine," *International Security* 29 (Spring 2005): 140–153. For a discussion of the missionary tradition in U.S. foreign policy, see Walter Russell Mead, *Special Providence: American Foreign Policy and How It Changed the World* (New York: Alfred A. Knopf, 2001), pp. 139–162.

58. Niall Ferguson, "The Unconscious Colossus: Limits of (and Alternatives to) American Empire," *Daedalus* 134 (Spring 2005): 23.

59. The empirical tracing of America's diplomatic swings between periods of introversion (isolationism) and extroversion (internationalism) is documented in Frank L. Klingberg, *Cyclical Trends in American Foreign Policy Moods: The Unfolding of America's World Role* (Lanham, MD: University Press of America, 1983). Also see Stephen E. Ambrose and Douglas G. Brinkley, *Rise to Globalism: American Foreign Policy since 1938*, 8th ed. (New York: Penguin, 1997).
60. George Liska, *Imperial America: The International Politics of Primacy* (Baltimore: Johns Hopkins University Press, 1967) and *Career of Empire: America and Imperial Expansion Over Land and Sea* (Baltimore: Johns Hopkins University Press, 1978); Robert W. Tucker, *Nation or Empire? The Debate over American Foreign Policy* (Baltimore: Johns Hopkins University Press, 1966); Raymond Aaron, *The Imperial Republic: The United States and the World* (Cambridge, MA: Winthrop, 1974). Also important was Stanley Hoffmann, *Primacy or World Order: American Foreign Policy Since the Cold War* (New York: McGraw-Hill, 1978); Harry Magdoff, *The Age of Imperialism* (New York: Monthly Review Press, 1969); Gabriel Kolko, *The Roots of American Foreign Policy* (Boston: Beacon, 1969); William H. Blanchard, *Aggression American Style* (Santa Monica, CA: Goodyear Publishing Company, 1978); and Amaury de Riencourt, *The American Empire* (New York: Dell Publishing, 1968).
61. J. William Fulbright, *The Arrogance of Power* (New York: Vintage, 1966).
62. Hans J. Morgenthau, "The Intellectual, Political, and Moral Roots of U.S. Failure in Vietnam," in William D. Coplin and Charles W. Kegley, Jr., *A Multi-Method Introduction to International Politics* (Chicago: Markham, 1971), pp. 16–31. Also see his *A New Foreign Policy for the United States* (New York: Praeger, 1969).
63. For example, see Henry Brandon, *The Retreat of American Power* (New York: Doubleday, 1993).
64. Richard Rosecrance, *America as an Ordinary Country: U.S. Foreign Policy and the Future* (Ithaca, NY: Cornell University Press, 1976).
65. See, for example, Samuel P. Huntington, "The United States—Decline or Renewal?," *Foreign Affairs* 67 (Winter 1988–1989): 76–96; Bruce Russett, "The Mysterious Case of Vanishing Hegemony, or Is Mark Twain Really Dead?," *International Organization* 39 (Spring 1988): 207–232; and Henry R. Nau, *The Myth of America's Decline* (New York: Oxford University Press, 1990).
66. Stephen Peter Rosen, "An Empire, If You Can Keep It," *The National Interest* 71 (Spring 2003): 51. An example of this position can be found in Samuel P. Huntington's contention that "A world without U.S. primacy will be a world with more violence and disorder and less democracy and economic growth." See his "Why International Primacy Matters," *International Security* 17 (Spring 1993): 83.
67. James Kurth, "Migration and the Dynamics of Empire," *The National Interest* 71 (Spring 2003): 5.
68. Paul T. McCartney, "American Nationalism and U.S. Foreign Policy from September 11 to the Iraq War," *Political Science Quarterly* 119 (Fall 2004): 403. Also see Omar G. Encarnación, "The Follies of Democratic Imperialism," *World Policy Journal* 22 (Spring 2005): 47–60.
69. Walter A. McDougall, *Promised Land, Crusader State* (Boston: Houghton Mifflin, 1997), p. 221. On this characterization, see also Henri Lévy, *American Vertigo*,

translated by Charlotte Mandell (New York: Random House, 2006). Ironically, by acting as a supreme, self-appointed global judge, the United States seems to be deviating from its own Declaration of Independence, which stressed the importance of harboring "a decent respect for the opinions of humankind."

70. In Brian Urquhart, "World Order and Mr. Bush," *The New York Review of Books* 50 (October 9, 2003): 8.

71. Thusly summarized by Dana Villa, *Socratic Citizenship* (Princeton, NJ: Princeton University Press, 2001), p. 34. Also see Pratap Bhanu Mehta, "Empire and Moral Identity," *Ethics and International Affairs* 17 (No. 2, 2003): 49.

4

American Preponderance and Military Peril

We can generate more military power per square inch than anybody else on Earth, and everybody knows it.

—General John Abizaid,
Head of U.S. Central Command

The United States stands at the pinnacle of world power. It possesses overwhelming military might as well as unsurpassed national wealth and cultural influence. America thus would seem to be more secure than any great power in history. No challenger can even contemplate defeating the United States in a set-piece battle; America is invincible in conventional warfare.

Accompanying America's ascent to the summit of world power is the widely held myth that preeminent states in unipolar systems can attain national security singlehandedly, using military muscle to bend others to their will.[1] Cowed by American preponderance, allies purportedly would acquiesce to Washington's desires, adversaries would back away from confrontations, and previously nonaligned countries would partner with the United States for protection and profit.

Myths in the field of national security serve various purposes: they describe potential threats in clear, simplified terms; they prescribe how aggressive, menacing foes should be combated; they help rally domestic support for costly, protracted military campaigns; and they preserve public perceptions of national virtue during dire, tempestuous times. Of course, the difficulty with myths is that they are a complex mixture of fact and fantasy that distort reality in ways that may not be immediately evident. Psychologically comforting, they blur the differences between harsh international realities and idealized self-images.

Perhaps the greatest distortion in the mythology surrounding unipolar power lies in confusing invincibility with invulnerability. American military might, amassed to defend the country's territory and vital interests, may truly be unbeatable in conventional engagements; however, it elicits fear and resentment among the leaders of state and nonstate actors whose political ambitions clash with Washington's foreign policy goals. Concerned that this awesome power could be used against them, some of America's adversaries have sought nuclear weapons to deter the United States as well as to cripple it if deterrence fails; others, lacking fissile material, have adopted terrorist tactics to unnerve Americans at home as well as to contest their presence abroad. In short, Washington's unparalleled strength in ground, naval, and air forces has *not* led its adversaries to accommodate themselves to the American Imperium; instead, they have challenged the United States at the far ends of the conflict spectrum, countering America's conventional superiority with nuclear threats at one extreme and with irregular warfare at the other.

Contrary to the mythology regarding unipolar power, preponderance alone cannot guarantee U.S. national security. Overwhelming military might does not automatically provide protection against unconventional threats. The paradox of American security policy today is that the United States has become increasingly vulnerable at the very moment of its greatest strength. Tempting as it might be for the world's only superpower to rely on the military instruments of statecraft, the United States cannot afford to be seduced by the fantasy that the weak inevitably accede to the strong.[2] As one veteran observer of American defense policy concludes, running roughshod over others "will redound to the country's detriment." In a world where many people do not share America's benevolent self-image, U.S. leaders must be able to translate their enormous military capability into political influence that can be brought to bear when and where national security threats emerge. While the United States cannot shrink from using military force when its vital interests are at stake, America "must keep its powder dry."[3]

Security Risks and Policy Responses

America's vulnerabilities were starkly revealed by the September 11, 2001, terrorist attacks on Washington and New York. The difficulties in defending open, democratic societies against unconventional attacks were further underscored by the March 11, 2004, Madrid and July 7, 2005, London bombings. The openness of the United States gives freedom of movement to those planning such operations, allowing them to reconnoiter potential target sites and find their weaknesses. With 7,000 miles of land borders and some 95,000 miles of shoreline, there are ample opportunities for small, tenacious groups of conspirators to infiltrate the United States and unleash mayhem on American soil. "From water and food supplies; refineries, energy grids, and pipelines; bridges, tunnels, trains, trucks, and cargo containers; to the cyber backbone that underpins the information age," warns a student of U.S. homeland security, the measures Washington has been "cobbling together are hardly fit to deter amateur thieves, vandals, and hackers, never mind determined terrorists."[4] Historically protected by vast oceans and innocuous neighbors, America's traditional security concern has been vying with other great powers; since September 11, it has become warding off insidious enemies who use irregular forces and unconventional means to fight asymmetrical wars.

Nonstate Actors and Asymmetrical Warfare

The concept of "asymmetrical warfare" refers to organized violence conducted between political units of vastly unequal military capability, where each side practices different methods of fighting and follows different rules of engagement.[5] The ill-fated Scythian campaign of ancient Persia's King Darius, described in Chapter 2, exemplifies this form of warfare. The Scythians used stealth and surprise to frustrate a superior Persian army. Rather than engage Darius in the massive, climactic battle that he wanted, Scythian warriors used their mobility to strike when and where they had an advantage. Demoralized and exhausted, the Persians were eventually compelled to withdraw from Europe by an agile, determined adversary.

Belligerents in asymmetrical wars may be states, or they may involve some combination of state and nonstate actors. When Osama bin Laden, the son of a wealthy Saudi construction magnate, announced his 1996 "Declaration of War Against Americans Occupying the Land of the Two Holy Places" and issued a *fatwa* (religious ruling) two years later calling for Americans to be killed anywhere in the world, he laid the foundation for asymmetrical warfare between the United States and Al Qaeda (or "Base"), the shadowy network of terrorist cells and front organizations that seeks the destruction of Israel, the end of Western influence in the Muslim world, and the establishment of a fundamentalist, pan-Islamic Caliphate.

Al Qaeda's origins can be traced to the Afghan Service Bureau (*Maktab al-Khidmat*), an organization created by bin Laden and Abdullah Azzam to assist Muslims from across the globe who had been recruited during the 1980s to fight a holy war (*jihad*) against the Soviet occupation of Afghanistan. Following the Soviet withdrawal from Afghanistan in 1989, bin Laden formed Al Qaeda to wage an international jihad, using his inheritance (which may have been as much as $300 million) to fund training camps and provide logistical support for terrorist operations. He and core members of Al Qaeda briefly resided in Saudi Arabia (1989–1991) and Sudan (1991–1996), but ultimately returned to Afghanistan, where they were given refuge by the Taliban regime in exchange for financial support.

Over the past decade, Al Qaeda has conducted a series of attacks on U.S. citizens and facilities, including suicide truck bombings of the Khobar Towers military housing complex near Dharran, Saudi Arabia (1996), and the American embassies in Nairobi, Kenya, and Dar es Salaam, Tanzania (1998), as well as a suicide boat bombing of the *U.S.S. Cole* in Aden, Yemen (2000), and the suicide aircraft hijacking attacks on the World Trade Center and the Pentagon (2001).

Al Qaeda's spectacular attacks are part of a multipronged effort to compel the United States to disengage from Muslim land stretching from North Africa to South Asia. Without an American presence in the region, bin Laden and his followers believe that Israel and corrupt, spiritually bankrupt Arab regimes could be swept away. Islamic militants have traditionally emphasized rooting out apostates, heretics, and other internal enemies. Bin Laden has urged Muslims to suspend their intramural quarrels and concentrate on punishing the United States—the invidious infidel state he charges with responsibility for myriad problems within the Islamic community. "Tracking down the Americans and the Jews is not impossible," insists his top lieutenant, Ayman al Zawahiri. "With available means, small groups [of jihadists] could prove to be a frightening horror for the Americans and the Jews."[6]

Pointing to the withdrawal of U.S. military forces from Lebanon following the 1983 bombing of the Marine barracks in Beirut and their withdrawal from Somalia a decade later after losses sustained while fighting in Mogadishu, bin Laden sees terror as a proven instrument in waging asymmetrical warfare against the United States. Just as the mujahadeen evicted the Soviet Union from Afghanistan through a combination of resourcefulness, resolve, and unrelenting pressure, so too will a legion of holy warriors oust the United States from the realm of Islam. Every highly visible attack bin Laden engineers increases his prestige, and every major incidence of collateral damage from retaliatory strikes has the potential to add new recruits to his movement. "When people see a strong horse and a weak horse," bin Laden once quipped while explaining his strategy, "by nature they will like a strong horse."[7]

Loosely tied together by the Internet, e-mail, and cellular telephones, Al Qaeda's organizational structure originally resembled a hub-and-spoke organization: bin Laden and a small core of loyalists from the war against the Soviet Union provided strategic direction and aid to a franchise of affiliated terrorist cells.[8] Rather than serving as a commander, bin Laden functioned as a coordinator who, in addition to organizing dramatic, high-casualty attacks, solicited and supported proposals for other operations from like-minded Islamic militants.

Following the defeat of the Taliban regime by the American military and its partners in the Northern Alliance in Afghanistan, Al Qaeda underwent a structural change. Combined with the loss of a safe haven in Afghanistan, the killing or capture of roughly one third of Al Qaeda's leadership transformed the organization into an entity that resembled a chain. Bin Laden and his close associates continued offering ideological inspiration to small, disparate cells scattered around the world, but as the activities of Abu Mousab al-Zarqawi in Iraq exemplified before his death, they no longer are directly involved in the planning and execution of most of the armed attacks undertaken in the name of Al Qaeda. Operating independently, without the training, financing, and logistical infrastructure previously available through a central headquarters, Al Qaeda's diffuse underground cells have attacked "soft" targets, sometimes in conjunction with sympathetic local forces. The October 2002 nightclub bombing in Bali, Indonesia, the May 2003 suicide attacks in Casablanca, Morocco, the July 2005 resort bombings in Sharm el Sheikh, Egypt, and the November 2005 hotel bombings in Amman, Jordan, illustrate this new globalized pattern of activity. More worrisome, however, is the possibility the Al Qaeda will acquire weapons of mass destruction. In May 2003, bin Laden obtained a *fatwa* from the Saudi cleric Hamid bin Fahd that justifies the use of nuclear weapons against the United States, allegedly as a reciprocal response for Muslim deaths attributed to American military action.[9] "We have the right," asserts Al Qaeda member Suleiman Abu Gheith, "to kill 4 million Americans—2 million of them children—and to exile twice as many and wound and cripple hundreds of thousands."[10]

Threat Assessment and the Framing of National Security Decisions

As decision makers in Washington cast their eyes across the global landscape, their duty is to identify and extinguish smoldering anti-American hostilities before groups like Al Qaeda can ignite larger conflagrations. But decision makers are not clairvoyant. Even the most vigilant can misperceive emerging threats, as the differences that frequently arise among the assessments provided by national intelligence agencies indicate. Research in cognitive psychology reminds us that all people tend to view the world according to their prior expectations. Moreover, they give disproportionate weight to readily available evidence that confirms these expectations, they interpret ambiguous data in ways that support what they expect to see, and they ignore anything that is inconsistent with their most central beliefs.[11] Thus, how decision makers frame potential security problems affects the policy responses they ultimately adopt. Threats they expect, or can easily imagine, generally anchor these frames of reference. But when policymakers become wedded to a certain way of seeing the world, they accentuate some threats and overlook others.[12]

How have Al Qaeda's attacks and the wars in Afghanistan and Iraq framed American expectations about future security threats? To what extent are Washington's apprehensions about asymmetrical warfare warranted? Do they justify what historian Arthur Schlesinger, Jr. calls an "extraordinary reversal of the direction of American foreign policy,"[13] or are they an understandable overreaction to the trauma the country experienced over the past few years? Are these experiences such imprinting events that they will structure policy reactions long after the war in Iraq fades from the international scene? Indeed, will current fears become an obsession that diverts attention from other foreign policy challenges that will someday imperil America if they are not met?

To answer these questions, we shall look first at the traditional security threats that the United States has confronted. Then we shall examine what some commentators call the "new face of war"[14] and assess the unprecedented threat that transnational networks of fanatical adversaries pose to the American Imperium.

The Old Face of War

In a world undergoing constant change, a grim continuity stands out: organized armed conflict among human communities. According to one authoritative account, a total of 118 armed conflicts broke out in 80 locations during the period between the thawing of the Cold War in 1989 and 2004.[15] As shown in Figure 4.1, the vast majority were civil wars *within* countries. To put this pattern in perspective, compare it to the trends in civil, international, and major-power war over the century and a half prior to 1989, displayed in Figure 4.2. Whereas both international and civil wars occurred frequently between 1816 and 1989, civil wars have become far more prominent since the end of the Cold War. Counting only civil wars with more than 1,000 fatalities, approximately one country in eight is embroiled in internal civil strife.[16] Meanwhile, wars between major powers have disappeared over the past 50 years. These changes in where wars are fought, by whom, and the issues at stake are thought by some to mark a turning point in the evolution of warfare, which is fostering a "dramatic if not revolutionary change in how wars are conducted."[17]

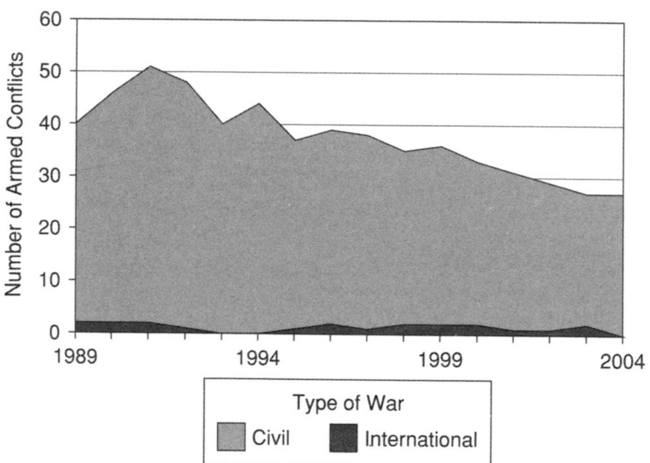

Figure 4.1 The Incidence of Civil and International Wars, 1989–2004 *Source: Lotta Harbom and Peter Wallensteen, "Armed Conflict and Its International Dimensions, 1946–2004,"* Journal of Peace Research *42 (September 2005): 624. A description of the data can be found in Håvard Strand, Joachim Carlson, Nils Petter Gleditsch, Håvard Hegre, Christin Ormhaug, and Lars Wilhelmsen, with Peter Wallensteen, Margareta Sollenberg, Mikael Eriksson, Lotta Harbom, and Halvard Buhaug and Jan Ketil Rød,* Armed Conflict Dataset Codebook, *version 3–2005, at http://www.prio.no/cscw/armed-conflict.*

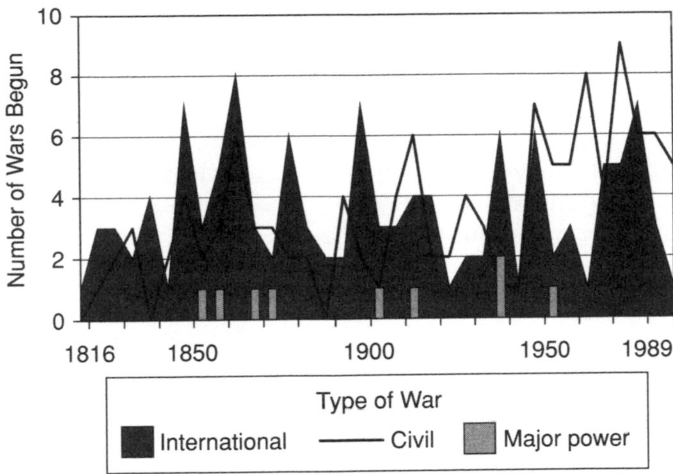

Figure 4.2 The Frequency of War, 1816–1989 *Source: Version 3.0 of the Correlates of War data set, as reported in Melvin Small and J. David Singer,* Resort to Arms: International and Civil Wars, 1816–1980 *(Beverly Hills, CA: Sage, 1982); and Meredith Reid Sarkees, "The Correlates of War Data on War: An Update to 1997,"* Conflict Management and Peace Science *18 (No. 2, 2000): 123–144. Data aggregated by half-decade.*

Three Generations of Modern Warfare

The conduct of war has undergone several "generational" changes since the Peace of Westphalia (1648) brought the Thirty Years' War to a close and gave birth to the modern state system.[18] A product of wrenching changes spawned by the cultural Renaissance and religious Reformation that swept through Europe in the twilight of the medieval era, the Thirty Years' War was one of history's watershed events. The peace treaties negotiated at the Westphalian cities of Münster and Osnabrück not only ended one of the most grisly periods in human experience, they transformed the organizing principles on which world politics was based, replacing the vertical order of supranational Church authority with a horizontal order of sovereign nation-states.[19] Although unequal in size and strength, hereafter all states were considered equal before international law in the sense that they possessed the same sovereign rights and duties. In addition to possessing exclusive jurisdiction over their respective territories, sovereignty meant that national governments could act as independent, autonomous agents in foreign affairs, negotiating treaties, forming alliances, and even waging war when perceived national interests seemed to justify military action.

In what has been called the "first generation of modern warfare," which extended from the Peace of Westphalia to the American Civil War, soldiers armed with smooth-bore muskets were normally deployed in tight linear formations to coordinate volleys from relatively inaccurate weapons. Once weapons with greater accuracy and rates of fire became available, formation battle on open ground lost its effectiveness. A comparison of the Napoleonic era (1799–1815) with the period immediately preceding the First World War illustrates the problem weapons modernization created for armies relying upon first-generation tactics. Whereas an infantry battalion in 1812 could project 2,000 musket balls to an effective range of 100 yards every minute, in 1912 a battalion armed with magazine rifles and four machine guns could project more than 21,000 rounds to an effective range of 1,000 yards within the same time frame. While a massed frontal assault during Napoleon's day would encounter muzzle-loading cannons that could deliver a 12-pound ball a distance of 1,000 yards every 30 seconds, attacking soldiers a century later would face breach-loading artillery capable of delivering 18-pound shells more than 12,000 yards every 10 seconds.[20] Advances in weapons technology thus made line-and-column tactics obsolete, which led to a new generation of tactics that emphasized massive firepower to annihilate fixed-fortification defenses.

The second generation of modern land warfare substituted massed artillery for massed infantry. During the First World War, machine guns, barbed wire, minefields, and entrenched defenses strung along continuous fronts stymied the precise, geometric lines of attack typical of early modern warfare.[21] In response, artillery barrages from the rear were used to breach fortified positions, allowing infantry units to overrun crippled defenses. "The artillery conquers, the infantry occupies," proclaimed a popular early twentieth-century French military slogan. Marshal Ferdinand Foch likened the strategy to a parrot climbing the bars in its cage, systematically using beak and claws in an alternating sequence of bite-and-hold moves.[22]

Although lengthy preparatory barrages could shatter fixed positions, they alerted the other side to where the subsequent infantry assault would occur. By extending defenses in greater depth and maintaining significant reserve forces, defenders could counterattack before advancing foot soldiers were able to break through. However, improvements in transportation and communication technology provided a way to deal with these tactics. Drawing upon their country's experience of combining suppressive fire with movement during the spring offenses of 1918, German officers like Heinz Guderian and Erich von Manstein envisioned a third generation of warfare that accentuated speed and surprise rather than firepower and attrition. Tracked-armored vehicles and tactical air power, they reasoned, enabled an attacker to concentrate mobile forces at a decisive point along the front, penetrate deep into enemy territory, and roll the opposition up from the rear in battles of encirclement.

In sum, three generations in the conduct of war evolved from the Peace of Westphalia through the end of the Cold War. The first emphasized linear troop formations; the second, massed firepower; and the third, combined arms and maneuver. Despite taking different approaches to the conduct of war, each generation assumed that a war's outcome hinged on battles fought by the militaries of sovereign, territorial states.

Fourth-Generation Warfare

Since the end of the Cold War, the threat of the United States being attacked by the conventional military forces of another nation-state has greatly receded.[23] Instead, a new form of warfare has emerged in which nation-states are pitted against sovereignty-free, nonterritorial actors in hostilities that lack front lines and clear distinctions between soldiers and civilians. In this so-called fourth generation in the evolution of modern war, the irregular forces of militant transnational organizations, often operating out of strife-ridden "failed states" and using unconventional tactics, pose the most immediate security threat to the United States. Unable to defeat U.S. troops on the field of battle, they focus instead on America's political will, using patience, ingenuity, and gruesome acts of violence to compel political leaders in Washington to weigh the mounting costs of continuing a long, drawn-out struggle with tactics that injure U.S. ideals.[24] As shown in Figure 4.3, the scope of the problem is enormous, with some 2 billion people living in 60 states at risk of collapse. Reflecting

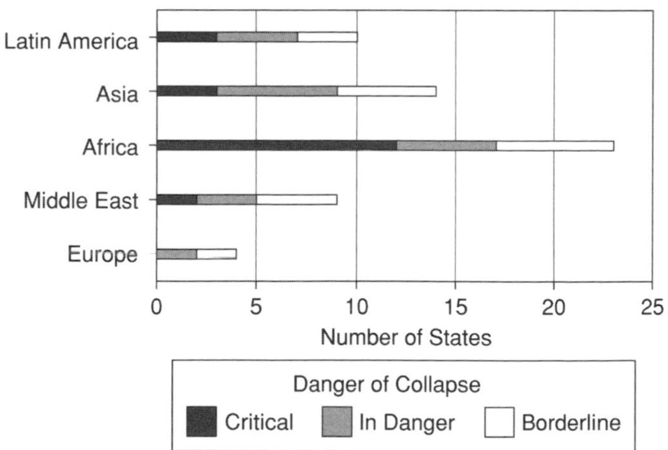

Figure 4.3 States on the Brink of Failure The index of at-risk states is based on a composite of 12 social, economic, political, and military indicators derived from data sources from 2004. For a discussion of these indicators, see http://www.fundforpeace.org. *Source: "Failed States Index,"* Foreign Policy *149 (July/August 2005): 59.*

on the acute crises that have erupted in Somalia, Haiti, Bosnia, Cambodia, and elsewhere since the end of the Cold War, Francis Fukuyama concludes that weak and failing states are now "the single most important problem for international order." Besides committing human rights abuses, provoking humanitarian disasters, driving massive waves of immigration, "they shelter international terrorists who can do significant damage to the United States and other developed countries."[25]

Defense establishments, it is often observed, generally "prepare for the problems that they prefer to solve, rather than those that a cunning enemy might pose."[26] Although some military leaders may see fourth-generation warfare as an annoyance that detracts from preparing for combat against other conventionally armed and professionally trained adversaries, determined enemies will not fight in ways that favor American military strengths.

Can the United States adapt to this strategic reality? Policymakers attempting to cope with unconventional security threats find it difficult to cast off old habits of mind, yet it is imperative that they do so. The new kind of wars on the horizon will be difficult to wage and to win. As the American experience with the Iraqi insurgency following the defeat of Saddam Hussein's regular army attests, they will be conducted against elusive adversaries who rely upon terrorist tactics to erode American morale, which they believe will eventually compel Washington to reduce its commitments abroad. Unlike the earlier generations of wars between the militaries of sovereign states, fourth-generation conflicts will involve protracted, low-intensity operations that yield piecemeal, localized victories. The evolution of warfare away from decisive, large-scale engagements should not be mistaken for the end of war. Low-intensity operations may target irregular combatants, but to quote General John Abizaid, "it's war however you describe it."[27]

The New Face of War

During the mid-1990s, two notorious individuals were apprehended, tried, and convicted for acts of political terrorism. The first, Ramírez Sánchez (alias Carlos the Jackal), epitomized a form of terrorism that was based on a secular agenda, a relatively hierarchical command structure, and a desire to have a lot of people watching, not a lot of people dead.[28] The second, Ramzi Ahmed Yousef, represented a form of terrorism based on a religious agenda, a more horizontal organizational structure, and a desire to kill as many people as possible. Their capture symbolized an important transition in terrorist strategy. Whereas the former was steeped in older paramilitary doctrines geared to expelling a colonial power or overthrowing an incumbent regime, the latter embodied newer ideas that suggest terrorist tactics were potent weapons in an asymmetrical struggle against the American Imperium.

The conventional view of terrorism as a rare and relatively remote threat to the United States was challenged by the events of September 11, 2001. In one horrific morning, those absent towers in New York became the symbol for the shapelessness of an apparent new world *dis*order. "The prospect of another attack," warned Vice-President Dick Cheney "is not a matter of if, but when."[29] "America is full of fear," proclaimed a jubilant Osama bin Laden. "Nobody in the United States will feel safe."[30]

"Night fell on a different world," lamented President George W. Bush in the aftermath of the September 11 attacks.[31] Terrorism was no longer a marginal menace in other countries to be watched on the evening news. The United States faced a relentless enemy that recognized no moral restraints and claimed to be poised to strike anyone, anywhere, anytime. Moreover, its tactics were "relatively inexpensive to conduct, and devilishly difficult to counter."[32] According to the president, 9/11 inaugurated the first war of the twenty-first century, a war that his administration estimated would cost as much as $160 billion annually to wage.

Defining the Terrorist Threat

Although political terrorism is one of the most widely discussed security problems of the early twenty-first century, a firm consensus has yet to materialize on its character, causes, and cure (see Table 4.1). Polemics and divergent interpretations abound. The phenomenon of terrorism, complains one frustrated legal scholar, is similar to pornography: "You know it when you see it, but it is impossible to come up with a universally-agreed-upon definition."[33] On the one hand, the term frequently is used as a shrill, pejorative label for one's enemies. On the other hand, explanations for why it occurs and how to control it are often based on clichés and anecdotes rather than on empirical evidence. Without a clear conception of the nature of the terrorist threat they hope to defeat, efforts by U.S. leaders to realize that ambitious goal are unlikely to succeed. According to a former senior U.S. intelligence officer, as long as discussions of political terrorism remain rife with impassioned rhetoric and crude impressionism, efforts to identify those committed to using terrorist tactics and attempts to understand their motives will suffer.[34]

Political terrorism entails the deliberate use or threat of violence against noncombatants, calculated to instill fear, alarm, and ultimately a feeling of helplessness in an audience beyond the immediate victims. Because the perpetrators of terrorism often strike symbolic targets in a horrific manner, the psychological impact of an attack can exceed the physical damage. The campaign of assassinations in Judea conducted by the Sicarii during the first century C.E. illustrates the atmosphere of collective vulnerability that can be created by terrorism. As Flavius Josephus wrote in *The Jewish War*: "The state of fear engendered was more distressing than the calamity itself. . . . [H]ourly each man expected death. People kept watch at a distance from their enemies and did not trust even an approaching friend."[35] Political terrorism is thus "defined by the nature of the act, not the identity of the perpetrators or the nature of the cause."[36] A mixture of drama and dread, terrorism is not senseless violence; it

Table 4.1 Disagreements Over the Nature of Political Terroism

IS TERRORISM AFTER 9/11 FUNDAMENTALLY DIFFERENT FROM ITS HISTORICAL PRECEDENTS?

Yes: "What we are up against is apocalyptic nihilism. The nihilism of [the terrorists'] means—the indifferences to human costs—take their actions not only out of the realm of politics, but even out of the realm of war itself. The apocalyptic nature of their goals makes it absurd to believe they are making political demands at all. [The terrorists who waged the 9/11 attacks were] seeking the violent transformation of an irremediably sinful and unjust world. [This new] terror does not express a politics, but a metaphysics, a desire to give ultimate meaning to time and history through ever-escalating acts of violence which culminate in a final battle between good and evil."

—Michael Ignatieff

No: "The looped footage of the collapse of the towers . . . take[s] on the feelings of déjà vu. . . . In my view 9/11 is a combination of new and old forms of conflict, including: the rhetoric of holy war from both sides; a virtual network war in the media and on the internet; a high-tech surveillance war overseas but also in our airports, our cities, and even our homes; and a dirty war of counter-terrorism and counter-insurgency, using an air campaign and limited special operations to kill the leadership and intimidate the supporters of al Qaeda and the Taliban."

—James Der Derian

ARE REVOLUTIONARY TERROR AND REGIME TERROR DIFFERENT?

Yes: "While all terrorism has a political purpose, it certainly is distinguishable—technically and morally—from civil dissidence. Terrorism remains distinguishable from legitimate methods of political struggle. . . . Unlike [state] armies which employ force against other armed parties, terrorists distinguish themselves by targeting civilians, the unarmed, and the innocent."

—Christopher C. Harmon

No: "Terrorism is not a philosophy or a movement. It is a method. . . . Terrorism is the systematic use of coercive intimidation, usually to service political ends. . . . Terrorism may be used in its own or as part of a wider unconventional war. It can be employed by desperate minorities, by states as a tool of domestic and foreign policy, or by belligerents as an accompaniment . . . in all types and stages of warfare."

—Paul Wilkinson

IS STATE SUPPORT A COMPONENT OF GLOBAL TERRORISM?

Yes: "We are not going to cripple terrorists completely by depriving them of state support, but the sanctuary states provide is very important. Extirpating state support will reduce [terrorism], which is the best we can do."

—Richard Perle

No: "We will . . . still have a major terrorism problem for decades even if we sharply reduce state support. . . . If we end state sanctuary, three-quarters of the task will be left for the long haul."

—Joseph S. Nye

IS VIOLENCE A NECESSARY ELEMENT OF TERRORISM?

Yes: "All terrorist acts involve violence or the threat of violence. . . . We may therefore define terrorism as the creation and exploitation of fear through violence or the threat of violence in pursuit of political change."

—Bruce Hoffman

No: "Terror . . . does not necessarily include violence; just as some violence involves no terror, some terror (e.g. intimidation) requires no violence."

—Alexander Dallin and G. W. Breslauer

springs from a premeditated, coldly calculated strategy of extortion that attempts to present people with a danger that seems ubiquitous, unavoidable, and unpredictable.

Terrorism can be employed to support or change the political status quo. Repressive terror, also known as establishment or state terror, is wielded by governments as well as by vigilantes to sustain an existing political order. From the Committee of General Security in Jacobin France to the so-called "death squads" operating in some Latin American countries in recent decades, repressive terror seeks to strengthen established governments by eliminating political opponents and intimidating virtually everyone else.

Dissident terror, which seeks to change the status quo, has been employed for a wide array of purposes. Some groups, like the MPLA (Popular Movement for the Liberation of Angola), used terrorism to expel colonial rulers; others, such as ETA (Euzkadi Ta Askatasuna, or Basque Homeland and Liberty), adopted terrorism as part of an ethnonational separatist struggle; still others, including the Islamic Jihad, the Christian Identity Movement, the Sikh group Babbar Khalsa, and Jewish militants belonging to Kach, placed terror in the service of what they saw as religious imperatives; finally, groups such as the Japanese Red Army and the Italian Black Order turned to terrorism for left- or right-wing ideological reasons. In short, dissident terror may be grounded in anticolonialism, separatism, religion, or secular ideology.

The Objectives of Terrorism

Although the ultimate goals of dissidents who use terrorism differ, they seek similar intermediate objectives as a means of attaining their goals. The *agitational objectives* of terrorism include promoting the dissident group, advertizing its agenda, and discrediting rivals. Shocking behavior makes people take heed, especially when performed at a time and place imbued with symbolism. Nineteenth-century anarchists like Johan Most and Pyotr Kropotkin were among the first to emphasize the propaganda value of terrorism. A single stunning act, they believed, would draw more attention than a thousand leaflets.

Once groups win notoriety and have their cause widely acknowledged, they can exert leverage over established authorities. The primary *coercive objectives* of terrorism include disorienting a target population, inflating the perceived power of the dissident group, wringing concessions from authorities, and provoking a heavy-handed overreaction from the police and military. Launching vicious, indiscriminate attacks at markets, cafes, resorts, and other normally tranquil locations can create a paralyzing sense of foreboding within the general public. Anything, it seems, can happen to anyone at any time. As doubts about the ability of the government to protect innocent civilians spread, civil society becomes atomized. Communal life gives way to isolated, demoralized individuals who feel exposed to arbitrary, capricious dangers. Believing they are alone, people easily exaggerate the strengths of terrorists. At first, political leaders may give in to terrorist demands. But once the demands escalate, the government may respond with brutal oppression, which the terrorists hope will drive the population to their side of the struggle.

The *organizational objectives* of terrorism include acquiring resources, forging group cohesion, and maintaining an underground network of supporters. Although terrorist groups are not all alike, they face common problems stemming from their need for secrecy. To guard against infiltration, they are usually compartmentalized into small, clandestine cells. Command and control within such decentralized structures are difficult; however, terrorism can fortify these groups in several ways. First, it can finance training and logistical support for field operations when used to rob banks, obtain ransom for hostages, and collect protection money from businesses. Second, it can elevate morale, particularly when employed to win the release of imprisoned group members. Third, since high initiation costs tend to lower group defections, it can increase allegiance when recruits are required to participate in violent acts. Finally, terrorism can enforce obedience when used to punish anyone who collaborates with the enemy.

The Evolution of Terrorism

Although the roots of political terrorism can be traced back to the Sicarii and Zealot uprising in 6 C.E. against Roman rule in Palestine, modern dissident terrorism originated in the nineteenth century and has evolved over time in motives and tactics. Daggers, poisons, and pistols were terrorism's primary weapons until the invention of dynamite in 1867. More stable than nitroglycerin and requiring smaller amounts than black powder, dynamite seemed to be the answer to the German radical Karl Heinzen's call for an instrument by which a few militants could destroy thousands of reactionaries.[37]

Over the next century and a half, terrorist tactics changed in response to new technologies and new targets of opportunity. The most common tactics involved bombing with blast and fragmentation devices, though assaults, hijacking, and kidnaping were used as well. In most cases, the perpetrators engaged in selective, discriminate acts of violence. During the 1990s, however, various observers noticed the emergence of a new trend, which Bruce Hoffman suggested would mean "nothing less than a sea-change in our thinking about terrorism and the policies required to counter it. . . ."[38] Extremists motivated by religious convictions were initiating undiscriminating, mass-casualty attacks.

What makes these groups more lethal then their older, secular counterparts is their propensity to conceptualize acts of terror on two levels. At one level, terrorism is a means to change the political status quo by punishing those countries and corporations believed culpable for felt wrongs. At another level, terrorism is an end in itself, a sacrament performed for its own sake in an eschatological confrontation between good and evil.[39] Functioning only on the first level, most secular terrorist groups tend not to mount suicide campaigns.[40] Operating on both levels, religious and millenarian terrorist groups see worldly gain as well as transcendent importance in a martyr's death. As a result, groups like Hezbollah in Lebanon and Hamas in Palestine have not shied away from suicide attacks. Ramadan Shalah of the Palestinian Jihad is reported to have explained the military logic of suicide missions in asymmetrical wars in the following way: "Our enemy possesses the most sophisticated weapons in the world and its army is trained to a very high standard. . . . We have nothing with which to repel killing and thuggery against us except the weapon of martyrdom. It is easy and it costs us only our lives . . . human bombs cannot be defeated."[41]

For the United States, the acquisition of WMDs by religious fanatics or extremists with an apocalyptic world view would present the greatest security threat. Nuclear armaments are the ultimate terror weapons. Their blast, thermal, and ionizing radiation effects are catastrophic, even if produced by small atomic demolition munitions in the form of "suitcase" bombs. Consider the impact of a 10-kiloton nuclear bomb detonated in the heart of New York City:

> The blast would generate temperatures reaching the tens of millions of degrees Fahrenheit. The resulting fireball and blast wave would destroy instantaneously the theater district, the New York Times building, Grand Central Terminal, and every other structure within a third of a mile of the point of detonation. The ensuing firestorm would engulf Rockefeller Center, Carnegie Hall, the Empire State Building, and Madison Square Garden, leaving a landscape resembling the World Trade Center site. From the United Nations headquarters on the East River and the Lincoln Tunnel under the Hudson River, to the Metropolitan Museum in the eighties and the Flatiron Building in the twenties, structures would remind one of the Alfred P. Murrah Federal Building following the Oklahoma City bombing.
>
> On a normal workday, more than half a million people crowd the area within a half-mile radius of Times Square. A noon detonation in midtown Manhattan could kill them all. Hundreds of thousands of others would die from collapsing buildings, fire, and fallout in the ensuing hours. The electromagnetic pulse generated by the blast would fry cell phones, radios, and other electronic communications. Hospitals, doctors, and emergency services would be overwhelmed by the wounded. Firefighters would be battling an uncontrolled ring of fires for many days thereafter.[42]

The long-term consequences of such an attack would be equally staggering.

> The financial and cultural center of the United States would cease to exist. The metropolitan area would be uninhabitable, living only in the nation's imagination and in aerial footage of the blast zone. America's GDP would fall by 3 percent immediately, and one of its major ports would be closed indefinitely. A successful attack would embolden our enemies and weaken our society. Americans would lose confidence in their social and political institutions. The potential for a breakdown in public order would necessitate the suspension of civil liberties. People would clamor for a major retaliatory strike—but against whom? Populations would desert major urban areas. The vast number of wounded and traumatized people from the New York region, and the shattered national sense of physical security would precipitate an unprecedented and long-lasting public health crisis.[43]

Of course, terrorists who possessed a nuclear weapon could choose a different target. They might select Washington, Chicago, Los Angeles, or any other American city. Besides devastating everything within a one and one-half mile radius of the epicenter, the blast would stun the entire nation. Dreading the possibility that additional weapons might have been smuggled into other metropolitan areas, the residents of many urban neighborhoods would panic. Coping with the aftermath of a nuclear terrorist attack would place an unimaginable strain on the country's disaster relief infrastructure. Given the inept response of the Federal Emergency Management Agency (FEMA) to the destruction and chaos wreaked by Hurricane Katrina (a disaster for which there was prior warning), one can only wonder how Washington would react when taken by surprise.

While most people fear nuclear terrorism, they often forget that radiological, chemical, and biological weapons pose extraordinary dangers. Crude radiological dispersion devices (RDDs) can be fabricated by combining ordinary explosives with nuclear waste or radioactive isotopes, which can be stolen from hospitals, industrial facilities, or research laboratories. Rudimentary chemical weapons can be made from herbicides, pesticides, and other toxic substances that are available commercially. Primitive biological weapons based on foodborne pathogens are also easy to concoct. Weapons based on viral agents are more difficult to produce, although the dispersal of anthrax spores through the mail during the fall of 2001 illustrated that low-technology attacks with bacterial agents in powder form are a frightening possibility.

Beyond the dangers posed by weapons of mass destruction, cyberterrorism presents yet another threat to the United States. Not only can the Internet be used by extremists as a recruiting tool and as a means of coordinating their activities with like-minded groups, but it allows them to "case" potential targets by hacking into a foe's computer system. Viruses and other weapons of "information warfare" would cause havoc if they disabled financial institutions, power grids, air traffic control systems, or other key elements within any country's communication infrastructure, but the mayhem would be enormous in digital America. Disrupting vital streams of data flowing between and within highly interdependent societies offers extremist groups an attractive, inexpensive way to besiege their more powerful enemies.

In summary, the type of warfare confronting the American Imperium for the foreseeable future will pit powerful, conventional units of the U.S. military against fluid, loosely structured irregular forces that come in swarms. Operatives from the dispersed nodes of terrorist networks will converge stealthily on a target, and then rapidly disperse after their attack.[44] These attacks will be difficult to contain because the new face of war is:

- *Global,* in the sense that national borders no longer serve as barriers to terrorism
- *Lethal,* because now terrorists have shifted their tactics from theatrical violence aimed at gaining publicity to the destruction of civilian targets in order to kill as many people as possible

- *Novel,* in terms of the sheer size, destructiveness, and professionally coordinated planning involved
- *Sophisticated,* employing some of the most advanced technology available
- *Networked,* involving unprecedented levels of communication and coordination among terrorist cells located in many countries
- *Fanatical,* pursued by extremists driven by hatred who are willing to sacrifice their own lives in suicide attacks, which are extremely difficult to deter or prevent
- *Diffuse,* in the sense that these attacks can be orchestrated from different locations and do not emanate from the territory of a single country

These conditions require a new strategic compass to guide the United States through an unfamiliar strategic landscape, one that has prompted the United States to experiment with new approaches for dealing with global terrorism. As Paul Wilkinson has lamented: "Fighting terrorism is like being a goalkeeper. You can make a hundred brilliant saves but the only shot that people remember is the one that gets past you."[45]

The New Global Terrorism and U.S. Foreign Policy

American political leaders are understandably obsessed by the fear that a catastrophic terrorist attack will again strike the homeland. The danger has been painted in stark terms, which made the Bush administration's linkage of Saddam Hussein with 9/11 seem compelling to many Americans, despite an absence of supporting evidence. Toppling Iraq's Baathist regime proved relatively easy, but as Secretary of Defense Donald Rumsfeld admitted, securing the country would be "a long, hard slog." Asked when America's worldwide battle against terrorism might be over by a U.S. soldier who inquired if he should get his three-year-old ready for air assault school, Rumsfeld candidly replied: "I wish I could give you a date, but I can't. That would be like estimating when a town will no longer need firefighters or police."[46]

To put the terrorist threat faced by the United States into historical perspective, consider the trends in terrorist episodes over the past few decades (see Figure 4.4). Since the U.S. Department of State's Office of the Coordinator for Counterterrorism began to keep statistics in 1968, the frequency in terrorist activity has displayed wide variation from one year to the next, with the lowest incidence (174) in 1968 and the highest (665) in 1987, after which the level gradually but erratically declined, until 2004, when the new National Counter Terrorism Center (NCTC) was given responsibility by the White House for counting the number of international terrorist incidents. To the administration's chagrin, its claim that the war on global terrorism was being won did not look convincing, since the number climbed in 2004 to 655 incidents.[47]

In addition to the upswing in frequency, terrorism is also growing in lethality, as the death toll in 2004 was near the highs in 1995, 1989, and 2001, when

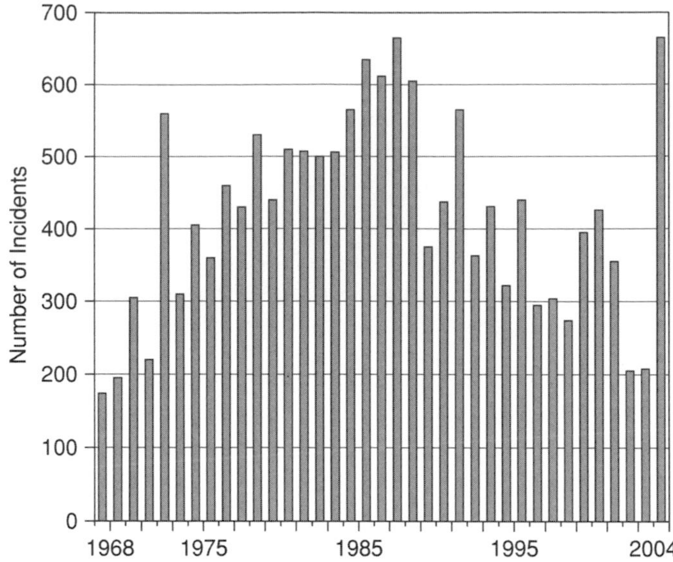

Figure 4.4 The Incidence of International Terrorism, 1968–2004 The data are based on conceptualizing terrorism as "premeditated, politically motivated violence perpetrated against noncombatant targets by subnational groups or clandestine agents," where noncombatants are defined as "civilians [and] military personnel (whether or not armed or on duty) who are not deployed in a war zone or a war-like setting." *Source: United States Department of State, Office of the Coordinator for Counterterrorism,* Country Reports on Terrorism 2004 *(Washington, DC: U.S. Department of State, 2005), p. 1, and National Counter-Terrorism Center (NCTC) at www.the_counterterrorism_blog.*

the number of people killed by terrorists rose exponentially. The mounting waves of terrorist suicide bombing in Iraq and Afghanistan in mid-July 2005 cast doubt on the success of the U.S. military occupation of those countries. "The war is helping, not hurting, the terrorists," Paul Krugman lamented. "Before the war, opponents warned that it could strengthen, not weaken, terrorism. And so it has: a C.I.A. report warns that since the U.S. invasion Iraq has become what Afghanistan was under Soviet occupation, only more so: a magnet and training ground for Islamic extremists, who will eventually threaten other countries."[48]

The issue that confronts American policymakers is that, regardless of the number of victims, global terrorist actions always exert a powerful symbolic impact, which commands heightened public attention every time a major attack occurs, elevated by the seeming lack of effective countermeasures. As Secretary of State Colin Powell lamented six days after 9/11: "I was raised a soldier and you are trained: There is the enemy occupying a piece of ground. We can define it in time, space and other dimensions, and you can assemble forces and go after it. This is different."[49]

A key difference lies in the likelihood that America's psychological trauma will not vanish, even if the number of terrorist acts declines. The death toll of U.S. soldiers and Iraqi civilians at the hands of elusive suicide bombers and fanatical insurgents suggests that America's awesome conventional military might is not currently configured to fight asymmetrical, fourth-generation wars. Preponderant power is not reducing global terrorism. Even though wars between states have radically declined, civil wars within failing states continue to be a major problem for the international community, creating breeding grounds and training sites for a new generation of terrorists. Unless the United States can harness *both* soft and hard power to meet the menace posed by ruthless nonstate actors like Al Qaeda, its security policies are likely to create difficult new problems, making the future one of increasing peril.

To what purposes is the United States putting its uncontested military strength? How is America wielding its unipolar power? Is that awesome capability being exercised wisely? Or is the new code of conduct that the United States has embraced creating a dangerous precedent for others to follow in the wake of the Iraq War? What would be the consequences if other states adopt policies similar to those pursued by the United States? In the next chapter we will address these questions by analyzing the security policies that the Bush administration formulated after the September 11 terrorist attacks on New York and Washington.

Notes

1. Nancy Soderberg, *The Superpower Myth: The Use and Misuse of American Might* (New York: John Wiley, 2005); Robert Jay Lifton, *The Superpower Syndrome* (New York: Basic Books, 2003), pp. 187–188; Ronald Steel, *Temptations of a Superpower* (Cambridge, MA: Harvard University Press, 1995).
2. One of the earliest expressions of this myth can be found in the ancient fable of the hawk and the nightingale. "Why scream?" asked the hawk, after he had snatched the nightingale in his talons. "Your master has you. You shall go wherever I take you. . . . He is a fool who tries to match his strength with the stronger. He will lose his battle, and with shame will be hurt also." Hesiod, *The Works and Days*, translated by Richmond Lattimore (Ann Arbor: University of Michigan Press, 1959), p. 43.
3. Robert J. Art, *A Grand Strategy for America* (Ithaca, NY: Cornell University Press, 2003), p. 11.
4. Stephen Flynn, *America the Vulnerable: How Our Government Is Failing to Protect Us from Terrorism* (New York: HarperCollins, 2004), p. 2. To illustrate the problems involved in securing America's borders, Flynn points out that in 2002, "over 400 million people, 122 million cars, eleven million trucks, 2.4 million rail freight cars, approximately eight million maritime containers, and 59,995 vessels entered the United States at more than 3,700 terminals and 301 ports of entry" (p. 12). In addition, at least 11 million illegal migrants are currently estimated to be living in the United States, with some 10,000 entering the country monthly.

5. Roger W. Barnett, *Asymmetrical Warfare: Today's Challenge to U.S. Military Power* (Washington, DC: Brassey's, 2003), pp. 17–18. Also see Lloyd Matthews, ed., *Challenging the United States Symmetrically and Asymmetrically: Can America Be Defeated?* (Carlisle Barracks, PA: Strategic Studies Institute, U.S. Army War College, 1998); T. V. Paul, *Asymmetric Conflicts: War Initiation by Weaker Powers* (Cambridge: Cambridge University Press, 1994).
6. Ayman al Zawahiri, "Knights Under the Prophet's Banner," in Walter Laqueur, ed., *Voices of Terror* (New York: Reed Press, 2004), p. 432.
7. Cited in Michael Hirsh, "Bush and the World," Foreign Affairs Editors' Choice, in *The War on Terror* (New York: Council on Foreign Relations, 2002), p. 175.
8. For descriptions of Al Qaeda's structure, see Marc Sageman, *Understanding Terror Networks* (Philadelphia: University of Pennsylvania Press, 2004); Rohan Gunaratna, *Inside al Qaeda: Global Network of Terror* (New York: Columbia University Press, 2002); and Simon Reeve, *The New Jackals: Ramzi Yousef, Osama Bin Laden and the Future of Terrorism* (Boston: Northeastern University Press, 1999).
9. Mia Bloom, *Dying to Kill: The Allure of Suicide Terror* (New York: Columbia University Press, 2005), p. 173. See also Robert A. Pape, *Dying to Win: The Strategic Logic of Suicide Terror* (New York: Random House, 2005).
10. Cited in Graham T. Allison, *Nuclear Terrorism: The Ultimate Preventable Catastrophe* (New York: Times Books, 2004), p. 12.
11. The classic work in this area is Leon Festinger, *A Theory of Cognitive Dissonance* (Evanston, IL: Row, Peterson, 1957). Also see Jon Hurwitz and Mark Peffley, "How Are Foreign Policy Attitudes Structured?" *American Political Science Review* 81 (December 1987): 1099–1120.
12. Robert Jervis, *Perception and Misperception in International Politics* (Princeton, NJ: Princeton University Press, 1976), pp. 187–191. Other significant literature on decision-making biases includes Philip E. Tetlock, *Expert Political Judgment: How Good Is It? How Can We Know?* (Princeton, NJ: Princeton University Press, 2005); Richard Nisbett and Lee Ross, *Human Inferences: Strategies and Shortcomings of Social Judgment* (Englewood Cliffs, NJ: Prentice-Hall, 1980); and the following summary articles by Amos Tversky and Daniel Kahneman: "The Framing of Decisions and the Psychology of Choice," *Science* 211 (January 30, 1981): 453–458, and "Judgment Under Uncertainty: Heuristics and Biases," *Science* 185 (September 27, 1974): 1124–1131.
13. Arthur Schlesinger, Jr., "Eyeless in Iraq," *New York Review of Books* 50 (October 9, 2003): 25.
14. See Bruce Berkowitz, *The New Face of War: How War Will Be Fought in the 21st Century* (New York: Free Press, 2003); also see Nicolaus Mills and Kira Brunner, eds., *The New Killing Fields* (New York: Basic Books, 2003), and Mary Kaldor, *New and Old Wars: Organized Violence in a Global Era* (Cambridge, MA: Polity Press, 1999).
15. Lotta Harbom and Peter Wallensteen, "Armed Conflict and Its International Dimensions, 1946–2004," *Journal of Peace Research* 42 (September 2005): 623. Although different procedures for measuring organized, armed conflict produce somewhat different totals, they all depict high levels of global violence over the past half century. See the Stockholm International Peace Research's annual, *SIPRI Yearbook 2005* (New York: Oxford University Press, 2005) and previous *SIPRI Yearbooks*

for methodological discussions of issues related to the measurement of the frequency of armed conflict.

16. "The Global Menace of Local Strife," *The Economist* (May 26, 2003): 23. See also Ann Hironaka, *Neverending Wars: The International Community, Weak States, and the Perpetuation of Civil War* (Cambridge, MA: Harvard University Press, 2005).
17. Jack S. Levy, Thomas C. Walker, and Martin S. Edwards, "Continuity and Change in the Evolution of Warfare," in Zeev Maoz and Azar Gat, eds., *War in a Changing World* (Ann Arbor: University of Michigan Press, 2001), p. 15.
18. William S. Lind, Keith Knightengale, John F. Schmitt, Joseph W. Sutton, and Gary I. Wilson, "The Changing Face of War: Into the Fourth Generation," *Marine Corps Gazette* 73 (October 1989): 22–26.
19. For an analysis of the international normative order engendered by the Thirty Years' War and Peace of Westphalia, see Charles W. Kegley, Jr. and Gregory A. Raymond, *Exorcising the Ghost of Westphalia: Building World Order in the New Millennium* (Upper Saddle River, NJ: Prentice-Hall, 2002).
20. Stephen Biddle, "Land Warfare: Theory and Practice," in John Baylis, James Wirtz, Eliot Cohen, and Colin S. Gray, eds., *Strategy in the Contemporary World* (Oxford: Oxford University Press, 2002), p. 94.
21. Two revealing examples of the geometric conceptualization of military strategy that underpinned first-generation warfare can be found in Adam Heinrich Dietrich von Buelow's *Geist des neuern Kriegssystems*, originally published in 1799, and Antoine-Henri Jomini's *Précis de l'art de la guerre*, which appeared 39 years later. See J. D. Hittle, ed., *Jomini and His Summary of the Art of War* (Harrisburg, PA: Military Service Publishing Company, 1947).
22. Cited in Stefan T. Possony and Etienne Mantoux, "Du Picq and Foch: The French School," in Edward Mead Earle, ed., *Makers of Modern Strategy* (Princeton, NJ: Princeton University Press, 1943), pp. 231–232.
23. Human Security Center, the University of British Columbia; for trend data, see James Traub, "Wonderful World? Since the Cold War, the Earth Has Become More Peaceful: Why Doesn't It Feel That Way?" *New York Times Magazine* (March 19, 2006): 13–14.
24. Thomas X. Hammes, *The Sling and the Stone: On War in the 21st Century* (St. Paul, MN: Zenith Press, 2004), pp. 207–224.
25. Francis Fukuyama, *State-Building: Governance and World Order in the 21st Century* (Ithaca, NY: Cornell University Press, 2004), pp. 92–93.
26. Colin S. Gray, "How Has War Changed Since the End of the Cold War?" Paper prepared for the Global Trends 2020 Project of the U.S. National Intelligence Council (May 2004): 2. Reassessing standard ways of problem solving is difficult, especially for large organizations like defense establishments. Miyamoto Musashi's 17th-century treatise *A Book of Five Rings* is a classic statement on the importance of constantly adjusting military strategy to the novel threats posed by new adversaries. Rather than relying on what worked against previous opponents, he argued for taking a fresh approach that responds to the circumstances of the moment. See Miyamato Musashi, *A Book of Five Rings: The Classic Guide to Strategy*, translated by Victor Harris (Woodstock, NY: Overlook Press, 1974).

27. Cited in *The State* (Columbia, SC), July 20, 2003, p. D3. Even small victories by irregular forces in a limited geographic theater, argues one critic of American foreign policy, can have a powerful demonstration effect that ultimately weakens the U.S. position elsewhere. Walden Bello, *Dilemmas of Domination: The Unmaking of the American Empire* (New York: Metropolitan Books, 2005), p. 76.
28. Brian M. Jenkins, "International Terrorism: The Other World War," in Charles W. Kegley, Jr., ed., *The New Global Terrorism: Characteristics, Causes, Controls* (Upper Saddle River, NJ: Prentice-Hall, 2003), pp. 20–23.
29. Cheney warned, "If we make the wrong choice, then the danger is that we'll get hit again and we'll be hit in a way that will be devastating." Comments by Vice President Dick Cheney in Des Moines, Iowa, on September 7, 2004, retrieved at http://www.whitehouse.gov/news/releases/2004/09/20040907-8.html. This may be hyperbole, but the fear is widely shared; two of every three Americans surveyed in March 2006 reported that they believed the United States would suffer a "major terrorist attack" by March 2007. *Harper's* (May 2006): 19.
30. Videotaped statement broadcast on al-Jazeera television (Qatar), retrieved at http://www.cnn.com/2001/WORLD/asiapcf/central/10/07/bin.laden.statement.
31. Address to a joint session of Congress on September 20, 2001, retrieved at http://www.whitehouse.gov/news/releases/2001/09/20010920=8.html.
32. L. Paul Bremer, III, "A New Strategy for the New Face of Terrorism," *The National Interest* 65-S (Special Issue, Thanksgiving 2001): 25.
33. Christopher C. Joyner, "In Search of an Anti-Terrorism Policy," *Terrorism: An International Journal* 2 (No. 1, 1988): 30. Indeed, more than 100 contending definitions can be found in the literature on terrorism. Alex P. Schmid, *Political Terrorism* (Amsterdam: North Holland Publishing Co., 1983), pp. 119–158. For discussions of the difficulties of achieving a widely accepted definition of political terrorism, see Alex P. Schmid, "Frameworks for Conceptualizing Terrorism," *Terrorism and Political Violence* 16 (Summer 2004): 197–221; and Peter C. Sederberg, *Terrorist Myths: Illusion, Rhetoric, and Reality* (Englewood Cliffs, NJ: Prentice-Hall, 1989), pp. 25–40.
34. See Anonymous [Michael Scheuer], *Through Our Enemies' Eyes: Osama bin Laden, Radical Islam, and the Future of America* (Washington, DC: Brassey's, 2003).
35. Nahum N. Glatzer, ed., *Jerusalem and Rome: The Writings of Josephus* (New York: Meridian, 1960), p. 159. According to one source, whereas the Sicarii (named after a short dagger, or *sica)* generally targeted Jews who collaborated with the Romans, several Zealot organizations (named after the zeal or righteous rage exemplified by Phineas, a High Priest during the Exodus) focused their attacks on Roman legionnaires and functionaries. See David C. Rapoport, "Fear and Trembling: Terror in Three Religious Traditions," *American Political Science Review* 78 (September 1984): 658–677.
36. Bruce Hoffman, "Terrorism Trends and Prospects," in Ian O. Lesser et al., *Countering the New Terrorism* (Santa Monica, CA: RAND, 1999), p. 11n.
37. See Karl Heinzen, "Murder," in Walter Laqueur, ed., *The Terrorism Reader* (New York: Meridian, 1978), p. 59.
38. Bruce Hoffman, *Inside Terrorism* (New York: Columbia University Press, 1998), p. 212. Also see Walter Laqueur, *The New Terrorism* (Oxford: Oxford University Press, 1999); Jessica Stern, *The Ultimate Terrorists* (Cambridge, MA: Harvard University

Press, 1999); and Harvey W. Kushner, ed., *The Future of Terrorism* (Thousand Oaks, CA: Sage, 1998).

39. Mark Juergensmeyer, *Terror in the Mind of God: The Rise of Religious Violence* (Berkeley: University of California Press, 2000), pp. 145–163; Jessica Stern, *Terror in the Name of God: Why Religious Militants Kill* (New York: HarperCollins, 2003), pp. 281–283. Interestingly, many jihadists do not fit Western stereotypes about fundamentalism. Educated, multilingual, and from middle or upper-middle class backgrounds, young Islamic radicals often are a product of the globalized world they violently oppose. Oliver Roy, *Globalized Islam: The Search for a New Ummah* (New York: Columbia University Press, 2004).
40. The Liberation Tigers of Eelam in Sri Lanka and the Kurdistan Workers Party (PKK) in Turkey are examples of secular groups that have participated in suicide terror campaigns.
41. Cited in Ehud Sprinzak, "Rational Fanatics," *Foreign Policy* 120 (September/October 2000): 68. Based on an analysis of 315 suicide terrorist attacks since 1980, Pape concludes that groups such as Al Qaeda, Hamas, and Hezbollah believe not only that their conventional inferiority necessitates suicide attacks, but that the United States is vulnerable to coercive punishment allegedly because, like all democratic governments, it has a low threshold for accepting casualties. Suicide terrorism, he concludes, "is a strategy for national liberation from foreign military occupation by a democratic state." Robert Pape, *Dying to Win: The Strategic Logic of Suicide Terrorism* (New York: Random House, 2005), p. 45.
42. Graham T. Allison, *Nuclear Terrorism* (New York: Times Books, 2004), pp. 3–4.
43. Daniel Benjamin and Steven Simon, *The Age of Sacred Terror* (New York: Random House, 2002), pp. 398–399.
44. For an elaboration on this form of conflict, see John Arquilla and David Ronfeldt, *The Advent of Netwar* (Santa Monica, CA: RAND, 1996).
45. Cited in Pamala L. Griset and Sue Mahan, *Terrorism in Perspective* (Thousand Oaks, CA: Sage, 2003), p. 191. Because "it takes just *one* well-timed and publicized incident to put terrorism back in the public eye, terrorists can reverse all perceptions of counterterrorist progress with a single attack." Jeffrey D. Simon, *The Terrorist Trap: America's Experience with Terrorism*, 2nd ed. (Bloomington: Indiana University Press, 2001), p. 24.
46. Matt Kelly, "Pentagon Digs in for Long War on Terror," *The State* (Columbia, SC) (October 26, 2003): A9. "I worry about being excessively optimistic," Rumsfeld confessed on March 29, 2005. "Insurgencies tend to go on five, six, eight, 10, 12 years," he later added. *The New York Times* (July 3, 2005): 12.
47. Data retrieved at http://www.counterterror.typepad.com/the_counterterrorism_blog, April 14, 2004; and Jonathan S. Landay, "Number of Attacks in 2004 is Record, Data Show," *The State* (Columbia, SC), April 27, 2005, p. A4. According to Alan Krueger and David Laitin, the decline through 2003 was a result of the State Department combining significant (loss of life, serious injury, or major property damage) and nonsignificant attacks. When only significant attacks are counted, terrorist activity increased eightfold over the past two decades. Andrew Mack, *Human Security Report: War and Peace in the 21st Century* (New York: Oxford University Press, 2005), pp. 42–43. Also see Anne Sabastenski, ed., *Patterns of Global Terrorism, 1985–2004* (Great Barrington, MA: Berkshire, 2005).

48. Paul Krugman, "America Held Hostage," *The State* (Columbia, SC), July 1, 2005, p. A19. A recent content analysis of Islamist internet sites reveals that the war in Iraq has not only given extremists greater focus, but it has also fostered more sophisticated strategic thinking about their perceived enemies and how they can be defeated. See Thomas Hegghammer, "Global Jihadism: After the Iraq War," *Middle East Journal* 60 (Winter 2006): 11–32.

49. *USA Today* (September 17, 2001): p. 2. The intractable problem of terrorist violence, and the proposition that the Bush administration's post–9/11 policies have inadvertently led to an increase of international terrorism, is advanced by Daniel Benjamin and Stephan Simon, *The Next Attack: The Failure of the War on Terror and a Strategy for Getting It Right* (New York: Henry Holt, 2005). On the thesis that the U.S. military's capability has been reduced by preparations to wage yesterday's wars, see Robert D. Kaplan, *Imperial Grunts: The American Military on the Ground* (New York: Random House, 2006).

5

The Changing Purposes of American Military Power

Detached reflection cannot be demanded in the presence of an uplifted knife.

—Oliver Wendell Holmes

In the immediate aftermath of the September 11, 2001, attacks on the World Trade Center and the Pentagon, demands for revenge reverberated across the United States. Essayist Lance Morrow gave voice to the nation's fury when he advocated a foreign policy of fierce and relentless retaliation against Osama bin Laden's Al Qaeda terrorist network. "Let's have rage," he thundered. "Enemies are enemies. You find them and put them out of business."[1]

Cries for vengeance were not surprising. Anger often follows in the wake of moral outrage. The vocabulary we use when discussing how to deal with perpetrators of grievous offenses is permeated with metaphors about debt ("repaying a wrong") and balance ("getting even") that underscore the central place of retribution in our conceptions of justice. What was surprising, however, was the Bush administration's abrupt shift from a national security strategy based on deterring enemies through the threat of retaliation to one that emphasized preemptive military action. As Secretary of Defense Donald Rumsfeld put it: "This isn't punishment. We've got the wrong models in our minds if we're thinking about punishment."[2] For Rumsfeld and other key members of the Bush administration, the aim was not to deter future attacks by vowing retribution; it was striking a menace *before* it was fully formed, even if the United States had to act unilaterally.

The Bush Doctrine

During his first campaign for the presidency, George W. Bush promised that if elected, he would be "very careful" when committing U.S. troops abroad; his administration would "refuse the crown of empire" and avoid using the military in nation-building operations. "If we're an arrogant nation," he asserted while debating Vice President Al Gore, "they'll resent us. If we're a humble nation but strong, they'll welcome us." According to candidate Bush, "one way for us to end up being viewed as the ugly American is for us to go around the world saying, 'We do it this way, so should you.'"[3]

The events of 9/11 radically altered Bush's worldview. Gone were exhortations on the need to be humble with power. The United States had to extinguish a new kind of security threat, the newly elected president told the country. "We have found our mission." Americans did not yet have the distance of history from Al Qaeda's deadly attacks, he said. "But our responsibility to history is already clear: to answer these attacks and rid the world of evil."[4]

President George W. Bush first sketched the contours of his administration's new national security strategy during his commencement address at West Point on June 1, 2002. "We face a threat with no precedent," he told the graduates. On the one hand, modern technology allows shadowy terrorist networks to launch catastrophic attacks against the United States. On the other hand, these networks cannot be deterred by traditional military means because they have no fixed territory or populace to defend. "We must take the battle to the enemy," he exhorted, "and confront the worst threats before they emerge." After urging Americans to be "forward-looking and resolute," Bush concluded by calling upon them "to be ready for preemptive action."[5]

Washington's current embrace of military preemption has roots in the strategic debates of the 1980s. At that time, America's primary concern was a nuclear attack by the Soviet Union. Hawks like Richard Perle, Donald Rumsfeld, and Richard Armitage urged President Ronald Reagan to jettison the "passive" policy of mutual assured destruction (MAD) in favor of a more assertive nuclear utilization strategy (NUTS), which would prevent the Soviets from striking the United States by destroying their weapons before they could be launched. Whereas deterrence under MAD hinged on a credible threat of punishment, NUTS would replace retaliation with damage denial, that is, by taking preemptive action upon learning that an enemy attack would soon commence.[6]

Paralleling the controversy over the possible role of preemption in American nuclear doctrine was a debate over how it might be used in responding to threats at the lower end of the conflict spectrum. In a January 1986 address at the National Defense University, Secretary of State George Shultz proclaimed America's legal right to be proactive in its use of military force against states that supported, trained, or harbored terrorists. Similar sentiments were expressed by other members of the Reagan administration, including National Security Advisor Robert "Bud" McFarlane in a speech to the National Strategy Information Center on March 25, 1985, and Ambassador Vernon Walters in a report to the United Nations on April 15, 1986. All of these officials saw overt and covert preemptive attacks as an effective way to suppress terrorist activity. In effect, they had accepted an old Talmudic injunction: "If someone comes to kill you, rise and kill him first."

Even after the end of the Cold War, preemption remained part of the national security discourse in Washington. During the administration of George H. W. Bush, for example, then-Secretary of Defense Cheney's *Defense Planning Guidance* document linked preemption to the problem of nuclear proliferation, asserting that the United States must be prepared to use force to deal with the spread of weapons of mass destruction and should be "postured to act independently when collective action cannot be orchestrated."[7]

The strategy of military preemption was revived after September 11, when administration officials began worrying that terrorist organizations with global reach might obtain WMDs and use them against the United States. As shown in Figure 5.1, the threats of great-power nuclear and conventional attacks were perceived as remote. In contrast, the threats of terrorist strikes and limited conventional wars with lesser powers were seen as more probable, with terrorist attacks using nuclear, biological, or chemical weapons posing calamitous risks.

The call for acting preemptively against terrorists and the rogue states that harbored them was underscored in President Bush's September 17, 2002, report, *The National Security Strategy of the United States of America* (NSS). Building on the proposition that "nations need not suffer an attack before they can lawfully take action to defend themselves against forces that present an imminent danger,"[8] the report argued that the acquisition of WMDs by terrorists with global

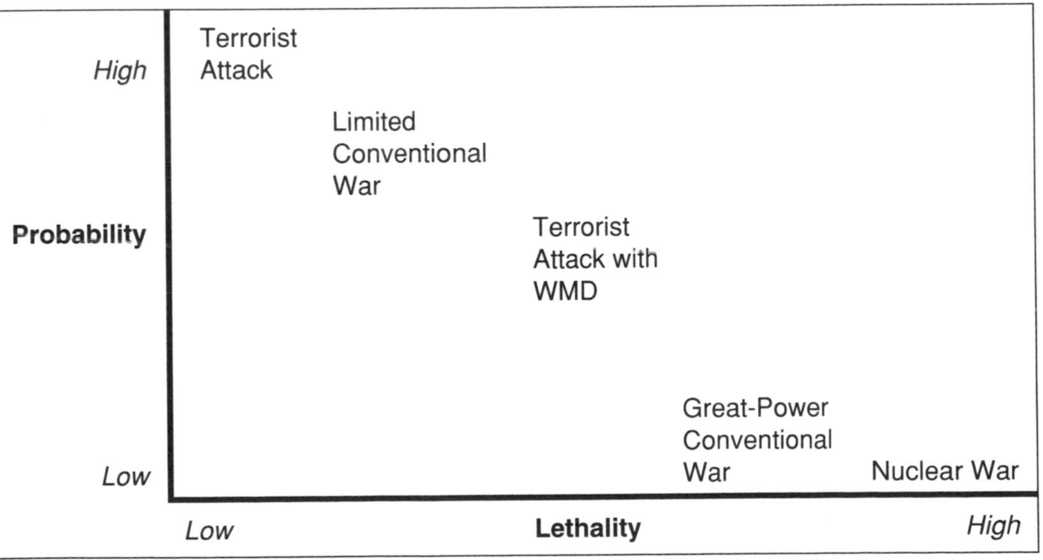

Figure 5.1 The Bush Administration's Perceptions of the Security Threats Facing the United States

reach provided the United States with a compelling case for engaging in anticipatory self-defense, even if it was not clear when and where an enemy might attack. It was a theme that the president returned to frequently in subsequent weeks when talking about Saddam Hussein. Speaking in Cincinnati on October 7, 2002, for example, he warned that grave dangers were gathering in Iraq. "We have every reason to assume the worst, and we have an urgent duty to prevent the worst from happening." Something had to be done to stop Hussein from acquiring and using WMDs and sharing them with groups like Al Qaeda. Regime change was imperative, and preemption was the mechanism for removing the Iraqi leader from office. America, Bush insisted, must be assertive; it "cannot wait for the final proof—the smoking gun—that could come in the form of a mushroom cloud."[9]

By avowing that the United States could not wait for UN inspectors to find a "smoking gun," Bush was laying the groundwork for a fundamental change in U.S. policy governing the use of force. The president was not "reserving a right" to counter imminent threats, noted one observer.[10] He was "seeking an extension of the right of self-defense to include action against potential future dangers." As Secretary of State Colin Powell explained: "If you recognize a clear and present threat that is undeterrable by the means you have at hand, then you must deal with it. You do not wait for it to strike; you do not allow future attacks to happen before you take action." Waiting for dangers to fully materialize is waiting too long. A security policy that accepts the legitimacy of anticipatory self-defense instills anxiety in one's adversaries, suggested Powell. It "increases the likelihood that they will cease activity or make mistakes and be caught."[11]

In summary, through a series of speeches, interviews, and publications over the months following the September 11 attacks, the president and his foreign policy advisors sketched a new security strategy that has since been called the "Bush Doctrine." Although there is some disagreement as to what it entails, the doctrine is generally thought to rest on the following propositions:

1. Political extremists with potential access to weapons of mass destruction present a unique, ominous, and undeterrable threat to American security
2. The United States draws no distinction between the extremists who use terrorist tactics and the failing and rogue states that harbor and back them
3. By changing the regimes in failing and rogue states, the United States can significantly decrease the support given to transnational terrorist networks
4. The United States has the legal right on the grounds of anticipatory self-defense to take "preemptive" action against these networks and their accomplices; and
5. Because the United States may have to act unilaterally when it engages in "preemption", it will keep its military strength beyond challenge.

The essence of the Bush Doctrine was not to eliminate prevailing normative limits on the use of force; instead, the doctrine "tried to carve out an exception" for America's behavior."[12] As one of the architects of the Bush NSS attests: "The world is a messy place, and someone has to clean it up."[13]

The Logic of Anticipatory Self-Defense

Self-defense is one of the "fundamental principles" of international law.[14] Since the earliest days of the modern state system, legal authorities have characterized it as a "natural right," one that every sovereign political entity possesses in order to preserve itself in the rough and tumble anarchy of world politics.[15] In a classic statement of this point of view, natural law theorist Samuel von Pufendorf advised political leaders that "no other obligation ought to outweigh . . . [a state's] own safety."[16]

Although states have a widely recognized right to defend themselves against aggression, legal scholarship has not reached a consensus on when that right may be invoked. Traditionally, the right of self-defense has been understood as allowing states recourse to force when repelling actual as well as imminent armed attacks. As expressed by U.S. Secretary of State Daniel Webster in the 1837 *Caroline* incident, to exercise this right a state must face an "instant, overwhelming necessity . . . leaving no choice of means, and no moment for deliberation."[17] In addition, the defensive reaction must be proportionate to the danger, should not sacrifice others to minimize one's own risk, and cannot serve as a reprisal. Self-defense is thus restricted to protection, not excessive or punitive measures aimed at redressing injuries.

Following the promulgation of the United Nations Charter, appeals to this customary right of self-defense became more controversial. The Charter addresses self-defense in two places. First, Article 2(4) stipulates that "all members shall refrain in their international relations from the threat or use of force against the territorial integrity or political independence of any State, or in any other manner inconsistent with the purposes of the United Nations."[18] Second, Article 51 states that "Nothing in the present Charter shall impair the inherent right of individual or collective self-defense if an armed attack occurs against a Member of the United Nations, until the Security Council has taken the measures necessary to maintain international peace and security." One school of thought about the Charter interprets Articles 2(4) and 51 as superseding customary law, and thus limiting forcible self-defense to cases where the Security Council has not yet responded to an armed attack. A second school of thought disagrees. Highlighting the concept of "inherent right" in Article 51, it argues that pre-Charter, customary rules of self-defense continue in place. Some support for the second school can be found in the *travaux préparatoires* of the Charter[19] and in the position taken by the International Court of Justice in the *Nicaragua* case. "Article 51 of the Charter is only meaningful on the basis that there is a 'natural' or 'inherent' right of self-defense and it is hard to see how this can be other than of a customary nature," reasoned the

Court. "It cannot, therefore, be held that Article 51 is a provision which 'subsumes and supervenes' customary international law."

The language of the Charter, concludes legal scholar Anthony Clark Arend, "admits to two interpretations about the permissibility of preemptive force."[20] International practice, however, is unambiguous: states regularly claim an independent right to use military force in an anticipatory manner, and their claims tend to be accepted as long as the criteria of necessity, proportionality, and protection are met. Where they encounter difficulties is justifying when a situation rises to the level of what Webster called an "overwhelming necessity."

Throughout the ages, statesmen have tried to justify various kinds of foreign policy undertakings by appealing to the exigencies of necessity. Indeed, the concept of necessity is so "deeply rooted in the consciousness of the members of the international community" that judge Robert Ago of the International Court of Justice once joked that if it was "driven out of the door it would return through the window."[21] The rhetorical strategy behind these appeals is to frame situations of limited options as situations where no alternatives exist. However, the dictates of necessity do not provide clear, objective criteria for determining how a state should act in a particular situation. National leaders rarely have one unavoidable course of action at their disposal. When leaders resort to the argument from necessity, they are generally using it to bolster a personal preference grounded in expediency. Rather than following an absolute strategic imperative that makes it practically impossible to do anything else, they are attempting to buttress a policy option that they believe is more advantageous than any other alternative.

Although appeals to necessity have been used by unscrupulous leaders "as a pretext for committing all sorts of unconscionable acts,"[22] when clear, convincing evidence exists of an attack being mounted, the international community generally accepts that the victim need not wait until the perpetrators have crossed the border.[23] But what if an attack is foreseeable rather than imminent? Are preemptive actions a military necessity when, in the words of the Bush NSS, "uncertainty remains as to the time and place of the enemy's attack?" In the absence of incontrovertible proof that an armed attack is imminent, can forcible measures be justified legally in order to prevent a state from acquiring the means of launching an attack sometime in the more distant future? At what point does the language of preemption simply mask a more radical policy of prevention?

From Preemption to Prevention

The concepts of preemptive and preventive motivations for war are used by people in many different ways.[24] For our purposes, a *preemptive* military attack entails the use of force to quell or mitigate an impending strike by an adversary. A *preventive* military attack entails the use of force to eliminate any possible future strike, even when there is no reason to believe that aggression is planned or the capability to launch such an attack is operational. Whereas the grounds for preemption lie in evidence of a credible, imminent threat, the basis for prevention rests on charges of an incipient, contingent threat.[25]

To illustrate the differences between military actions grounded in preemptive versus preventive motivations, let us briefly compare two historical cases. The Six Day War between Israel and an alliance of Egypt, Syria, Jordan, and Iraq was a classic case of preemption. Tensions between Israel and its Arab neighbors had been growing throughout the spring of 1967 and reached their zenith in May, when Egyptian President Gamal Abdel Nasser undertook a series of actions that raised fears in Tel Aviv of an imminent attack. Besides mobilizing his troops and cementing military ties with Syria, Jordan, and Iraq, Nasser ordered the UN Emergency Force to leave the Sinai, where they had been deployed since the 1956 Suez War as a buffer between Egypt and Israel. Furthermore, he announced a blockade of the Straits of Tiran, Israel's vital waterway to the Red Sea and Indian Ocean, and proclaimed that his goal in any future war with Israel would be the destruction of the Jewish state. Assuming that an invasion was forthcoming and survival was doubtful if the other side landed the first blow, the Israelis launched a surprise attack on June 5, which enabled them to win a decisive victory.

Whereas the Six Day War exemplifies preemption, the Third Punic War between Rome and Carthage (149–146 B.C.E.) illustrates preventive warfare. Although reduced to the status of a minor power by losses to the Romans in two previous wars, Carthage had undergone an economic resurgence during the first half of the second century B.C.E., which led some Roman leaders to worry about its future ambitions. Consumed with the fear that Carthage would regain its former strength and eventually threaten Rome, Marcus Porcius Cato ended every speech to the Roman Senate by proclaiming: "Carthage must be destroyed!"[26] Heeding his advice, Rome annihilated Carthage in a brutal, unprovoked military campaign. In contrast to the Israelis, who saw an immediate Egyptian threat in 1967, the Romans attacked on the outside chance that someday Carthage might become a threat. Israeli preemption involved striking a clear and present danger when the cost of inaction would have been devastating. Roman prevention entailed fighting a winnable war straightaway in order to avoid the risk of clashing under less favorable circumstances later.

The Preemptive Pretext for Preventive War

On May 29, 2002, former U.S. Secretary of State George P. Shultz delivered an address at the National Foreign Affairs Training Center in Arlington, Virginia. Reiterating an argument that he had made following the 1983 bombing of the American Marine barracks at the Beirut airport, Shultz called for the United States to adopt a policy of preemption. Declaring that effective counterterrorist policies were "not a matter of law enforcement," he insisted that

U.S. leaders should "prevent acts of terror through intelligence that enables [American forces] to preempt and ultimately eliminate" terrorists with global reach. "We have a war to win," he exclaimed. "Every tool available must be used aggressively."[27]

Shultz's speech was warmly received by Vice President Dick Cheney, who remarked that it was Shultz at "his wisest and best."[28] Having made similar recommendations, Cheney appreciated Shultz's proactive approach to dealing with nameless, faceless enemies who seemed able to strike almost anywhere at any time. In effect, the two men were reiterating the advice that Cardinal Richelieu had once given King Louis XIII of France: nothing, the cardinal impressed upon the king, is more valuable than foresight. "Just as a doctor who knows how to prevent illness is more esteemed than one who works cures, so too . . . it is more important to anticipate the future than to dwell upon the present, since with the enemies of the state, as with diseases, it is better to advance to the attack than to wait and drive them out after they have invaded."[29] Vigilance is crucial, since it allows national leaders to forestall security problems that can only be remedied with great difficulty afterwards.

The temptation to attack an adversary who may attack sometime in the future is often overwhelming. "An ounce of prevention is worth a pound of cure," so a popular cliché advises. "Better to be rid at once of someone who does not yet threaten you," quipped the protagonist in Umberto Eco's *Baudolino*, "than leave him alive so that he may threaten you one day."[30] Indeed, some historians see anxiety over increasing strategic vulnerability as an important variable in explaining the frequency of war in an anarchical, self-help state system.[31] It is "the right of every sovereign state to protect itself by preventing a condition of affairs in which it will be too late to protect itself," counseled former U.S. Secretary of State Elihu Root.[32]

While we acknowledge that military preemption is justifiable whenever an attack is truly impending, what is problematic with the Bush administration's new security strategy is its framing of preventive military action as preemption. Needless to say, the 2003 decision by President Bush to launch a preventive war against Saddam Hussein's Iraq under the guise of preemption has antecedents in political rhetoric. In fact, it is hard to find many cases of states that did not claim that in initiating war they were merely acting in anticipatory self-defense. Yet preventive strikes couched in the idiom of preemption do not always yield positive long-term results. To illustrate this point, let us consider two noteworthy examples.

One of the most frequently cited cases of preventive motivations for military action is Japan's December 7, 1941, surprise attack on Pearl Harbor. Designed to weaken the United States before it could someday turn its superior military capabilities against Japan, the attack destroyed most of the U.S. Pacific fleet and thereby shifted the Japanese–American balance of power, at least in the short run. But preventive military action hardly proved practical in the long run, awakening America from its isolationism and dedicating it to winning Tokyo's unconditional surrender.

Another commonly cited case of preventive military action can be found in Israel's June 1981 raid on the Osiraq nuclear reactor in Iraq. The type of reactor Baghdad acquired, its purchase of fuel that could be used in weapons manufacturing, and the termination of inspections by the International Atomic Energy Agency provided strong circumstantial evidence that Iraq was seeking a military nuclear capability.[33] Given the vehement hostility expressed by Iraqi leaders towards Israel, as well as the vulnerability of Israel's population centers and nuclear arsenal to a first strike, the Israelis concluded that Saddam Hussein could not be deterred; Iraq's reactor had to be destroyed before it became operational.[34] Although Israeli Prime Minister Menachem Begin regarded Osiraq as a threat to Israel's survival, the rest of the world condemned the raid as an act of aggression. The Reagan administration criticized the strike, France pronounced it unacceptable, and Great Britain denounced it as a grave breach of international law. While some observers claim that the attack worked, others remained skeptical, arguing that it "is hard to determine in fact whether the strike against Osiraq retarded Iraq's nuclear program or spurred it."[35]

Our purpose in highlighting these two examples is to suggest that serious problems can be created by preventive wars. Among other things, they may strengthen the determination of the target state and elicit international condemnation. Drawbacks such as these raise questions about building a national security strategy on a foundation of preventive military action. Moreover, some scholars contend that such a strategy would represent a significant departure from American diplomatic tradition. For instance, Richard F. Grimmett of the U.S. Congressional Research Service maintains that prior to the war in Iraq, the United States had never engaged in this type of action against another nation. Nor had "the United States ever attacked another nation militarily prior to its first having been attacked or prior to U.S. citizens or interests first having been attacked, with the singular exception of the Spanish-American War. . . . In all of [the] varied instances of the use of military force by the United States, such military action was a 'response,' after the fact."[36] While other scholars disagree, pointing to Andrew Jackson's invasion of Spanish Florida in 1818, Woodrow Wilson's occupation of Haiti in 1915, and Ronald Reagan's invasion of Grenada in 1983, most concur that no American leader prior to President Bush has so explicitly elevated the practice of preventive military action from an implicit policy option to a declaratory doctrine.[37]

It is certain that the advantages and disadvantages of preventive war will continue to generate heated debate. This is illustrated by the rhetoric from the White House on the need to keep "all options open" to prevent Iran from developing nuclear weapons. Aside from concerns that Tehran might use those weapons against Israel or some other state, many fear that a fledgling nuclear arsenal might encourage Iran's leaders to adopt a bolder, more aggressive foreign policy, thus triggering efforts by surrounding states to acquire their own nuclear weapons. For understandable reasons, these fears heightened tensions with the United States. Furthermore, in some Washington circles, they spawned discussions about preventive military strikes against Iranian nuclear facilities.

Hints of this possibility surfaced when the 2006 *National Security Strategy* labeled Iran the most serious challenge to the United States, and when journalist Seymour Hersh reported that the Bush administration had drawn up plans for attacking Iran and that U.S. military personnel had entered the country covertly to gather targeting data on its widely dispersed and hardened nuclear sites. According to Hersh, the administration was even considering the use of bunker-buster tactical nuclear weapons, like the B61-11, to eliminate Iran's underground laboratories and centrifuge plant at Natanz.[38]

The obstacles to a successful first strike are many, however. To begin with, Iran could retaliate by disrupting the supply of oil from the Persian Gulf. During their spring 2006 war games, for example, the Iranians unveiled a naval vessel that they said is undetectable by radar and capable of launching a high-speed torpedo, apparently based on the Russian VA-111 Shkval. They also claimed to have successfully tested the Fajir-3, a missile that allegedly can carry multiple warheads. Regardless of whether these new weapons possess the capabilities that the Iranians describe, Iran's military poses a credible threat against Persian Gulf petroleum facilities and tankers. According to some estimates, closure of the Strait of Hormuz for several months could result in a 4–5 percent decrease in America's gross domestic product.

Further complicating matters would be the difficulty of garnering support for a preventive war against Iran. Given the painful American experience in Iraq, it would be hard for the president to rally domestic public opinion and secure international backing for a military campaign. While it remains uncertain whether such an attack could do anything more than delay Iran's nuclear progress, it would ignite a firestorm of condemnation. As a result of the war in Iraq, the United States is less able to flex its military muscles in Iran. A first strike could easily backfire, strengthening support for the Ahmadinejad government and inviting a wave of terrorist reprisals against the United States and its interests worldwide. In the light of these short-run difficulties and long-term risks, the United States is less well positioned than before the Iraq war to undertake preventive military action.

Caveat Preemptor

On September 11, 1941, President Franklin Roosevelt delivered one of his renowned fireside chats to the nation. Nazi submarines had recently attacked the U.S. destroyer *Greer* off the coast of Greenland. The attack was not a localized incident, he noted. It was part of a larger pattern of aggressive German behavior in the North Atlantic. Calling upon Americans to be far-sighted and recognize that now was the time for the United States to take preventive action, Roosevelt explained that "when you see a rattlesnake poised to strike, you do not wait until he has struck before you crush him."[39]

According to President George W. Bush, terrorist networks and the states that support them constitute an evil that also must be crushed by preventive military action. Because Al Qaeda, its associated groups, and states such as Iran and North Korea are pictured as ruthless adversaries bent on aggression, he has described U.S. resistance to evil as America's mission. The "war on terror is not a figure of speech," he insists, "it is an inescapable calling."[40] But as legal scholar April Morgan points out, "identifying someone as evil tends to forestall the possibility of redemption."[41] Viewing world politics in Manichaean terms as a cosmic battle between the forces of light and darkness greatly simplifies questions of national strategy. If all of your enemies are perceived as wicked beyond reform, there is no point in differentiating among them to identify which ones are truly incorrigible. Since they are all evil, they must be destroyed. Preventive war, from this perspective, is a moral obligation, an ineluctable duty.

Yet even some people who supported the war in Iraq worry that "[a]ny doctrine that allowed states to use force to prevent merely the potential development of a threat would wreak havoc on international security."[42] Nevertheless, the president remains committed to preventive military action. As expressed in the February 2006 *Quadrennial Defense Review Report*, the Bush administration believes that it is critically important for the United States to increase its "freedom of action" in order to take "early, preventive measures" against irregular and catastrophic security challenges."[43] "We do not rule out the use of force before attacks occur," declares the March 2006 *National Security Strategy of the United States*. America "cannot afford to stand idly by as grave dangers materialize."[44]

The aftereffect of a national security policy that embraces preventive military action will be felt for decades, long after U.S. military occupation forces depart from Iraq. The decisions made after 9/11 are certain to cast a long shadow. Even now, as noted, they have stretched American military forces thin, reducing the U.S. capacity to deal with new dangers such as a nuclear-armed Iran and a threatening North Korea. The question is thus raised: Is America stronger, or weaker, as a result of its new strategic doctrine? Has American security increased, or decreased? After Iraq, how will the American Imperium fare?

The Bush administration's shift from a security strategy based on containment and deterrence to one anchored in preventive warfare thus raises anew timeless moral and legal issues about the conditions under which, and the purposes for which, anticipatory self-defense is permissible to counter potential threats to national and international security. What are the obligations of the powerful? How should they behave in asymmetrical conflicts? Does strategic necessity absolve them from observing prevailing normative limits on the use of military force? Or, do preventive-war strategies run the risk of casting those who use them as aggressors? What will be the likely long-term effects of initiating a preventive war in Iraq? What does the new U.S. security strategy portend about how the rest of the world will perceive America and how it will respond to future efforts by Washington to exert global leadership? It is to these questions that we turn in the next chapter.

Notes

1. Lance Morrow, "The Case for Rage and Retribution," *Time* (September 2001, Special Issue): 48.
2. Seymour M. Hersh, "Manhunt: The Bush Administration's New Strategy in the War Against Terrorism," *The New Yorker* (December 23 & 30, 2002): 70. According to Rumsfeld, anyone who called for "perfect evidence" to justify preemptive military action was "back in the 20th century and still thinking in pre-9/11 terms." Cited in John Newhouse, *Imperial America: The Bush Assault on the World Order* (New York: Alfred A. Knopf, 2003), p. 47.
3. Quotations from the 2000 campaign taken from the following sources: November 19, 1999, speech at the Ronald Reagan Presidential Library, cited in Stefan Halper and Jonathan Clarke, *America Alone: The Neo-Conservatives and the Global Order* (Cambridge: Cambridge University Press, 2004), p. 133; Presidential Debate I, October 3, 2000, retrieved at http://www.c-span.org/campaign2000/transcript/debate.100300.asp; and Presidential Debate II, October 11, 2000, retrieved at http://www.c-span.org/campaign2000/transcript/debate.101100.asp.
4. Cited in Gary Hart, *The Fourth Power: A Grand Strategy for the United States in the Twenty-First Century* (Oxford: Oxford University Press, 2004), p. 133. Bush later expanded the mission to include promoting democracy abroad, even though democratization, humanitarian intervention, and human rights "became more of an after-the-fact justification only when it turned out that there were no WMD or prewar links to international terrorism," argues Kenneth Roth, executive director of Human Rights Watch. *Time* (March 27, 2006): 31. In his second inaugural address he proclaimed: "It is the policy of the United States to seek and support the growth of democratic movements and institutions in every nation and culture, with the ultimate goal of ending tyranny in our world." Critics, however, point out that "[m]ilitary interventions have sometimes installed democracies by force, but they have more often failed, and the successes have been immensely expensive in lives and treasure." Bruce Russett, "Bushwhacking the Democratic Peace," *International Studies Perspectives* 6 (November 2005): 405. Interestingly, many of the so-called "realists" who had worked in the administration of Bush's father criticized efforts to democratize other countries through military intervention. See Jeffrey Goldberg, "Breaking Ranks: What Turned Brent Scowcroft Against the Bush Administration?" *The New Yorker* (October 31, 2005): 52–65.
5. Speech delivered by President George W. Bush at West Point on June 1, 2002, retrieved at http://whitehouse.gov/news/releases/2002/06/print/20020601-3.html.
6. See Spurgeon M. Keeny, Jr., and Wolfgang K. H. Panofsky, "MAD Versus NUTS: Can Doctrine or Weaponry Remedy the Mutual Hostage Relationship of the Superpowers?" *Foreign Affairs* 60 (Winter 1981/1982): 287–304.
7. S. R. Weisman, "Iraq War Entrenches Policy of Pre-Emption," *New York Times* (March 23, 2003): B5.
8. *The National Security Strategy of the United States of America* (Washington, DC: The White House, September 17, 2002), p. 15.
9. Speech delivered by President George W. Bush in Cincinnati on October 7, 2002, retrieved at http://www.whitehouse.gov/news/releases/2002/10/print/20021007-8.html. In his support of the president's position on being proactive, former Deputy

Secretary of Defense Paul Wolfowitz noted: "There is a constant bias toward inaction, because the risks are less obvious. But you must also consider the costs of inaction." Quoted in Mark Bowden, "Wolfowitz: The Exit Interviews," *The Atlantic* 296 (July/August 2005): 120.

10. Michael Byers, "Jumping the Gun," *London Review of Books* (July 25, 2002): 5.
11. Colin L. Powell, "A Strategy of Partnerships," *Foreign Affairs* 83 (January/February 2004): 24. Because they assume the threat of military preemption will intimidate terrorists, some members of the Bush administration occasionally call it "forward deterrence." Others have labeled it "forward engagement" and "active counterproliferation." Benjamin R. Barber, *Fear's Empire: War, Terrorism, and Democracy* (New York: Norton, 2003), pp. 89, 95. While a successful record of preventive military action may have deterrent value, it can also prompt potential adversaries to become more secretive, thus complicating future efforts to thwart their plans.
12. Peter Dombrowski and Roger A. Payne, "Global Debate and the Limits of the Bush Doctrine," *International Studies Perspectives* 4 (November 2003): 396.
13. Condoleezza Rice as cited in Jeffrey Goldberg, "Breaking Ranks," *The New Yorker* (October 31, 2005): 59. Rice's role in formulating the Bush NSS is discussed in James Mann, *The Rise of the Vulcans: The History of Bush's War Cabinet* (New York: Viking Penguin, 2004), pp. 315, 367.
14. Georg Schwarzenberger, "The Fundamental Principles of International Law," *Recueil des Cours*, Vol. 1 (Leyden: A.W. Sijthoff, 1955), pp. 195–383. For an overview of legal opinions on this principle that take the 9/11 attacks into consideration, see Mary Ellen O'Connell, *International Law and the Use of Force* (New York: Foundation Press, 2005).
15. See Derek W. Bowett, *Self-Defense in International Law* (New York: Praeger, 1958). Although the right of self-defense has long been used as a justification for war, Rodin has argued that attempts to model international law on domestic law are misconceived; there is no valid analogy, he submits, between national defense and personal rights of self-defense. David Rodin, *War and Self-Defense* (New York: Oxford University Press, 2003).
16. Samuel von Pufendorf, *The Law of Nature and Nations*, 5th ed., translated by Basil Kennet (London: Bonwicke, 1749), p. 200. The ancient Hindu writer Sukra goes even further. In the *Nitisara,* he argues that to preserve his state a leader may have to wage a treacherous war, where ordinary limits on the conduct of hostilities do not apply. C. Joseph Chacko, "India's Contribution to the Field of International Law Concepts," *Recueil des Cours*, Vol. 1 (Leyden: A.W. Sijthoff, 1958), pp. 132, 140.
17. The *Caroline* was an American ship that had been supplying Canadian rebels during an insurrection against the British in 1837. British forces attacked the vessel while it was docked in an American port on the Niagara River. The British claimed their actions were a justified act of self-defense. Daniel Webster responded by arguing that acts of self-defense must entail necessity, proportionality, and immediacy.
18. Since 1945, the UN General Assembly has applied the Charter's prohibition on the use of military force to international terrorism. The 1970 *Declaration on Principles of International Law Concerning Friendly Relations and Co-operation Among States in Accordance with the Charter of the United Nations* proclaims that terror cannot be used to coerce other states. The 1987 *Declaration on the Enhancement of the Effectiveness of the Principle of Refraining from the Threat or Use of Force in International Relations*

refines that proscription by calling upon states to refrain from "organizing, instigating, or assisting or participating in paramilitary, terrorist or subversive acts, including the acts of mercenaries."

19. J. L. Brierly, *The Law of Nations*, 6th ed., edited by Humphrey Waldock (Oxford: Oxford University Press, 1963), p. 417. Advocates of this position frequently cite the ruling of the Permanent Court of International Justice in the 1927 *Lotus* case, which held that "restrictions upon the independence of States cannot . . . be presumed." States, it was argued, have "a wide measure of discretion which is only limited in certain cases by prohibitive rules." According to this view, a state's actions are legal unless they are explicitly prohibited by an international legal rule.
20. Anthony Clark Arend, "International Law and the Preemptive Use of Military Force," *Washington Quarterly* 26 (Spring 2003): 93. Also see Steven C. Welsh, "Preemptive War and International Law," *Columbia International Affairs Online* (New York: Columbia University Press, 2004), retrieved at http://www.ciaonet.org/wps/wes05/index.html.
21. "Addendum to the Eighth Report on State Responsibility," Document A/CN.4/318/ADD.5-7, *Yearbook of the International Law Commission, 1980*, Vol. 2 (New York: United Nations, 1982), p. 51.
22. David Little, "Morality and National Security," in Kenneth M. Jensen and Elizabeth P. Faulkner, eds., *Morality and Foreign Policy: Realpolitik Revisited* (Washington, DC: United States Institute of Peace, 1991), p. 11.
23. C. H. M. Waldock, "The Regulation of the Use of Force by Individual States in International Law," *Recueil des Cours*, Vol. 2 (Paris: Sirey, 1952), p. 498.
24. For example, some scholars distinguish between preemption based on interceptive self-defense and prevention based on anticipatory self-defense. Others use precautionary self-defense when referring to actions taken to ensure that certain threats never materialize. Yoram Dinstein cited in Barry E. Carter and Phillip R. Trimble, *International Law* (Boston: Little, Brown, 1991), p. 1243; Mark A. Drumbl, "Self-Defense and the Use of Force: Breaking the Rules, Making the Rules, or Both?" *International Studies Perspectives* 4 (November 2003): 422. Still others criticize these types of distinctions, arguing that a preemptive attack is simply a form of preventive war, with the crucial point being that some preventive strikes may be justified while others may not be justified. Robert W. Tucker, *The Just War: A Study in Contemporary American Doctrine* (Baltimore: The Johns Hopkins Press, 1960), p. 144. Michael Walzer proposes three criteria for identifying a threat sufficient to justify a first strike: (1) "a manifest intent to injure" demonstrated by explicit threats rather than boastful tirades; (2) "a degree of active preparation that makes the intent a positive danger;" and (3) "a general situation in which waiting, or doing anything other than fighting, greatly magnifies the risk" to one's political independence or territorial integrity. Michael Walzer, *Just and Unjust Wars: A Moral Argument with Historical Illustrations* (New York: Basic Books, 1977), pp. 80–82. However, applying criteria such as these often generates further scholarly disagreement.
25. Major contributions to the literature on preemptive and preventive motivations for the use of military force include Douglas Lemke, "Investigating the Preventive Motive for War," *International Interactions* 29 (October 2003): 273–292; Jack S. Levy and Joseph R. Gochal, "Democracy and Preventive War: Israel and the 1956 Sinai

Campaign," *Security Studies* 11 (Winter 2001/02): 1–49; Dale Copeland, *The Origins of Major War* (Ithaca, NY: Cornell University Press, 2000); Stephen Van Evera, *Causes of War: Power and the Roots of Conflict* (Ithaca, NY: Cornell University Press, 1999); Dan Reiter, "Exploding the Powder Keg Myth: Preemptive Wars Almost Never Happen," *International Security* 20 (Fall 1995): 5–34; Randal Schweller, "Domestic Structure and Preventive War: Are Democracies More Pacific?" *World Politics* 44 (January 1992): 235–269; Jack S. Levy, "Declining Power and the Preventive Motivation for War," *World Politics* 40 (October 1987): 82–107; and Robert E. Harkavy, "Preemption and Two-Front Conventional War: A Comparison of the 1967 Israeli Strategy with the Pre-World War One German Schlieffen Plan," *Jerusalem Papers on Peace Problems*, No. 23 (Jerusalem: Leonard Davis Institute for International Relations, The Hebrew University, 1977).

26. For a further discussion of the Third Punic War, see Charles W. Kegley, Jr. and Gregory A. Raymond, *How Nations Make Peace* (New York: St. Martin's/Worth, 1999), pp. 70–93.

27. George P. Shultz, "The Work of Diplomacy," speech delivered on May 29, 2002, in Arlington, Virginia, retrieved at http://www.statew.gov/secretary/rm/2002/10564pf.htm.

28. Cited in Bob Woodward, *Plan of Attack* (New York: Simon & Schuster, 2004), p. 129.

29. Armand Jean du Plessis, *The Political Testament of Cardinal Richelieu*, translated by Henry Bertram Hill (Madison: University of Wisconsin Press, 1961), p. 80. Machiavelli also used a medical metaphor when urging political leaders to guard against looming dangers. "Foreseen they can be easily remedied," he insisted, "but if one waits till they are in hand, the medicine is no longer in time as the malady has become incurable." Niccolò Machiavelli, *The Prince*, translated by Luigi Ricci and revised by E. R. P. Vincent (New York: Modern Library, 1950), pp. 10–11.

30. Umberto Eco, *Baudolino* (New York: Harcourt, 2000), pp. 250–251.

31. See, for example, A. J. P. Taylor, *The Struggle for Mastery in Europe, 1848–1918* (New York: Oxford University Press, 1954), p. 166.

32. Cited in Charles G. Fenwick, *International Law*, 4th ed. (New York: Appleton-Century-Crofts, 1965), p. 275.

33. Shai Feldman, "The Bombing of Osiraq—Revisited," *International Security* 7 (Fall 1982): 18.

34. Shlomo Nakdimon, *First Strike*, translated by Peretz Kidron (New York: Summit Books, 1987); Jack C. Snyder, "The Road to Osiraq—Baghdad's Quest for the Bomb," *Middle East Journal* 37 (Autumn 1983): 565–593.

35. Richard K. Betts, "Striking First: A History of Thankfully Lost Opportunities," *Ethics & International Affairs* 17 (Winter 2003): 20.

36. Richard F. Grimmett, *U.S. Use of Preemptive Military Force: The Historical Record* (Washington, DC: Congressional Research Service, 2003), pp. 1–2.

37. Melvin P. Leffler, "Bush's Foreign Policy," *Foreign Policy* 144 (September/October 2004): 23; Philip Zelikow, "The Transformation of National Security: Five Redefinitions," *The National Interest* 71 (Spring 2003): 26.

38. Seymour M. Hersh, "The War Plans," *The New Yorker* (April 17, 2006): 30–37. For a discussion of the difficulties of eradicating Iran's nuclear program by military

means, see Ilan Berman, *Tehran Rising: Iran's Challenge to the United States* (Lanham, MD: Rowman & Littlefield, 2005), pp. 113–117. On the likelihood that a U.S. preventive attack would cause an upsurge in anti-Americanism and increased terrorist attacks, see *New York Times* (April 16, 2006): 13.

39. Radio address by Franklin Delano Roosevelt on September 11, 1941, retrieved at http://www.usmm.org/fdr/rattlesnake.html. For a discussion of the historical context of this episode, see David Palkki, "Preventive War Theory and the Irrelevance of Regime Type," paper presented at the annual meeting of the Pacific Northwest Political Science Association, November 6, 2004, Portland, Oregon.

40. Speech delivered by President George W. Bush in the East Room of the White House on March 19, 2004, retrieved at http://www.whitehouse.gov/news/releases/2004/03/20040319-3.html. For the thesis that America's crusade against evil and evildoers throughout the world has striking parallels with Islamists who call for a global jihad, see Robert Jewitt and John Shelton Lawrence, *Captain America and the Crusade Against Evil* (Grand Rapids, MI: Wm. B. Eerdmans, 2003).

41. April Morgan, "The War on Terrorism: Time for a New 'Wise War' Framework?" in Howard M. Hensel, ed., *The Law of Armed Conflict: Constraints on the Contemporary Use of Military Force* (Aldershot, England: Ashgate, 2005), pp. 210–211. Also see Robin Wright, "War on Evil," *Foreign Policy* 144 (September/October 2004): 34. An earlier example of this eschatological perspective on world politics can be seen in some of the public statements former U.S. Secretary of State John Foster Dulles made about nonaligned countries during the Cold War. To remain neutral in the face of the evil represented by the Soviet Union, he once declared, is "immoral and shortsighted." Cited in Laurence W. Martin, "Introduction: The Emergence of the New States," in Laurence W. Martin, ed., *Neutralism and Nonalignment: The New States in World Affairs* (Westport, CT: Greenwood, 1962), p. xviii.

42. Abraham D. Sofaer, "On the Legality of Preemption," *Hoover Digest* 2 (2003), retrieved at http://www-hoover.stanford.edu/publications/digest/032/sofaer.html.

43. U.S. Department of Defense, *Quadrennial Defense Review Report* (February 6, 2006), pp. 2–3.

44. *National Security Strategy of the United States* (Washington DC: The White House, March 16, 2006), p. 23.

6

America's Strategic Choices and Their International Consequences

> Persons who regard any sort of fear as a just ground for precautionary killing . . . are themselves greatly deceived.
>
> —Hugo Grotius

The Bush Doctrine has been described as "a radical new twist on the traditional idea of self-defense."[1] Built on the premise that victims rarely know when terrorists are about to strike, the doctrine calls for taking preventive military action against "grave and gathering" dangers, rather than waiting for evidence of an imminent attack. "Did we know on September 10 that September 11 was imminent?" National Security Advisor Condoleezza Rice asked rhetorically when defending the new Bush strategy.[2] "If we had such a strategy in place years earlier," added General Tommy Franks, "we might have been given the authority to remove the Taliban from power, and destroy al Qaeda in Afghanistan, before the terrorist attack of 9/11."[3] Challenging the notion that the world's most powerful state was obliged to get authorization from the United Nations in order to defend itself, one senior advisor to President Bush reportedly boasted: "we're an empire now, and when we act we create our own reality."[4]

Scholars from several different research traditions agree that powerful states shape the international environment. The "rules of the system," they concur, "tend to be established during periods of high capability concentration and the leadership/dominance of a single state."[5] Given America's awesome capabilities, how the United States acts exerts an enormous influence on setting the rules that affect the behavior of others. When the dominant member of the state system promotes a new code of conduct, it alters the normative frame of reference for virtually everyone else. What the strongest do in world politics eventually shapes what others do, and when that practice becomes common, it tends to take on an aura of obligation. Especially in novel situations, when most states are uncertain about how they should respond to events, the actions of the powerful provide social cues about acceptable behavior, which others subsequently emulate. In short, rules *of* behavior in international affairs presage rules *for* behavior, and those rules are most influenced by the actions taken by a reigning superpower, such as the United States at this historical moment.[6]

Global Primacy and Normative Order

The first written records of interstate relations date from the middle of the third millennium B.C.E., when the Sumerians established city-states on the alluvial plain near the confluence of the Tigris and Euphrates Rivers. Conflicts over boundaries and water rights were incessant. Yet inscriptions on steles and cuneiform tablets indicate that these states possessed a code of conduct that mitigated the most pernicious aspects of their anarchic environment. Even in the absence of a supreme overarching authority, Sumerian leaders shared a canon that framed how they thought about themselves and what they might do to one another. The rules for behavior within this canon communicated the scope of each state's entitlements, the extent of its obligations, and the range of its jurisdiction.

General standards for behavior have existed among all autonomous, independent political entities engaged in sustained interaction. Frequently they are reflected in explicit conventions that solve coordination problems among actors with common interests or common aversions. Occasionally they are mirrored in tacit agreements among mutually dependent actors that possess divergent interests. In both cases these behavioral standards emanate from calculations based on expediency. Formal and informal ground rules allow everyone to navigate through delicate situations and avoid outcomes that no one desires.

When, as in the case of the ancient Sumerians, independent political entities share a canon of fundamental values, they are more than members of a state system that observe rules of prudence; they are participants in a rudimentary international *society*, whose behavior is guided by international norms.[7] Simply put, international norms express socially sanctioned injunctions that prescribe certain actions and proscribe others. Rather than representing "average" or modal behavior in a statistical sense, they entail a collective evaluation of behavior by members of the state system in terms of what ought to be done, as well as a collective expectation as to what will be done. Communicated through a rich lexicon of legal symbols and reinforced by diplomatic ritual, international norms are intersubjectively shared understandings about the obligations of international actors to behave in specified ways. Conformity with a norm's instructions elicits approval from nearly all other relevant international actors—deviance, disapproval. Moreover, these voices of praise and protest encourage abidance by influencing every actor's image of itself and its reputation among others.

International norms do not exist in isolation. They fit together in a complex mosaic to form a normative order. Underpinning every normative order is a set of foundational norms that define its axiology or value orientation. At any given time, the prevailing "rules of the game" within the state system are anchored in an axiology that ranges from permissive to restrictive. A *permissive normative order* gives national leaders considerable latitude to do whatever they believe must be done to protect the state and advance its position within the global hierarchy, no matter how repugnant such acts might seem in the light of those moral dictates that guide the behavior of people in their private, interpersonal lives. Conversely, a *restrictive normative order* gives national leaders far less leeway. Demarcation lines remove certain areas from interstate competition, and specific criteria delineate when it is appropriate to wage war and how to fight. In addition, procedures exist for settling disputes through third-party intercession, as well as for upholding any accords that are reached.

Table 6.1 lists some of the key differences between permissive and restrictive normative orders. Although each type of order has been championed by different theorists and policymakers as conducive to peace, a growing body of historical evidence suggests that permissive normative orders are associated with international strife.[8] Restrictive orders, by way of contrast, offer political leaders principles and procedures for diffusing confrontations and containing human costs when conflict resolution fails. The greater the strength of a restrictive order, the lower the probability that conflicts of interest will become militarized disputes and that militarized disputes will eventually escalate to wars.[9]

In summary, the behavior of the powerful exerts a significant impact on whether prevailing international norms are permissive or restrictive. At the

Table 6.1 Characteristics of Two Ideal Normative Orders

PERMISSIVE ORDER	RESTRICTIVE ORDER
International politics is driven by the quest for power and position	International politics is driven by the quest for stability and mutual gains
Diplomacy is status and hierarchy oriented	Diplomacy is task and solution oriented
States are believed to have no obligation beyond their own parochial interests	States are believed to have obligations that transcend their immediate self-interests
Changed circumstances allow the nonperformance of promissory obligations	Agreements are binding; barring inadequate performance by one side, they cannot be repudiated prior to their expiration without agreement by the parties
Force and the threat of force are required to elicit compliance with interstate agreements	Legal regimes based on voluntary consent elicit compliance with interstate agreements
Security is based on self-help	Security is based on rules that confine the geographic scope of state competition, limit the use of force, promote collective problem solving, and build reciprocity-based trust

extreme, in making state autonomy and autarky supreme values, permissive normative orders subordinate all other political considerations to freedom, giving states license to define national interests without regard to community consensus. By condoning the unbridled pursuit of national advantage, permissive orders have historically fostered a climate of mistrust. Ever suspicious about the intentions of others, political leaders in permissive normative orders are prone to gravitate toward unilateralist foreign policies, overestimate the utility of military power for solving political problems, and exaggerate the susceptibility of their opponents to ultimata. Alternatively, by curbing untrammeled self-help, restrictive orders encourage reciprocal cooperative exchanges, which induce moderation and foster trust. Of course, cooperation can take place without trust, and treachery can occur among those who trust one another; however, the prospects for mutually beneficial problem solving increase within an atmosphere of trust since information is readily shared, the cost of undertaking cross-border transactions is low, and scarce resources do not have to be expended to assure compliance with promises.[10] Trust permits habits of collaboration to develop and expand—a process of learning that builds still new levels of trust.

Before we analyze the likely impact of the Bush administration's security policies on the evolution of the international normative order, let us put the current situation within a larger historical context by examining fluctuations over the past two centuries in the degree of support for permissive versus restrictive norms regarding the use of force. When viewed through the lens of history, we can ascertain whether current policies represent a significant departure from recent trends and whether they will strengthen or erode international trust.

Trends in International Norms Regarding the Use of Force

Throughout history, attempts have been made to establish a code of conduct that would regulate the use of military force. The belief that there are right and wrong ways to wage war is an ancient one. Formal efforts to prescribe rules of warfare can be found in such diverse sources as the Book of Deuteronomy, the Hindu Code of *Manu*, the law of *Szu-ma* during China's Chou dynasty, the proclamation of Caliph Abu Bakr, and the exhortations of the Second Lateran Council. Examples of informal efforts include the principles of feudal chivalry in medieval Europe, the *Rajput* code in India following the Gupta period, and the dictates of *bushido* that arose in Japan after the twelfth-century civil war between the Taira and Minamoto clans. Since the emergence of the modern state system, the international legal community has also attempted to craft rules to delineate when it is legitimate for states to employ deadly force, how it should be used, and against whom it may be applied. Furthermore, it has specified when it is acceptable to intervene militarily into the domestic affairs of another sovereign state.[11] Although some observers assert that its work has focused on "procedural minutiae and superficial issues,"[12] others see it as an important factor in making international life less dangerous than a Hobbesian state of nature. "Violated or ignored as they are," notes Telford Taylor, "enough of the rules are observed enough of the time so that mankind is very much better off with them than without them."[13]

Periodic attempts are made to circumvent these normative restraints by citing the exigencies of military necessity. Appeals to necessity challenge the wrongfulness of an act on the basis that it was the only means of safeguarding an essential interest against a serious threat. It was this meaning that the British had in mind when they defended their 1807 bombardment of Copenhagen by claiming that the danger they faced "was certain, urgent and extreme, as to create a case of urgent, paramount necessity, leaving his Majesty's ministeres no choice."[14] Their sentiments were echoed shortly thereafter by U.S. Secretary of State John Quincy Adams, when he defended American military actions in Spanish western Florida during 1818.

Military necessity has been invoked by political and military leaders alike in order to sidestep normative limitations on the use of force. Chancellor von Bethmann-Hollweg of Germany, President McKinley of the United States, as well as such famous commanders in the field as Napoleon and Sheridan are among those who have drawn upon the logic of military necessity to justify their actions. References to the doctrine have appeared in international treaties (e.g., Article 23 [g] of the Hague Convention IV), the judgments of international tribunals (e.g., the Hardman incident of 1910 [*Great Britain v. the United States*]), military field manuals (e.g., *Kriegsbrauch im Landkriege*, General Staff of the German Army, 1902), and diplomatic notes (e.g., letter of September 6, 1814, from U.S. Secretary of State Monroe to British Vice-Admiral Cochrane regarding the burning of the village of Newark in Upper Canada). Since it may absolve a state from the nonobservance of international obligations, pleas of military necessity have been advanced to excuse behavior ranging from belligerent measures taken against an enemy to egregious breaches of neutral rights. For example, military necessity was invoked in 1854 by the United States to defend the bombardment of Greytown, Nicaragua; it was employed by Prussia to excuse the sinking of British colliers in the Seine during the Franco-Prussian War; it was used by Great Britain to justify mining the North Sea during World War I; and it was conjured up by Germany to excuse the devastation of the Somme region during the retreat of 1917.[15] In each of these episodes the defense mounted represented a variant of the maxim, *necessitas non subditur legi* (necessity is not subject to the law). Foreign policy, it was argued, unfolds in "a realm of moral approximations, tentative compromises, and, occasionally, choices among lesser evils."[16] Leaders responsible for national security cannot always abide by a set of Marquis of Queensberry rules; violations of restrictions

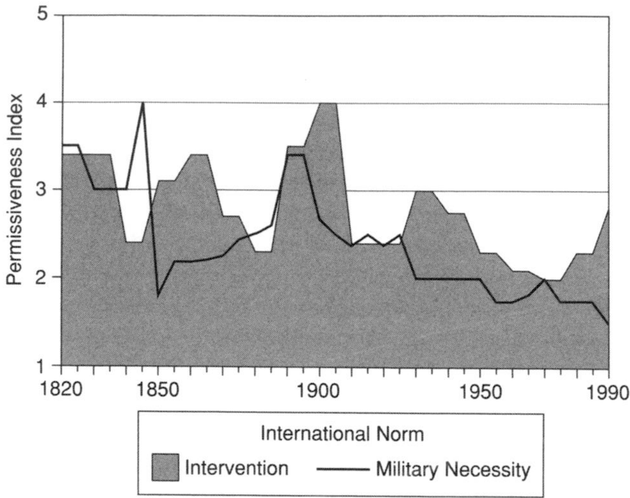

Figure 6.1 The Changing Level of Support for Intervention and Military Necessity Whereas acceptance of intervention has risen in recent years, acceptance of military necessity has declined, as measured by changes in international law (see Appendix, pp. 105–107).

on the use of force may be unavoidable, even when it means intervening in the internal affairs of another state.

In order to trace changes over time in international norms that pertain to military necessity and intervention, 275 legal treatises written between 1815 and 1999 were content analyzed under the auspices of the Transnational Rules Indicators Project (see Chapter Appendix). To gauge the degree to which prevailing norms were perceived by the authors of these works as supporting a permissive definition of military necessity, each treatise was coded on a 5-point scale, ranging from 1.00 (rejection of the necessity defense) to 5.00 (acceptance of the necessity defense without reservations), with intermediate positions indicating various levels of qualified backing. Normative support for military intervention as a tool of statecraft was also measured on a 5-point scale, ranging from 1.00 (no support for intervention) to 5.00 (strong support), with intermediary positions again designating degrees of qualified backing.

Once every treatise in a particular half-decade was coded, the mean value was calculated for each successive recording period to create time-series data. The higher the score on each index, the more prevailing legal norms supported a permissive interpretation of the norm in question; the lower the score, the more they restricted military necessity and intervention. Figure 6.1 shows the fluctuations in normative support for military necessity and intervention over the past two centuries. Inspection of the trend lines suggests that the period of the Concert of Europe during the early decades of the nineteenth century was among the most permissive eras in the time frame under investigation.

The Concert of Europe

The French Revolution and the Napoleonic Wars battered Europe for almost a quarter-century, leaving over two and a half million combatants dead. The carnage galvanized a consensus among the victors who met at the Congress of Vienna in 1815 about the need for rules that would govern their future relations and prevent another great-power death struggle. Three months after the Battle of Waterloo, Austria, Prussia, and Russia signed the Treaty of the Holy Alliance, in which they vowed to "remain united by the bonds of a true and indissoluble fraternity" and "on all occasions and in all places, lend each other aid and assistance." Less than a month later they concluded a Quadruple Alliance with Great Britain to renew the pledges of cooperation against French aggression that all four had previously made in the Treaty of Chaumont. In addition, they resolved to hold periodic conferences "for the purpose of consulting upon their common interests."

From these agreements emerged the Concert of Europe, an oligarchic system of great-power consultation and policy coordination. Since revolutionary France had overturned the constitutions of conservative states, reactionary statesmen like Klemens von Metternich and Friedrich Gentz now envisioned preventive military intervention as a strategic necessity to dampen liberal threats to monarchical legitimacy. At the Congress of Aix-la-Chapelle in 1818, Tsar Alexander I of Russia proposed an alliance to intervene on behalf of rulers who were threatened by revolutionary insurrection. A few years later, revolts in Spain and Naples led Russia, Austria, and Prussia to agree at the Congress of Troppau that force could be used against states "which have undergone in their internal structure an alteration brought on by revolt, whose consequences may be dangerous to other states." Subsequently, at the Congress of Laibach, the conservative continental powers backed Austria's intervention into Naples and Piedmont to suppress liberal revolts, and the following year at Verona, they agreed to a French proposal to crush Spanish rebels.

However, great-power unanimity on preventive intervention proved to be elusive. Great Britain generally resisted the argument that strategic necessities sanctioned intervention to regulate other states' domestic affairs. For example, Foreign Minister Viscount Castlereagh rejected the Protocol of Troppau, and the influential writer and philosopher John Stuart Mill condemned the use of military intervention to promote political change abroad. While the British were willing to help other great powers stem aggression that might destabilize the post-Napoleonic balance of power, they did not support intervention to prop up tottering autocrats. Nevertheless, they gradually began to support using intervention for other purposes, including the collection of debts and humanitarian aims.[17] Under Castlereagh's successor, George Canning, the threat of British sea power was used to support the independence movement in Spanish America; later, under Lord Palmerston, the British supported constitutionalist causes in Spain and Portugal. Intervention and forcible procedures, in other words, eventually became tools of liberal statecraft, championed by Great Britain, the most powerful member of the state system.

From the Revolutions of 1848 to World War I

The revolutions that swept through Europe in 1848 eroded the rules of international conduct that the continental monarchies had advocated. Normative support for a permissive conception of necessity plummeted. As military historian Geoffrey Best put it, this was the "golden decade" of restraints on warfare.[18] Concern over the plight of soldiers at Solferino during the Franco-Austrian War of 1859, which led to the Geneva Red Cross Conferences of 1864 and 1868, ushered in a more restrictive conception of military necessity. In addition, conferences were held in St. Petersburg (1868) and Brussels (1874) to regulate weapons that aggravated suffering on the battlefield. Despite these efforts to codify international humanitarian law, support for a permissive definition of necessity returned during the last quarter of the century, as the military establishments of various countries (e.g., Spain, 1882; Britain, 1884; France, 1884; Portugal, 1890; Russia, 1895; and Italy, 1896) began drafting field manuals, which reaffirmed the necessity defense. In addition, rulers like Bismarck, Cavour, and Napoleon II actively sought a new set of ground rules that would permit the major powers to intervene unilaterally. Interventions for the collection of debts and for humanitarian reasons, which had occurred during the Concert era, continued. Between 1902 and 1903, for example, Germany and Great Britain blockaded the Orinoco River, bombarded forts at Puerto Cabello, and sank several Venezuelan gunboats. France intervened in what is now Lebanon in 1860 to protect Maronite Christians, and Russia intervened in the Balkans a decade later to protect Orthodox Christians.

Disputes between the major powers intensified within this increasingly permissive normative order. Between 1882 and 1914, 38 wars between states erupted—more than twice the number of civil wars within states.[19] On the eve of the First World War, questioning of this permissive posture toward interventionism began to grow. Based on Argentine Foreign Minister Luis María Drago's insistence that insolvency should not be considered a form of misconduct, the parties to the Second Hague Peace Conference (1907) agreed to limit the use of military intervention to recover what was owed to foreign bondholders if the debtor state refused to arbitrate the financial dispute.

World War I Through the Cold War

Normative support for the necessity defense underwent a steady decline in the twentieth century. From the Hague Congresses (1899, 1907) onward, the situations under which appeals to military necessity would be accepted by the international community gradually diminished. The positions taken in the Geneva Protocol of 1925, the Nuremberg and Tokyo war crimes trials, the Geneva Convention of 1949 and Protocols of 1977, as well as in several United Nations documents (e.g., GA Doc. A/7720, November 20, 1969, and GA Doc. A/8052, September 18, 1970) testify to the growing restrictiveness of international legal norms.

The norms governing intervention also underwent significant changes after World War I, initially declining, rising during the Cold War, and then declining again until the end of the century. Thus, while the Bush administration's push for a more permissive interpretation of military necessity runs counter to the restrictive trend within the international normative order, its advocacy of intervention for the purpose of "regime change" presents a series of ambiguities about the prevailing consensus regarding the acceptability of using military force to promote democratic reforms.

Normative restrictions on intervention were frequently articulated in the aftermath of the Second World War. In addition to the limits expressed in Article 2 (7) of the Charter of the United Nations, several other of other international agreements prohibited military intervention, including such varied accords as the 1945 Act of Chapultepec and the 1975 Final Act of the Helsinki Conference on Security and Cooperation in Europe. The nonintervention norm, although widely viewed as legitimate by the international community, was nonetheless violated on repeated occasions during the Cold War. For example, the United States and the Soviet Union often used intervention as an instrument to influence the authority structures of governments within their spheres of influence. The U.S. interventions in Guatemala (1954) and the Dominican Republic (1965) and the Soviet Union's interventions in Hungary (1956) and Czechoslovakia (1968) illustrate this point. Toward the end of the Cold War, however, normative support for intervention began to increase as many world leaders called for military intervention to stop brutal governments from violating the human rights of their citizens. Furthermore, democratic governance was touted by some as a human rights entitlement. The June 1991 *Santiago Commitment to Democracy and Renewal of the Inter-American System*, for example, sketched out a interventionist policy for the Organization of American States to guarantee hemispheric democracy.

By the onset of the twenty-first century, state sovereignty was no longer seen as sacrosanct. During the conflicts in Bosnia and Kosovo, British Prime Minister Tony Blair, U.S. President Bill Clinton, and NATO Secretary General Javier Solana all spoke of humanitarian intervention as a moral imperative. Their argument hinged on three propositions:

1. Human rights are an international entitlement
2. Governments committing grave violations of human rights lose their legitimacy and thus forfeit protection under international law; and
3. The international community has a legal right and moral responsibility to stop human rights violations.[20]

Where the Bush administration has promoted more permissive norms than those advocated earlier in the Balkans is in asserting that preventive intervention should be authorized for security reasons, not merely to stop ongoing human rights abuses. For President Bush, regime change through military intervention is a necessary and effective tool in the asymmetrical war on terror.

Permissive International Norms and Asymmetrical Warfare

Calls for a more permissive interpretation of the laws of war arose from within the Bush administration during its military operations against the Taliban regime in Afghanistan and Saddam Hussein's Iraq. An example can be found in the March 2003 classified report on prisoner interrogation prepared for Secretary of Defense Rumsfeld. Bush administration lawyers argued that defensive necessity justified interrogation methods that violated the literal language of international law when they were undertaken to prevent further terrorist attacks on the United States. Terrorism, administration spokespersons insisted, posed a unique threat that required extraordinary countermeasures.[21]

As discussed in previous chapters, what makes these kinds of claims so compelling to U.S. national security policy makers is the prospect that terrorists with global reach will eventually gain access to WMDs. When a catastrophic terrorist attack seems inevitable, the urge to launch a preventive strike can feel overwhelming, especially since detecting the imminent use of such weapons by clandestine organizations is more difficult than observing the military build-up by a neighboring state prior to a conventional assault. Moreover, when an adversary possesses a "warrior" ethos and flouts the code of conduct observed by disciplined professional soldiers, it is easy to conclude that adhering to norms that restrict the use of force may be disadvantageous.[22] Believing the laws of war are the "least codified" part of international law,[23] and that what has been compiled is largely irrelevant for addressing the new security threats posed by global terrorism, American policy makers have appealed to strategic necessities as a justification for subsuming preventive military action under the guise of anticipatory self-defense. As the 2002 *National Security Strategy of the United States* put it, "the best defense is a good offense."[24]

The strategic logic behind current thinking about preventive military action can be traced to the ancient Greek preference for fighting decisive engagements, meeting adversaries head on in the hope that a looming threat could be eliminated with a single blow.[25] Additionally, the argument that no tactics should be barred when fighting enemies who show little concern for legal niceties has roots in the double standard Romans adopted when dealing with different kinds of adversaries. Unlike in the Hellenistic world, where the Romans faced what they defined as "civilized" states, elsewhere they encountered "barbarian" tribes which were fought on other, less principled terms.[26] Between 150 and 130 B.C.E., for example, Roman leaders saw the inhabitants of the Iberian Peninsula as treacherous foes. Strategic necessity, they asserted, required Rome to be as brutal and duplicitous as their barbarian enemies.[27] Similar claims were made during the ferocious campaign of 15–16 C.E. led by Germanicus Caesar against Arminius, chief of the Cherusci and the architect of the massacre of three legions under the command of Publius Quintilius Varus in the Teutoburg Forest.[28] According to Robert Worley, Romans distinguished between two distinct forms of warfare: *bellum* was conducted against states under nascent laws of war; *guerra* was waged with few restraints against nonstate actors, including the irregular armed forces of barbarian tribes as well as marauding bands of pirates and brigands.[29]

Rome's *guerra* strategy represented an early approach to conducting asymmetrical warfare. Today various legal scholars question applying the term "war" to the use of military force against nonstate actors. International law has traditionally defined war as an armed conflict between sovereign states, and some people view the bloodshed perpetrated by transnational terrorist groups as crimes against humanity that should be prosecuted by law enforcement agencies and punished in national courts. Since 9/11, however, the concept of "armed attack" has been generally acknowledged to include acts of terror by nonstate actors that, taken singly or collectively, occur on a significant scale. From this perspective, small, isolated incursions across national frontiers do not pass the gravity threshold; conversely, massive assaults, as well as a pattern of smaller strikes that comprise a wider campaign of violence, tend to be seen as armed attacks covered by Article 51 of the UN Charter.[30] What remains controversial is whether the necessity defense can be invoked to legitimize preventive military actions as part of a twenty-first–century *guerra* strategy aimed at destroying transnational terrorist organizations and changing the regimes of those states that support them.

The Perils of Preventive Warfare

The war in Iraq is the first application of the Bush administration's declaratory policy of taking preventive military action against "gathering" dangers. By virtue of America's dominant position in the world, the words and deeds of its leaders are very likely to shape the content of the international normative order. With its emphasis on seizing the initiative in anticipation of an eventual menace, the Bush Doctrine promotes an exceptionally permissive interpretation of those norms that pertain to the use of force. What would be the consequences if such an interpretation gained widespread acceptance? Of what would a permissive normative order be a harbinger?

Debates over these questions are heated. Pointing to the heinous acts of Al Qaeda and its affiliates, one side believes that "half-measures will not suffice." As the world's only superpower, "America bears the responsibility to help guarantee . . . international stability, whether much of the world wants it or not."[31] In that regard, some supporters of the Bush Doctrine have expressed the desire to move beyond Iraq, contending that the next phase of the war on terror should include Iran and Syria, with Lebanon, North Korea, the Palestinian Authority, Saudi Arabia, Somalia, and Sudan also being named as possible targets.[32] It may be untidy, mused Secretary of Defense Rumsfeld, but anticipatory self-defense should not be "particularized to Iraq."[33]

Calling preventive warfare a "cockeyed,"[34] "confused and disturbing strategy,"[35] the other side in this debate complains that although the doctrine was originally directed at known terrorists whose location was uncertain, it has been applied to states with known locations but uncertain connections to actual aggression.[36] Declaring that there is a qualitative difference between a discrete strike aimed at a terrorist organization's facilities and a full-scale invasion aimed at regime change,[37] many critics of the Bush Doctrine maintain that states are not morally liable to be attacked unless they are involved in aggression, on the verge of assailing someone, or engaged in egregious human rights violations.[38]

Because the security threats facing the United States are embedded in the context of wider political issues, it is important to consider how the Bush administration's proposed solution of today's problems may generate new problems tomorrow. In judging the arguments on each side of the debate over the impact of an American-inspired shift from a restrictive to a permissive normative order, it is enlightening to recall Immanuel Kant's famous principle, the "categorical imperative." When contemplating an action or a policy, he urged considering what the consequences would be if everyone practiced that same conduct. Kant counseled that the only ethical activity is one that would be advantageous for humanity if it were to become a universal law practiced by all. Applying this principle to the policy of preventive war, we should ask: What is likely to result if the current practices of the United States become universal so that international norms permit all states to strike suspected threats in advance, before an enemy launches an attack or inflicts an injury? What if the new Bush strategic doctrine became every state's policy?

If other states act on the same rationale that the United States has proposed and accept preventive military action as a legitimate response to potential threats, a disorderly world would become more turbulent. Now that the United States has claimed that anticipatory self-defense justifies prophylactic military policies, what will stop others from doing the same? Indeed, since the Bush NSS was unveiled, Indian External Affairs Minister Yashwant Sinha, Iranian Defense Minister Ali Shamkhani, Israeli Defense Minister Shaul Mofaz, Japanese Prime Minister Junichiro Koizumi, and Russian President Vladimir Putin have all spoken about their right to engage in anticipatory self-defense.[39] The primary problem stems from the high probability that everyone who invokes this rationale for using force will define "grave and gathering" dangers in ways that fit their own particular adversaries, and that as a result "adoption of a policy by one government—particularly the sole remaining superpower—that accepts preventive wars could provide almost limitless rationales for other governments to embark on military actions against other states."[40] A second major problem is that widespread acceptance of preventive warfare will create an incentive for more states to acquire nuclear weapons as a deterrent.[41] Moreover, once some proportion of states obtains nuclear weapons, a threshold may be crossed for additional states, their acquisition being contingent on how many states already possess these weapons. Their subsequent acquisition, in turn, will cause another threshold to be crossed, and so on. Rather than preventive warfare dampening proliferation, it could easily trigger cascading increases in the number of nuclear-armed states.

Another problem with the Bush "nip-it-in-the-bud" strategy lies in its impact on longstanding *jus in bello* restrictions on the conduct of warfare. A policy of preventive war would not only undermine restraints on *when* states might use force, but also on *how* they may use force.[42] If the objective of an attack is to prevent the acquisition of WMDs, are pharmaceutical factories and nuclear power plants located in population centers fair game, even when targeting might cause collateral deaths among noncombatants? Adhering to the principle of discrimination and gauging proportionality is extraordinarily difficult in a preventive war. Any state acting in a discretionary, preventive manner against some hypothetical attack from a latent adversary must make a subjective judgment about how much force is needed to ensure a reasonable chance of success. Faced with such uncertainties, a reliance upon worst-case analysis is likely. Yet the devastation wrought by an unbridled first strike emanating from worst-case assumptions might outweigh whatever benefits the initiator hoped to gain. The short-term gain of neutralizing a possible threat would be eclipsed by the long-term rancor created by a disproportionate use of military might.

Still another problem with the Bush Doctrine lies in the demands it places on intelligence agencies. As historian Arthur Schlesinger, Jr. points out, "Preventive war is based on the proposition that it is possible to foretell with certainty what is to come."[43] But predicting another state's future behavior is difficult because leadership intentions are hard to discern. Information on an adversary's long-range goals may be obscured by its attempts to shroud policy planning in secrecy. Evidence on the options being considered for attaining those goals may be misinterpreted due to a carefully crafted deception campaign. Finally, signals of impending moves may be distorted by background noise. Abundant information can overload intelligence analysts, making it nearly impossible for them to determine what is important and what is not.

Acknowledging these difficulties, intelligence agencies often try to predict an adversary's future behavior by evaluating its military capabilities. However, capability estimates can be misleading as a guide to future intentions, especially when made over a long time horizon without reliable data on possible changes in training, command and control, maintenance, and logistics. Another drawback is divining whether projected capability enhancements are earmarked for offensive or defensive purposes. Weapons procurement by one state routinely provoke alarm in another, triggering round after round of countermeasures by each side, even when both have defensive motives. If prevailing international norms license preventive military action, these cycles of mutual suspicion could easily escalate to war.

The Bush administration's strategy thus raises important questions about the conditions under which, and the purposes for which, anticipatory self-defense is permissible to counter potential threats to national and international security. What does precaution warrant? Does strategic necessity absolve national leaders from observing the UN Charter's limitations on the use of force? Do unconventional security threats excuse behavior that would otherwise be morally repugnant?

Worse still, does this strategy run the risk of casting those who use it as aggressors? We contend that disregarding customary and Charter restraints on the use of force will herald the arrival of a new strain of American unilateralism and with it a new wave of anti-Americanism. Rather than simply reflecting the traditional American preference for autonomy in world affairs, it will establish rules for Washington that are different from those governing other members of the international community. Proclaiming an exclusive right to determine when anticipatory self-defense is legitimate impugns the legal principle that no one may be a judge in his own cause,[44] and thus will erode America's reputation and squander the "soft" power that is so critical for it to exercise global leadership. To quote an insightful commentary on the moral dilemma facing those who confront ruthless enemies: "As soon as men decide that all means are permitted to fight an evil, then their good becomes indistinguishable from the evil they set out to destroy."[45]

Foreign policy decision making cannot be divorced from the normative climate in which it occurs. During turbulent times, mistrust is endemic and suspicion, pervasive. Unsure of the aims of others, political leaders become fixated on the hostility they perceive, assume that decisive military action will yield a bandwagon of support, and frequently overlook the negative side effects of their national security policies.[46] Anticipatory self-defense is appealing to leaders in such circumstances. It seems prescient to defuse prospective threats. Yet, as Thomas Franck points out, the concept of anticipatory self-defense is rife with ambiguity.[47] When defined as preventive military action against what *could* happen or what *might* occur, it can encourage leaping through windows of opportunity that are shut. The long-term consequences of this kind of foreign policy folly can be so calamitous that earlier American statesmen such as George F. Kennan, Henry Stimson, George Marshall, and John Foster Dulles dismissed security strategies predicated upon preventive warfare as morally repugnant nonsense.[48] Indeed, after weighing the costs and benefits of the idea, U.S. President Dwight Eisenhower concluded that he "wouldn't even listen to anyone seriously that came in and talked about such a thing."[49]

The Bush administration has been vocal about the need to arrest foreign developments that may mature into attacks on the U.S. homeland and its interests abroad. It has been silent about the consequences that are likely to follow from a doctrine of preventive war couched in the idiom of anticipatory self-defense. Does countenancing military strikes against potential dangers enhance the security and moral reputation of the United States? Would it increase security in the world at large? While granting that preemption is justifiable whenever an attack is truly imminent, we contend that the permissive normative order engendered by the Bush strategy of preventive war will ultimately undermine national security. Preventive war, Otto von Bismarck is reputed to have said, is like committing suicide out of the fear of death. It causes the very thing one hopes to forestall. If the United States embraces preventive warfare, states currently locked in bitter rivalries from the Korean peninsula through South and Central Asia would have an inauspicious precedent to emulate. An American security strategy that cloaks preventive military action in the language of preemption would invite imitation. If a latent adversary's mere potential becomes a justifiable cause for preventive war, then every truculent, self-indulgent ruler will have rough-and-ready pretext for launching a first-strike.

In conclusion, America's unrivaled power gives it a unique opportunity to shape the international normative order. Depending on the policies it pursues, the United States can encourage the growth of permissive or restrictive norms and either the aggregation or sharing of power. What U.S. leaders do during the country's unipolar moment is important because it will help set the ground rules that affect how states will use military force in the years ahead.

As Solon allegedly warned King Croesus of Lydia in antiquity, the powerful often suffer from the illusion of omnipotence, believing that their preeminent position in the world is permanent. Yet history suggests otherwise: unipolar moments are fleeting; national fortunes rise and decline over time. The ground rules that the mighty entrench during their moment of primacy create the international realities within which they will live when they no longer hold overriding power.

Having examined the negative long-term consequences that are likely to arise from the current security policies of the American Imperium, let us turn in the final chapter to consider what can be done to avoid the perils that the nation will face as its preponderance erodes in the decades following the war in Iraq.

Appendix: Monitoring Change in the International Normative Order

International norms have interested international relations theorists since the birth of the modern state system. Acquiring reproducible evidence on their formation and decay has proven difficult, however, because they are not amenable to direct visual inspection. As intersubjectively shared understandings about right and wrong conduct, international norms are not tangible, materially based phenomena that can be measured in a straightforward manner, like one might do when counting the number of ships possessed by a country to determine the size of its fleet. Consequently, scholars have had to devise surrogate measures that allow them to monitor indirectly those changes that have occurred over time in the international normative order.

If international norms are conceptualized as "a form of communication" stored in "treaty collections, statute books . . . and treatises on international law" that conveys how states should or should not behave in certain situations,[50] then evidence on their prescriptions and proscriptions may be obtained by examining what publicists (or leading legal authorities) from different historical periods reported about the norms generally accepted by the international community at the times they were writing. Publicists have long sought to record what legal norms held sway at the time they wrote their treatises on international law. Indeed, some of them have had their works "quoted and requoted almost as if they were oracular pronouncements."[51] Although the role of publicists in actual law making may be nominal, their writings have traditionally been accepted by judicial tribunals as a subsidiary means of determining prevailing legal norms.[52] According to Malcolm Shaw, it is shortsighted to dismiss the value of publicists in legal research. "States in the presentation of their claims, national law officials in their opinions to their governments, the various international judicial and arbitral bodies in considering their decisions, and the judges of municipal courts when the need arises, all consult and quote the writings of leading juristic authorities."[53] As the only professional group dedicated to describing the substance of international legal norms, their narratives are a valuable information source. "If we turn to the most eminent publicists, and look for common agreement between them on some specific rule," recommends Ingrid Detter Delupis, "we will find considerable guidance as to the contents of international law on a specific problem."[54] Publicists are an "international guild whose bread and butter comes from expounding . . . what the law at any given moment actually is rather than what it ought to be or could have been."[55] The "selection of topics and the extent of their coverage" in a treatise reflects their "views as to the importance of each of them . . . since the text is intended to present a realistic picture of what the law is."[56]

In order to construct indicators that can gauge changes in the degree of normative support for various uses of military force, a content analysis was performed on what distinguished publicists since the Napoleonic era said about these norms. Content analysis is a data-making procedure that may be conducted on virtually any communication, from constitutions to comic strips. Devised for the study of social artifacts, it has proven extremely useful in longitudinal research designs for examining changes in the values and ideas of inaccessible subjects. International legal treatises are artifacts that document the commonly held expectations for state behavior that existed in their day. When these works are subjected to content analysis, the publicists are considered expert witnesses whose descriptions constitute observations that may be coded to make quantitative data on the directives contained in prevailing legal norms.

The major drawback of this procedure is that content analysis only deals with what explicitly appears in a document—its manifest, outward message. It does not reveal any deeper meaning that may be implied "between the lines" of the text. Fortunately, this liability does not invalidate the limited purpose for which we used content analysis in Chapter 6: namely, to extract information on generally held expectations about state behavior from a physical record of communication written for that very reason. While the memoirs of statesmen can also furnish this kind of information, these documents suffer from more drawbacks than legal treatises. Whereas treatises are comprehensive, systematic records that often go through multiple editions to reflect changes in norms, memoirs are produced episodically and may not address the topic of international norms. Because treatises provide a running historical record that is easily coded given their intent to inform others about the norms of the day, they offer a reasonable empirical proxy for monitoring the changes in the international legal order.

To trace the changes over time in the degree of support for interventionism and appeals to military necessity, 275 legal treatises were content analyzed under the auspices of the Transnational Rules Indicators Project (TRIP). The results are displayed in Figure 6.1. Of course, not all treatises are equally relevant for data-making purposes; hence, criteria are required for identifying those authoritative texts written by the most renowned publicists. The criteria used by TRIP was whether a work had gone through multiple revised editions or had been identified as authoritative by either independent scholarship (e.g., listed in the Association of Law Schools' bibliography of international law texts, the Hague Peace Palace Systematic Catalogue, etc.), a recognized legal body such as the International Court of Justice, or was cited in reports of Special Rapporteurs published in the *Yearbook of the International Law Commission.*

Notes

1. Speech by Senator Robert Byrd delivered on February 12, 2003. Also see his *Losing America: Confronting a Reckless and Arrogant Presidency* (New York: Norton, 2004), pp. 136–137.
2. Interview on March 14, 2004, with Tim Russert on NBC News "Meet the Press," retrieved at http://www.msnbc.msn.com/id/4515556/.
3. Tommy Franks, *American Soldier* (New York: HarperCollins, 2004), p. 404. Similarly, the *Wall Street Journal* editorialized on July 23, 2004, that "in a world of conflicting intelligence, uncertain consequences and potential foreign opposition, it is still sometimes necessary for America to attack an adversary before it attacks us." Additional support for a proactive military strategy is given by Tom McInerney and Paul Vallely, *Endgame: The Blueprint for Victory in the War on Terror* (Washington, DC: Regnery, 2004), p. 62.
4. Mark Danner, "What Are You Going to Do with That?" *New York Review of Books* (June 23, 2005): 53. The argument that existing international laws were inadequate for dealing with global terrorism was echoed by British Prime Minister Tony Blair in a speech in Sedgefield on March 5, 2004; Philippe Sands, *Lawless World: America and the Making and Breaking of Global Rules* (London: Allen Lane, 2005), p. 234. A stronger position has been articulated by U.S. Ambassador to the United Nations John Bolton. "It is a big mistake for us to grant any validity to international law even when it may seem in our short-term interest to do so," he argues, "because over

the long term, the goal of those who think that international law really means anything are those who want to constrict the United States." Quoted in *The New Yorker* (March 21, 2005): 23.

5. William R. Thompson, "Cycles, Capabilities, and War," in William R. Thompson, ed., *Contending Approaches to World System Analysis* (Beverly Hills, CA: Sage, 1983), p. 143. Immanuel Wallerstein's world-economy perspective, George Modelski's theory of the long cycle of world leadership, A. F. K. Organski's power transition theory, and Robert Gilpin's work on hegemonic war all reach similar conclusions about the relationship between power preponderance and norm formation. See Immanuel Wallenstein, *World-Systems Analysis* (Durham, NC: Duke University Press, 2005); George Modelski, ed., *Explaining Long Cycles* (Boulder, CO: Lynne Rienner, 1987); A. F. K. Organski, *World Politics*, 2nd edition (New York: Alfred A. Knopf, 1968); and Robert Gilpin, *War and Change in World Politics* (Cambridge, U.K.: Cambridge University Press, 1981).
6. Stanley Hoffmann, "International Law and the Control of Force," in Karl Deutsch and Stanley Hoffmann, eds., *The Relevance of International Law* (Garden City, NY: Doubleday-Anchor, 1971). Also see Ann Florini, "The Evolution of International Norms," *International Studies Quarterly* 40 (September 1996): 377–378; and Robert Axelrod, "An Evolutionary Approach to Norms," *American Political Science Review* 80 (Winter 1986): 1105, 1108. On the proposition that powerful states make the rules, see Robert O. Keohane and Joseph S. Nye, *Power and Interdependence*, 3rd edition (New York: Addison-Wesley-Longman, 2001).
7. Hedley Bull, *The Anarchical Society: A Study of Order in World Politics* (New York: Columbia University Press, 1977), p. 13. Also see Adam Watson, *The Evolution of International Society: A Comparative Historical Analysis* (London: Routledge, 1992); Hermann Mosler, *The International Society as a Legal Community* (Alphen aan den Rijn, The Netherlands: Sihthoff and Noordhoff, 1980); and Martin Wight, *Systems of States* (Leicester, U.K.: University of Leicester Press, 1977).
8. For a summary of these research findings, see Gregory A. Raymond, "Normative Orders and Peace," in John A. Vasquez, ed., *What Do We Know About War?* (Lanham, MD: Rowman and Littlefield, 2000), pp. 289–293.
9. Normative orders vary along several dimensions. They differ regarding (1) the amount of discrepancy between the order's professed principles and its applied rules; (2) the degree to which members of the state system have internalized those rules; and (3) whether the rules complement or contradict one another. Variations along these three dimensions affect the strength of a normative order. Those orders with high levels of normative consistency, consensus, and congruence have a greater probability of influencing international outcomes than those ranking lower on these dimensions.
10. Trust is a complex, multidimensional concept that blends risk with an expectation of forbearance. We accept the risk that someone could injure us at the very time we expect they will not take advantage of opportunities created by our acceptance of that risk. When trusting someone, we believe that (1) what they say is true, (2) they have concern for our welfare and are moved by the knowledge that we are counting on them, (3) they possess the capability to follow through on their pledges, and (4) there is consistency between their words and deeds. The stronger our beliefs along each of these dimensions, the greater our overall trust. To put it in more tech-

nical terms, trust can be conceptualized as a point on a distribution of expectations that represents the level of subjective probability with which we assess the other party will perform a particular act. The probability can range from complete trust to complete distrust of another party, and it is the product of our evaluation of the other party's credibility, good will, competence, and reliability. Trusting is thus a matter of degree. The magnitude of trust required for political leaders to accept different types of international agreements varies. The greater the potential injury arising from an act of betrayal, the higher a leader's subjective probability must be to reach a significant agreement with another state on a given issue. If transactions with that state stretch across many different issues, the degree of trust can be uniform, or it may vary from one issue-area to the next. Karen Jones, "Trust as an Affective Attitude," *Ethics* 107 (October 1996): 14; Aneil K. Mishra, "Organizational Responses to Crises: The Centrality of Trust," in Roderick M. Kramer and Tom R. Tyler, eds., *Trust in Organizations: Frontiers of Theory and Research* (London: Sage, 1996), pp. 264–269; Diego Gambetta, "Can We Trust?" in Diego Gambetta, ed., *Trust: Making an Breaking Co-Operative Relations* (Oxford, U.K.: Basil Blackwell, 1988), p. 218.

11. Ever since the Peace of Westphalia ended the Thirty Years' War in 1648, the twin principles of sovereignty and nonintervention have underpinned international relations. Following Rosenau, we define military intervention as an act undertaken by one state to modify the authority structure in a target state—either the way the target organizes itself for making decisions or the policies, internal or foreign, that emanate from the decision-making process of that structure. See James N. Rosenau, "Intervention as a Scientific Concept," *Journal of Conflict Resolution* 13 (March 1969): 149–171.

12. Kenneth L. Vaux, *Ethics and the Gulf War: Religion, Rhetoric, and Righteousness* (Boulder, CO: Westview, 1992), p. 30.

13. Telford Taylor, *Nuremberg and Vietnam: An American Tragedy* (New York: Bantam, 1970), p. 40. The importance of a code of conduct in warfare has been recognized for millennia. The *Ilioupersis,* a lost epic poem on the sack of Troy, is said by other ancient sources to describe the atrocities committed by some Achaian warriors. Divine retribution, as exemplified in the narrative of Ajax the Lesser's drowning by Poseidon in Book 4 of the *Odyssey*, signified that there were right and wrong ways to wage war, and those culpable for wrongdoing would be punished.

14. Ryoichi Taoka, *The Right of Self-Defense in International Law* (Osaka, Japan: Institute of Legal Study Research Series No. 1, Osaka University of Economics and Law, 1978), p. 39.

15. Giannantonio, Botti, *Lo "stato di necessita," nel diritto internazionale* (Ferrara: Universita di Ferrara, Facolta di Giurisprudenza, 1969); Edouard Hazan, *L'Etat de necessité en droit pénal interétatique et international* (Paris: Pedone, 1949); Burleigh Cushing Rodick, *The Doctrine of Necessity in International Law* (New York: Columbia University Press, 1928).

16. Alberto R. Coll, "Prudence and Foreign Policy," in Michael Cromartie, ed., *Might and Right After the Cold War: Can Foreign Policy Be Moral?* (Washington, DC: Ethics and Public Policy Center, 1993), pp. 3–4. The fate of Duke Hsiang of Sung is often used to illustrate the maxim that failure to circumvent generally acknowledged limits on the use of force in an emergency may prove catastrophic. In 638 B.C.E., the

duke refused to attack an army from the rival state of Ch'u while it was crossing the Hung River, even though his forces were outnumbered and would probably be vanquished if their adversaries made it to the other side. Believing that such an attack would be immoral, the duke waited until the army from Ch'u had forded the river. By not doing what was considered a military necessity, he was regarded as responsible for the terrible defeat suffered by Sung.

17. During this period the great powers began using military intervention to recover debts that other states owed their nationals as well as for humanitarian reasons. France, for example, landed troops in Vera Cruz in 1838 to collect debts owed by the Mexican government; Britain, France, and Russia intervened in 1827 to support the Greeks during their struggle for independence from Ottoman control.

18. Geoffrey Best, "Restraints on Land War," in Lawrence Freedman, ed., *War* (New York: Oxford University Press, 1994), p. 266.

19. Melvin Small and J. David Singer, *Resort to Arms: International and Civil Wars, 1816–1980* (Beverly Hills, CA: Sage, 1982).

20. Over the past 50 years, the United Nations has developed a detailed list of inherent, inalienable rights of all human beings. The most significant legal formulation of these rights is in the so-called International Bill of Human Rights, the informal name given to The Universal Declaration of Human Rights (passed by UN General Assembly in 1948), the International Covenant on Civil and Political Rights, and the International Covenant on Economic, Social, and Cultural Rights (both opened for signature in 1966 and entered into force a decade later). The legal rules governing these rights are regarded as *jus cogens*, peremptory norms from which no derogation is permitted. L. Hannikainen, *Peremptory Norms (Jus Cogens) in International Law* (Helsinki: Finnish Lawyers Publishing Company, 1988); Fernando R. Tesón, *Humanitarian Intervention: An Inquiry into Law and Morality* (New York: Transnational Publishers, 1988), p. 15.

21. *Wall Street Journal* (June 7, 2004): A17.

22. Robert D. Kaplan, *Warrior Politics: Why Leadership Demands a Pagan Ethos* (New York: Vintage, 2002), pp. 118–119, 128; Ralph Peters, "Winning Against Warriors," *Strategic Review* 24 (Summer 1996): 12–21.

23. U.S. Department of Defense, *Conduct of the Persian Gulf War: Final Report to Congress* (Washington, DC: Department of Defense, 1992), p. 616.

24. "A good defense is not enough," argued Vice President Cheney in an October 2003 speech to the Heritage Foundation. "We must stay on the offense," added National Security Advisor Condoleezza Rice a few months later in remarks delivered to the National Commission on Terrorist Attacks upon the United States. Http://www.whitehouse.gov/news/releases/2003/10/20031010-1.html; http://www.whitehouse.gov/news/releases/2004/04/20040408.html.

25. The ancient Greeks excelled at a style of shock combat based on the hoplite phalanx. A formation of massed heavy infantry, soldiers aligned shoulder-to-shoulder and weighted down with some 70 pounds of weapons and armor sprinted forward to overwhelm the enemy in a short, terrifying clash. Their legacy can be seen in the premium Western military strategists place on reducing an enemy's offensive capability with a single decisive stroke. J. E. Lendon, *Soldiers and Ghosts: A History of Battle in Classical Antiquity* (New Haven, CT: Yale University Press, 2005), pp. 39–

57; Victor Davis Hanson, *The Western War of War: Infantry Battle in Classical Greece* (Berkeley: University of California Press, 1989), pp. 9–18.

26. E. Badian, *Roman Imperialism in the Late Republic*, 2nd ed. (Ithaca, NY: Cornell University Press, 1968), pp. 4–11. Among the most important international norms influencing the use of force are those norms of inclusion/exclusion that enumerate what constitutes a "civilized" nation and how its members can treat "uncivilized" outsiders. Such norms frequently cast outsiders as unscrupulous adversaries against whom all necessary military means must be used. The philosopher David Hume, for example, argued that if a "civilized nation" was in a conflict with barbarians "who observed no rules even of war, the former must also suspend their observance of them . . . and must render every action . . . as bloody as possible." *A Treatise on Human Nature* (New York: Hafner, 1948), p. 188. Within the American diplomatic tradition, the Jacksonian school of thought recognizes two kinds of enemies: "Honorable enemies fight a clean fight and are entitled to be opposed in the same way; dishonorable enemies fight dirty wars and in that case rules don't apply." Walter Russell Mead, *Special Providence: American Foreign Policy and How It Changed the World* (New York: Alfred A. Knopf, 2001), p. 252.

27. The actions of Servius Sulpicis Galba and Licinius Lucullus in the Lusitanian War were especially vicious. See Appian, *Wars of the Romans in Iberia*, translated and edited by John S. Richardson (Oxford: Aris & Phillips, 2000). For contrasting interpretations of the rationale for Rome's brutality in Spain, see Tenney Frank, *Roman Imperialism* (New York: Macmillan, 1914) and Adolf Schulten, *Die Keltiberer und ihre Kriege mit Rom* (Munich: F. Bruckmann, 1914).

28. Caleb Carr, *The Lessons of Terror* (New York: Random House, 2003), pp. 38–42. For examples of Roman complaints about the perfidious behavior of Arminius, see Velleius Paterculus, *Compendium of Roman History*, translated by F.W. Shipley (Cambridge, MA: Loeb Classical Library, Harvard University Press, 1924) and Lucius Annaeus Florus, *Epitome of Roman History*, translated by E. S. Foster (Cambridge, MA: Loeb Classical Library, Harvard University Press, 1929).

29. Robert D. Worley, *Waging Ancient War: Limits on Preemptive Force* (Carlisle, PA: Strategic Studies Institute, U.S. Army War College, 2003), p. 1. Also see Marcus Tullius Cicero, *On Duties*, translated by Margaret Atkins and edited by M. T. Griffin and Margaret Atkins (Cambridge: Cambridge University Press, 1991), pp. 15–16, 141–142.

30. Kenneth Watkins, "Controlling the Use of Force: A Role for Human Rights Norms in Contemporary Armed Conflict," *American Journal of International Law* 98 (January 2004): 2–6; Carsten Stahn, "Terrorist Acts as 'Armed Attack': The Right to Self-Defense, Article 51½ of the UN Charter, and International Terrorism," *The Fletcher Forum of World Affairs* 27 (Summer/Fall 2003): 45–56.

31. Jean Bethke Elshtain, *Just War Against Terror: The Burden of American Power in a Violent World* (New York: Basic Books, 2003), pp. 169, 173.

32. For the target lists advocated by specific individuals, see Gary Dorrien, *Imperial Designs: Neoconservatism and the New Pax Americana* (New York: Routledge, 2004), pp. 242–244.

33. Cited in Bob Woodward, *Plan of Attack* (New York: Simon & Schuster, 2004), p. 138. Arguing for a highly selective use of preventive military action, Condoleezza Rice

professed that the number of cases in which anticipatory self-defense might be justified will be small. "The threat must be very grave," she insisted, and "the risks of waiting must far outweigh the risks of action." See her October 2002 Wriston Lecture at the Manhattan Institute for Policy Research, retrieved at http://www.whitehouse.gov/news/releases/2002/10/20021001_6.html.

34. George McGovern, *The Essential America: Our Founders and the Liberal Tradition* (New York: Simon & Schuster, 2004), p. 142.

35. Jimmy Carter, speech delivered to the Democratic National Convention on July 26, 2004, retrieved at http://www.cnn.com/2004/ALLPOLITICS/07/26/dems.carter.transcript/index.html. Also see his *Our Endangered Values: America's Moral Crisis* (New York: Simon & Schuster, 2005), p. 159.

36. Benjamin R. Barber, *Fear's Empire: War, Terrorism, and Democracy* (New York: Norton, 2003), p. 105.

37. See David Lubin, "Preventive War," *Philosophy & Public Affairs* 32 (No. 2, 2004): 214.

38. Allen Buchanan and Robert Keohane would include someone taking steps to create a dire risk of "sudden and very serious harms on a massive scale." See their "The Preventive Use of Force: A Cosmopolitan Institutional Proposal," *Ethics & International Affairs* 18 (No. 1, 2004): 5. For a critical appraisal of their suggestion, see Steven Lee, "A Moral Critique of the Cosmopolitan Institutional Proposal,"*Ethics & International Affairs* 19 (No. 2, 2005): 99–107.

39. See http://www.hindustantimes.com/news/181_232225,0008.htm; http://www.guardian.co.uk/iran/story/0,12858,1111570,00.html; http://www.smh.com.au/articles/2003/05/21/1053196642080.html; and http://www.chanelnewsasia.com/stories/afp_world/view/55514/1/.html. For a discussion of its incorporation into French defense strategy, see François Heisbourg, "A Work in Progress: The Bush Doctrine and Its Consequences," *The Washington Quarterly* 26 (Spring 2003): 83; and Tomas Valasek, "New Threats, New Rules: Revising the Law of War," *World Policy Journal* 20 (Spring 2003): 22.

40. Christopher C. Joyner, *International Law in the 21st Century* (Lanham, MD: Rowman & Littlefield, 2005), p. 170; Pierre Hassner, "The United States: The Empire of Force or the Force of Empire?" *Chaillot Papers*, No. 54 (Paris: European Union Institute for Security Studies, 2002), p. 41. As Richard Falk notes, the Bush administration's unwillingness to countenance any form of procedural accountability allows others to make the following argument from analogy, even when they face quite different circumstances than the United States: if Washington can mount preventive attacks without external scrutiny, so can we when confronting comparable threats to our security. See his *The Great Terror War* (New York: Olive Branch Press, 2003), pp. 97–98.

41. Joseph Cirincione, "Can Preventive War Cure Proliferation?" *Foreign Policy* 137 (July/August 2003): 68.

42. Mary Ellen O'Connell, *The Myth of Preventive Self-Defense* (Washington, DC: American Society of International Law, 2002), p. 19.

43. Arthur Schlesinger, Jr., "The Immorality of Preventive War" (2002). Retrieved at http://www.digitalnpq.org/archive/2002_fall/schlesinger.html. Without perfect information, decisions to launch preventive military actions rest on predictions that

carry high risks of what statisticians call "false positives" (incorrect predictions of future aggression by other states). A major policy dilemma facing political leaders who make preventive decisions concerns the ratio of false positives to false negatives. How can false positives be reduced without increasing false negatives? How can leaders avoid launching preventive wars against states that are wrongly believed to be planning aggression without foregoing action against states that are indeed planning aggression? For a discussion of the jurisprudence of preemption and preventive action, see Alan M. Dershowitz, *Preemption* (New York: Norton, 2006), pp. 11, 228–236.

44. An application of the legal principle *nemo debet esse index in propia sus causa* to preventive war can be found in the judgment of the 1945 International Military Tribunal of Nuremberg. According to the Tribunal, Germany wrongly asserted that it "alone could decide . . . whether preventive action was necessary, and that in making her decision her judgment was conclusive. But whether action taken under the claim of self-defense was in fact aggressive or defensive must ultimately be subject to investigation and adjudication if international law is ever to be enforced." Cited in Oscar Schachter, "Disputes Involving the Use of Force," in Lori F. Damrosch, ed., *The International Court of Justice at a Crossroads* (Dobbs Ferry, NY: Transnational Publishers, 1987), p. 230. Problems of this sort have led some legal scholars to describe justifications for preventive warfare as a "bottomless legal pit." Morton A. Kaplan and Nicholas deB. Katzenbach, *The Political Foundations of International Law* (New York: John Wiley, 1961), p. 213.

45. Christopher Dawson, *Dynamics of World History* (Wilmington, DE: ISI Books, 2002), xvii.

46. Jack Snyder cautions that preventive uses of military force expand rather than ameliorate security problems because they spark endless brushfire wars. Throughout history, "the preventive pacification of one turbulent frontier . . . has usually led to the creation of another, adjacent to the first." See his "Imperial Temptations," *The National Interest* 71 (Spring 2003): 30.

47. Thomas Franck, *Recourse to Force: State Action Against Threats and Armed Attacks* (Cambridge: Cambridge University Press, 2002), p. 107.

48. Richard Smoke, *National Security and the Nuclear Dilemma*, 3rd ed. (New York: McGraw-Hill, 1993), p. 51; Alfred Vagts, *Defense and Diplomacy: The Soldier and the Conduct of Foreign Relations* (New York: King's Crown Press, 1956), pp. 332–334.

49. Cited in John L. Gaddis, *Strategies of Containment* (New York: Oxford University Press, 1982), p. 149. These earlier calls for preventive U.S. military action generally focused on destroying the fledgling Soviet nuclear arsenal. In 1950, for example, the Commandant of the Air War College advocated a surprise first strike. "And when I went to Christ," he reportedly said, "I think I could explain to Him why I wanted to do it now before it's too late. I think I could explain to Him that I had saved civilization. With it [the A-bomb] used in time, we can immobilize a foe [and] reduce his crime before it happened." Cited in Jeffrey Record, "The Bush Doctrine and War with Iraq," *Parameters* 33 (Spring 2003): 19. For a discussion of calls for preventive action during the 1960s to destroy the emerging Chinese nuclear arsenal, see Lyle J. Goldstein, *Preventive Attack and Weapons of Mass Destruction: A Comparative Historical Analysis* (Stanford, CA: Stanford University Press, 2006), pp. 56–66.

50. Wesley L. Gould and Michael Barkun, *International Law and the Social Sciences* (Princeton, NJ: Princeton University Press, 1970), p. 136. Also see William D. Coplin, "International Law and Assumptions About the State System," *World Politics* 17 (July 1965): 618.
51. Nicholas Greenwood Onuf, "Global Law-Making and Legal Thought," in Nicholas Greenwood Onuf, *Lawmaking in the Global Community* (Durham: Carolina Academic Press, 1982), p. 21.
52. See *Paquete Habana, Lola*, 175 U.S. 677 [1900]; and Article 38 [1][d] of the Statute of the International Court of Justice.
53. Malcolm N. Shaw, *International Law*, 3rd ed. (Cambridge, U.K.: Cambridge University Press, 1991), pp. 92–93.
54. Ingrid Detter Delupis, *The International Legal Order* (Aldershot, U.K.: Dartmouth, 1994), p. 152; Shabtai Rosenne, *Practice and Methods of International Law* (London: Oceana, 1984), p. 119.
55. Geoffrey Best, *War and Law Since 1945* (Oxford: Clarendon Press, 1994), p. 406.
56. Gerhard von Glahn, *Law Among Nations: An Introduction to Public International Law*, 7th ed. (Boston: Allyn and Bacon, 1992), p. xii.

7

Ideals in the Pursuit of National Security Interests

> [The U.S.] fervent pursuit of war with Iraq is driving us to squander the international legitimacy that has been America's most potent weapon. . . . We have begun to dismantle the largest and most effective web of international relationships the world has ever known. Our current course will bring it instability and danger, not security.
>
> —U.S. diplomat John Brady Kiesling's letter of resignation to Secretary of State Colin L. Powell on February 27, 2003

Since the capture of Saddam Hussein in Tikrit on December 13, 2003, many Americans have wondered when the United States would be able to withdraw its troops from Iraq. Contrary to the assurances from the Bush administration that democratic governance and economic reconstruction would quickly get underway, Iraq has been overwhelmed by a torrent of violence that both shocks and bewilders. For most people, the February 2006 bombing of the Askariya mosque in Samarra, one of the holiest sites for Iraq's Shiite Muslims, symbolized the country's descent into a vicious civil war. Whether the Iraqis can construct a democracy in the years ahead remains highly uncertain. As the Chorus in Sophocles' tragic play *Ajax* reminds us, "Much may mortals learn by seeing, but before he sees it, none may read the future."[1]

Although we cannot read the future, it is possible to construct plausible forecasts of the alternative futures that could occur based on past patterns and unfolding trends. Our forecast in this concluding chapter warns of peril for the American Imperium. When seen in the light of what previous research has learned about the chaos characteristic of permissive international normative orders, the security policy followed by the Bush administration since the 9/11 terrorist attacks does not auger well for the United States. After the war in Iraq is over, policymakers in Washington will still be wrestling with the long-term effects of an ill-conceived grand strategy that complicates efforts to manage wrenching global power shifts.

Regime Change and Democratization

On the heels of 9/11, President George W. Bush announced a "forward strategy for freedom" whose objective was to bring about regime change in autocratic states that were regarded as hostile and dangerous.[2] U.S. national security, the president believed, would benefit if other countries had governments like the United States, an assumption derived from the ethnocentric opinion that America's political values were superior to others, and that all people naturally would like to be like Americans if they only could. "We are led, by events and common sense, to one conclusion," declared President Bush in January 2005 during his second inaugural address. "The survival of liberty in our land increasingly depends on the success of liberty in other lands." Spreading democracy throughout the entire world, he proclaimed, "is the urgent requirement of our nation's security, and the calling of our time." Therefore, "it is the policy of the United States to seek and support the growth of democratic movements and institutions *in every nation and culture*."[3]

Regime change, replacing the governing institutions of another country, was one of the Bush administration's primary goals in the Iraq War. In short order, the U.S. military removed Saddam Hussein from power, dismantled his security apparatus, and promptly set about in an effort to remake the Iraqi political system.[4] The aim was to create a secular democracy in a pivotal Arab state that would be a model for the region. Iraqis were ready for freedom, President Bush told the nation. Expel the dictator, draft a new constitution, hold elections, and Iraq will become a stable democracy.[5]

The Roots of American Interventionism

Military intervention has long been employed by the United States in an effort to liberalize the political institutions of other countries. Especially since World War II, U.S. presidents have overlooked the contradiction in using coercion to cultivate democracy, arguing, in the words of Richard Nixon, that it was "necessary to use American power and influence to defend and extend freedom in places thousands of miles away."[6]

Oddly enough, America's post-9/11 obsession with regime change borrows heavily from the Clinton administration's advocacy of enlarging democracy, which drew from the liberal beliefs of James Madison and Woodrow Wilson. Noting that democracies "don't attack each other," President Bill Clinton declared in his 1994 State of the Union address that "the best strategy to ensure our security and to build a durable peace is to support the advance of democracy elsewhere."[7] This argument was the cornerstone of his administration's widely publicized September 1993 *Bottom-Up Review*, which concluded that democratic "enlargement" would be a principal pillar of American foreign policy.[8] Clinton's first-term National Security Advisor, Anthony Lake, also advocated this policy priority, reiterating on many occasions that "The successor to a doctrine of containment must be a strategy of enlargement—enlargement of the world's free community."[9] Endorsing the same prescription, former Secretary of State Warren Christopher maintained that "securing and expanding the community of democratic nations and respect for human rights [is] critical to building a world where long-term stability is strengthened."[10] In fact, some supporters went so far as to insist that "when a people attempts to hold free elections and establish a constitutional democracy, the United States and the international community should not only assist but should 'guarantee' the result."[11]

President Bush's "forward strategy of freedom" thus gained initial traction in part because the active promotion of democracy had been recommended in some quarters for years.[12] As discussed in Chapter 6, the principle that states had an responsibility to intervene in the affairs of other states to stop human rights violations and to protect civil liberties had gained support throughout the 1990s.[13] By the time Bush took office, various members of the international legal community had come to see democracy as a "human right entitlement"[14] Once democracy was conceived as an entitlement, an international obligation to intervene in support of the alleged right of people to be ruled democratically surfaced as a corollary to the principle of civilian inviolability.[15] In this emerging climate of normative opinion, the Bush team found a practicable (though problematic) justification for viewing military intervention as a viable mechanism of regime change. It did so, however, only after 9/11, and only after the security goals of fighting global terrorism and disarming Saddam Hussein were advanced as rationales for the March 2003 invasion of Iraq, when evidence of Iraq's links to Al Qaeda and its possession of WMDs could not be produced.

The Impact of American Interventionism

Governments brought on the tips of bayonets have not historically inspired popular support. Are American bayonets different? What does the record tell us about the effectiveness, or lack thereof, of past U.S. military interventions in promoting regime change? Is there a pattern to what has happened in the political institutions of target countries as a result of U.S. interventions? Have their governments become more democratic?

In addressing these questions, the period after World War II is the most illuminating. By one estimate 115 overt U.S. interventions were undertaken between 1945 and 1996.[16] As shown in Figure 7.1, the rate at which these acts were initiated varied somewhat episodically over time (with peaks in the late 1950s and mid-1960s), but deviated within a narrow range (from none in nine different years to six in 1964), averaging slightly more than two per year (2.3) across the time span.

Most of these interventions were justified by pro-liberalization goals. As Mark Peceny points out, in nearly 80 percent of past U.S. interventions American power has been used to promote democratization in the target, in part because nearly all presidents authorizing the sending of troops abroad have

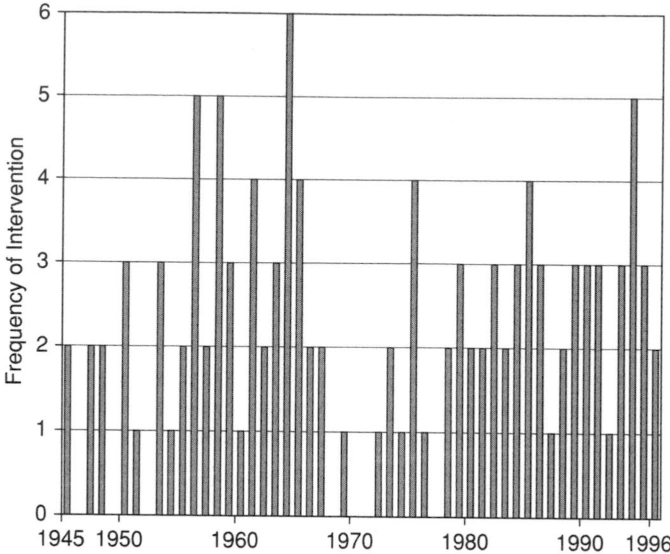

Figure 7.1 The U.S. Use of Military Intervention, 1945–1996 This inventory aggregates the separate U.S. military interventions identified by Frederic S. Pearson and Robert A. Baumann, "International Military Intervention, 1946–1988." *Sources: Inter-University Consortium for Political and Social Research, Data Collection 6035, University of Michigan, 1994; Herbert K. Tillema, "Foreign Overt Military Intervention in the Nuclear Age,"* Journal of Peace Research *26 (May 1989): 179–195; Herbert K. Tillema, "Foreign Overt Military Intervention in the Nuclear Age: A Clarification,"* Journal of Peace Research *26 (November 1989): 419–420; Herbert K. Tillema, "Cold War Alliance and Overt Military Intervention, 1945–1991,"* International Interactions *20 (No. 3, 1994): 249–278; and Jeffrey Pickering, "The Structural Shape of Peace,"* International Interactions *25 (No. 4, 1999): 363–391.*

found that rationale useful in building a consensus in both Congress and the American public about the ideals the involvement would serve, despite the risks. Indeed, since 1960 only the 1991 Persian Gulf War intervention was proclaimed by the United States as a justification for the use of force abroad for reasons that did not include bringing liberty to countries that did not benefit from it.[17]

The extent to which past U.S. interventions deserve applause or condemnation requires careful comparative evaluation. To our minds, this assessment is best conducted by evaluating their ultimate consequences.[18] Did U.S. interventions produce increases in the target's respect for representative governance? Or was repression more often the product?

The evidence as to whether U.S. military intervention can induce democratic reform is not encouraging. On the positive side, one study of 27 U.S. interventions during the post–World War II era, which measured whether the target country became more or less democratic one and three years after the intervention, found that "most nations retain[ed] their current level of democracy."[19] When, however, countries that had experienced a U.S. intervention were compared to those that had not, the latter were *less* likely to become more democratic. This evidence suggests to proponents of American interventionism that forcible regime change can be effective in promoting democracy.

On the negative side, a study of 89 interventions between 1945 and 1991 concluded that only 10 percent produced democratic changes in the target.[20] Countries that were members of the liberal democratic community at the beginning of the intervention tended to remain members after the withdrawal of U.S. armed forces; similarly, the countries that were nondemocratic tended to remain nondemocratic. Thus, if the maintenance of democratic institutions in the target is the reason for U.S. interventions, they have generally succeeded, which suggests that military intervention is better suited for the preservation of democratic governance abroad than it is for its promotion.

Other studies, which relied on different measurement techniques, have reached equally pessimistic conclusions about "reform" interventions. One analysis of U.S. interventions since 1945 found that not a single target country became more free.[21] Another investigation, which looked at American interventions since 1898, revealed a success rate of 26 percent, which drops to 17 percent when the U.S. intervened unilaterally.[22] Finally, in a study of U.S. interventions over the past century, the Carnegie Endowment for International Peace found that "in most instances where the United States used its military to help oust a government, democracy rarely followed." Germany and Japan after the Second World War and Panama after the ouster of Manuel Noriega in 1989 and Granada after the American invasion in 1983 were seen as the only successes. As Joseph Montville laments, Washington seems able to get itself "together enough to bomb somebody—that's not a problem. But after [America has] bombed everything usually becomes kind of a mess. The military doesn't want to play policeman, and the administration doesn't want to get involved in nation-building."[23] As a result, the United States often winds up backing dictators who trample on the civil rights of their own people, which provokes resistance movements that inevitably equate their oppression with American power. When America's client eventually falls, Washington has often faced a foreign enemy whose animus is directed at the United States.

Given these research findings, the flame of liberty is unlikely to burn brighter around the world as a result of additional U.S. military interventions. American efforts to engineer democratic transitions face substantial obstacles in countries that have had little or no experience with democratic rule. According to historian Niall Ferguson, previous attempts to overcome these obstacles have typically gone through the following stages:

1. Impressive initial military success
2. A flawed assessment of indigenous sentiment
3. A strategy of limited war and gradual escalation of forces
4. Domestic disillusionment in the face of protracted and nasty conflict
5. Premature democratization
6. The ascendancy of domestic economic considerations
7. Ultimate withdrawal[24]

The most successful U.S. interventions for regime change were those that (1) lasted less than a year, (2) involved *either* military support for a combatant but few U.S. troops beyond advisors *or* a large commitment of ground forces, but (3) did not rely on "gunboat diplomacy," (4) were backed by a consensus among the American foreign policy elite about the need to use force in the service of democratization, or (5) occurred in a time period when democracy was the political system of choice in the international arena.[25] But even under these conditions, America's success rate has been low, which suggests that future attempts at regime change will probably bring frustration and failure. After all of the noble talk about spreading democracy, U.S. military interventions frequently end with authoritarian clients in power. Rather than nurturing peace and justice, imposing democracy on culturally divided societies with weak political institutions often results in civil strife due to the inability of those institutions to handle rising demands for popular participation.

That, indeed, has been the sobering experience after three years of occupying Iraq. Born of false hopes for democraticization, the U.S. intervention delivered chaos; paradoxically, the overthrow of an oppressive, anti-American Sunni dictator has culminated in an electoral victory for militant Shiites, whose repressive anti-American militias appeared in the summer of 2006 to be gaining control over the country's security forces. In short, the American experience in Iraq has been no more encouraging than past efforts at intervention. Forceful regime change that fails to provide democracy, such as the CIA's 1953 overthrow of Prime Minister Mohammed Mossadegh in favor of the autocratic Shah of Iran, often results in a backlash against the United States after the regime that Washington has installed falls. The damage to America's international reputation is difficult to estimate; however, one consequence is clear: rather than being perceived as noble undertakings for high moral principles, U.S. armed interventions are seen as raw efforts to serve American interests. "We should expect ambivalence from other countries about democratic promotion," observes John Owen, because it "helps to keep America number one" and is interpreted by them as "purely and simply extending the American imperium."[26] From their perspective, the United States is no more honorable than any previous preponderant state; it puts power over principle, and seeks to expand its influence by enlarging the number of states cast in its image. Despite all of the rhetoric about democraticization, many conclude that forceful regime change is simply a means to an end—the preservation of American domination of world affairs.

American Interventionism and the Erosion of U.S. Moral Leadership

In view of the enormous difficulties in bringing democratic change to autocratic societies, why has the United States relied so heavily on military intervention rather than other means of realizing its foreign policy goals? It was not always so. In 1792, only the United States, Switzerland, and the French Republic could be safely classified as democracies. Hoping to discourage Europe's monarchies from stamping out liberal revolutions before they could spread, the United States became the most vocal proponent of the international legal prohibition against interference in the internal affairs of other states. A century later, however, Washington began to perceive its interests differently, seeing the nonintervention principle as an obstacle to projecting American power across the globe. Today, at the pinnacle of world power, the United States has taken the lead in promoting actions that it formerly opposed, insisting that the intrinsic justice of spreading democracy overrides the traditional legal prohibition against military intervention.[27]

Using preventive intervention to change regimes that may one day pose a threat to the United States has understandably renewed debate about the importance of international legitimacy in the conduct of American foreign policy. Emphasizing that no actor on the planet comes close to matching American military power, some policy analysts downplay its significance. The United States, they submit, would be severely constrained if it had to win approval from international institutions before undertaking a regime-change intervention. The "price demanded for the additional legitimacy," complains strategist Colin Gray, "would condemn the . . . [United States] to ineffectiveness."[28] "To be blunt," adds a former Defense Department official, the United States does not need the blessing of a UN Security Resolution and dressing of a few coalition partners; "in the end we'll be kicking down the door largely on our own."[29]

Other policy analysts worry that this headstrong, take-it-or-leave-it approach to foreign policy creates the impression that Washington wants one set of rules for itself and another for everyone else. Why, they ask rhetorically, was the United States unable to obtain broad international support for removing Saddam Hussein—a brutal dictator who had violated the human rights of his country's citizens, attacked neighboring countries, and ignored numerous UN Security Council resolutions? In the opinion of a former U.S. Assistant Secretary of State, the Bush administration's heavy-handed treatment of anyone questioning its plans for preventive war raised suspicions overseas about Washington's ulterior motives regarding Iraq.[30] In what Stephen Walt describes as a classic case of "soft balancing," France, Germany, and Russia were able to block UN Security Council authorization for the war and thus "deny the United States the legitimacy it had sought."[31] While America's sheer strength allowed it to invade Iraq anyway, the subsequent occupation and reconstruction of the country became more difficult without the international support that would have come with a UN endorsement. In short, the Bush administration failed to realize that legitimacy is the ultimate force multiplier.[32]

America's power is magnified when others interpret it as legitimate, as serving larger global interests as well as those of the United States. UN Security Council resolutions are a key source of that legitimacy; they help make "the brute fact of American hard power acceptable to other countries," giving "American values the heft of international law, rather than the stigma of a diktat from Washington."[33] But when the United States tries to impose its will on others, it "sacrifices its own legitimacy and undercuts the legitimacy of the liberal order it has sought to advance."[34] Acknowledging this dilemma, President Harry S Truman wisely counseled, "we all have to realize—no matter how great our strength—that we must deny ourselves the license to do always as we please."[35]

Rules for Rivals

Because fears about the arbitrary employment of American power can complicate the conduct of U.S. foreign policy, a few supporters of preventive military action have considered developing guidelines to govern its use. "The real issue may not be whether prevention is ever justified," mused Robert Kagan, "but rather who may do the preventing and who decides when, where, and how it is handled."[36]

In the previous chapter we discussed the risks associated with permissive normative orders forged by unilateralist, "might makes right" superpowers that countenance preventive warfare. We noted that in a global society in which many other states also adhered to Washington's self-proclaimed right to use military force unilaterally for *preventive* purposes, a climate of opinion would be created where mere fear is a justification for warfare. In such a world, uncertainty is likely to grow and international security erode as prevailing international norms license precautionary military interventions. However, there is an alternative scenario. Let us now sketch how we propose anticipatory self-defense by sovereign states be treated within a restrictive normative order.

Rule 1: All sovereign states have an inalienable right to use military force in self-defense.

Corollary 1.1: Sovereign states may engage in collective as well as individual self-defense. Concerted military action may be taken by several states against an aggressor, regardless of whether one, some, or all of them were attacked.

Corollary 1.2: When authorized by the United Nations, sovereign states may also undertake multilateral uses of force on behalf of the international community to defend a member of the UN against aggression.

Rule 2: Sovereign states may use military force in response to overt armed attacks, but their responses must be governed by the laws of war, which require every effort be made to employ force in proportion to the danger faced and to discriminate between combatants and noncombatants.

Rule 3: Sovereign states may use military force in response to a pattern of violent covert activities of such magnitude that they are tantamount to an armed attack, but their responses must be governed by the legal requirements of proportionality and discrimination.

Rule 4: Sovereign states may take military action to intercept an impending attack if (a) credible evidence of imminence exists, (b) there is no time for an effective nonmilitary response, and (c) the requirements of proportionality and discrimination are followed.

Rule 5: Sovereign states may launch discrete military strikes against state and nonstate actors that have taken significant, tangible steps toward implementing a plan of armed attack if (a) credible evidence of their aggressive intent and implementation efforts exists, (b) there is a grave danger that such an attack would cause substantial harm on a enormous scale, and (c) the strikes are proportionate and discriminatory. Every effort should be made to exhaust nonviolent alternatives before resorting to armed force and to obtain support from a competent, impartial international body that has responsibility for security matters within the targeted geographic region.

Corollary 5.1: A government harboring or supporting a genuine international terrorist threat to another state fails to meet its international legal obligations and therefore forfeits sovereign protection from limited external strikes directed at specific terrorist targets.

Corollary 5.2: A government that is either unable or unwilling to protect foreign nationals from life-threatening hostage situations forfeits sovereign protection from external military operations, which, as a last resort, may be initiated for the sole purpose of rescuing the threatened nationals.

Rule 6: Sovereign states may not wage a preventive war to weaken or change a regime that might conceivably pose a threat sometime in the future, but thus far is not an imminent danger that has done anything to make itself morally liable for intervention.

Though not a fully formed security regime, these rules suggest how a restrictive normative order can avoid the extremes of unbridled self-help on the one hand, and a blanket prohibition on robust uses of armed force on the other. The first three rules and their corollaries acknowledge the inherent right of individual and collective self-defense, but spell out guidelines for their use. Recognizing that there are times when preemptive military action is legitimate in an era of ballistic missiles and weapons of mass destruction, the next two rules and their corollaries describe the parameters that limit the scope of anticipatory self-defense. When judging when the first use of force is warranted it is important to consider the certainty of the threat, the magnitude and severity of the harm that will be suffered in the absence of preemption, the probability that preemptive military action will succeed, the costs that will be incurred, and the gravity of the consequences that may result from preemptive action. Reasonable people may disagree on how to weigh these factors in any given case, but the difficulty in judging when to use preemption does not mean it is never justified. Preventive military action, however, is another matter. To constrain the use of force based merely on conjecture about what might happen someday, the last rule proscribes preventive warfare.

As America searches for the means to deal with fourth-generation, asymmetrical warfare, there is ample reason to question whether preventive wars will enhance the prospects for twenty-first–century peace. Caution over the implications of a more permissive normative order is warranted, because many interventionary acts, inspired by noble intentions, not only exacerbate the very problems they try to solve, but their long-term repercussions can generate a welter of new problems. Whereas reconstructing Iraq, dealing with the Iranian and North Korean nuclear programs, and combating nonstate actors who employ terrorist tactics are the primary security concerns for the United States today, over the next several decades new and arguably more important challenges will originate from rising near-competitor states. Whether these challenges unfold within a permissive or a restrictive normative order will have a significant impact on the stability of an emerging multipolar future. As one student of world affairs has warned, if the United States continues to undermine international norms that restrict the use of force, sooner or later America itself "is certain to be victimized by the very weakness in the international system it is now causing."[37] The United States could accordingly be imperiled by its inability to set standards for international behavior that will serve its national interests when the time comes that America no longer stands unrivaled at the pinnacle of global power.

Power Trajectories Through the Coming Decades

Although the international system is anarchic, possessing no higher authority above the sovereign state, it is nonetheless stratified due to variations in the relative power of its members. At the summit of a unipolar system is the most powerful state, presently the United States, earlier Great Britain, and, in all probability, someday China. Just below are the major powers, followed in sequence by the middle, and then the minor powers.[38] If this international pecking order is clear, with the dominant state holding a substantial advantage over its nearest rival, then efforts to alter the rank order of states by force are unlikely. Conversely, if the capability advantage of the dominant state is eroding due to the rapid growth of one or more challengers, the probability of armed conflict increases.[39]

Recall from Chapter 2 that over two millennia ago Herodotus hypothesized that the trajectory of state power follows a cycle of ascendance and decline based on the ratio of its strength relative to others within the existing system. War, according to many contemporary scholars, is most likely at certain critical points along this cycle; namely, when shifts in the rate of growth or decline in a state's relative power create discontinuities between foreign policy expectations and diplomatic realities.[40] If the achieved status of a strong, growing state does not confer benefits commensurate with what it expects, add other scholars, the odds of war increase significantly. Peace, they aver, is preserved best by an imbalance of national capabilities between satisfied and dissatisfied states that favors those content with the international status quo. Their reading of the historical record suggests that major wars often result from rear-end collisions between rapidly rising dissatisfied states and dominant states, whose long-term interests are served by preserving the status quo. When, due to unequal rates of growth, the relative strengths of a revisionist challenger and the dominant state converge toward rough parity, armed conflict can erupt in two different ways. First, the dominant state may initiate a preventive war so as not to be overtaken by the challenger. Second, the challenger may strike first, confident that it can accelerate its climb to the apex of international power by beating the dominant state to the punch.[41]

As we have argued throughout this book, unipolar systems have not been durable in modern world politics. Dominant great powers conform to the law of gravity, that "what goes up must come down." No state has been able to sustain its preeminent position over a very long period. The United States, like the once-dominant powers that preceded it, will inevitably slip from its lofty perch as the current unipolar system gradually gives way to a world containing more than one center of power. This structural change may take decades, but now is the time to be prepared. The question looming before the next generation of American leaders will be how to manage this transition toward a multipolar future. "Major shifts of power between states," observes James Hoge, "occur infrequently and are rarely peaceful."[42] The policies Washington adopts will have an enormous impact on whether upcoming shifts harden into bitter rivalries that culminate in dangerous trials of strength. Since the early 1990s, various government officials have argued that the United States must focus on "precluding the emergence of any future global competitor."[43] By espousing a doctrine of unilateral preventive intervention and flaunting its military capacity for "shock and awe," has the Bush administration complicated efforts to convert aspiring global powers into prospective strategic partners? By embracing a grand strategy that promotes a permissive international normative order, has it inadvertently created future security perils for the United States? By standing tall, acting unilaterally, and dismissing the opinions of others, has America's declaratory policy of "Tell, Don't Ask" undermined relations with the countries most needed to combat the threat of global terrorism?

Rising Rivals or Prospective Partners?

One of the principal foreign policy challenges emanating from the war in Iraq, notes historian John Lewis Gaddis, is not to make that country the single lens through which the United States views the world. A defiant, nuclear-armed Iran may be the "wild card" of the next decade or so, but what happens in China, India, and elsewhere, he suggests, "may well be as important for the future of the international system as what transpires in the Middle East."[44] Indeed,

China's economic growth and energetic diplomacy are already causing huge global repercussions. The question is no longer whether China becomes strong, but how China will use its growing strength.[45]

When China began its market reforms in 1978, it accounted for less than 1 percent of the world economy, and its foreign trade totaled $20.6 billion. Since 1978, China has averaged 9.4 percent annual GDP growth and by 2005 accounted for 4.7 percent of the world economy, with its foreign trade increasing to $851 billion. Between 2000 and 2004 alone, gross domestic product climbed from $1.1 to $1.9 trillion (an estimated $6.4 trillion at purchasing-power parity), and foreign direct investment rose from $38 billion to $55 billion. Today China is the world's largest producer of steel, the largest exporter of information technology goods, the second largest consumer of energy, and is projected over the next half-decade to graduate four times the number of engineering doctorates as the United States. It also has one of the world's highest savings rates (roughly 40 percent of GDP) and foreign-exchange reserves of $845 billion, second in the world behind Japan.[46]

China's growing economic strength is expected to transform the twenty-first–century geopolitical landscape as dramatically as did America's rise at the end of the nineteenth century. The U.S. National Intelligence Council forecasts that China's gross domestic product will equal Germany's in 2009, Japan's in 2017, and the United States' in 2042.[47] "Once all of its potential is mobilized," predicts a prominent student of the Chinese economy, "its contribution to the world as an engine of growth will be unprecedented."[48]

Current projections notwithstanding, China's rise is not preordained; several obstacles could slow the pace of its economic development.[49] Some analysts are skeptical about China's capacity to move easily from low-cost manufacturing to technological innovation, from an economy based on producing commodities inexpensively to one that produces commodities that no one else has created. Others maintain that China's economic expansion will be hindered by its undeveloped capital markets, rickety banking system, and a shortage of skilled, internationally experienced managers. Still others point to unrest bred by inequalities between urban and rural areas, as well as by widening regional disparities. Finally, a last group of analysts highlight serious problems of resource degradation, scarcities of water, energy, and raw materials, and the growing cost of providing health care for an aging citizenry. Given its enormous population, China faces what have been called "division and multiplication" problems: "The division problem is that even large aggregate resources become small per capita resources when divided by 1.3 billion people," whereas the "multiplication problem is that even small problems become incredibly large when multiplied by 1.3 billion."[50]

Figure 7.2 shows the fluctuations in the material capabilities of China and the United States between the end of the Cold War and the 9/11 terrorist attacks, as measured by an index that combines their relative standing on energy consumption, iron and steel production, military expenditures, military personnel, total population, and urban population. The narrowing of the capability gap

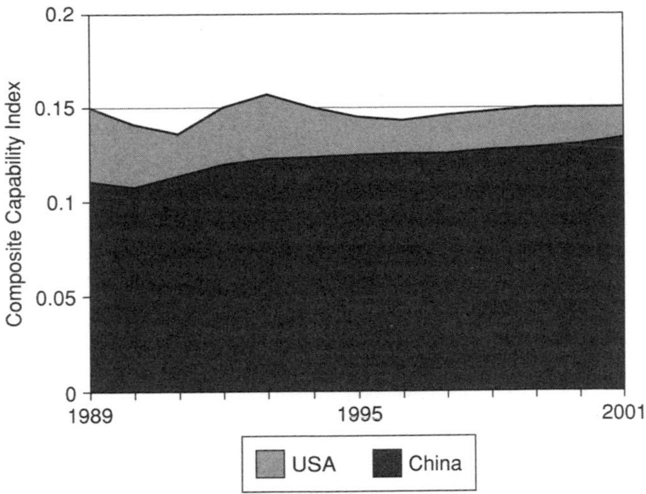

Figure 7.2 A Comparison of U.S. and Chinese Material Capabilities, 1989–2001 The Composite Index of National Capabilities (CINC) is the sum of all observations on each of six capability components for a given year (energy consumption, iron and steel production, military expenditures, military personnel, total population, and urban population), converting each state's absolute component to a share of the international system, and then averaging across the six components. *Source: Correlates of War project.*

between the two countries has led some observers to predict that China will eventually surmount the obstacles to its development and overtake the United States in military power. Such a power transition would probably unfold over several decades, which these analysts fear could be scarred by substantial instability.[51]

According to a recent Pentagon report, China has invested heavily in military programs designed to improve its power-projection capabilities. "The pace and scope of China's military build-up are, already, such as to put regional military balances at risk," warned the report. As its ambitious military modernizations continues, "China's leaders may be tempted to resort to force or coercion more quickly to press diplomatic advantage, advance security interests, or resolve disputes."[52] Chinese Foreign Minister Li Zhaoxing has dismissed these concerns as groundless, and Major General Zhu Chenghu, a dean at China's National Defense University, has expressed confidence that China and the United States would not fight one another in the near future, though he suggested that Beijing would respond to any U.S. attack on China with nuclear weapons.[53]

China's annual defense spending has been growing at a double-digit rate for the past decade, but most estimates place total expenditures somewhere between 14 and 19 percent of those of the United States. Currently, China has only 20 CSS-4 silo-based, liquid-fueled ICBMs, some 2,600 largely antiquated combat aircraft, and no aircraft carriers. Military modernization has enhanced China's coastal sea-denial capability but has not added a blue-water sea-control capability that challenges U.S. maritime supremacy.[54] Over the next two decades, however, China's defense budget could triple as the country continues to upgrade its conventional forces and deploys a credible, second-strike nuclear arsenal around solid-fueled DF-31 and DF-31A inter–continental ballistic missiles (ICBMs) and JL-2 submarine–launched ballistic missiles (SLBMs).

U.S. military confrontation with a more muscular China is, of course, not preordained. But avoiding friction that could spark conflict is certain to be more difficult in a permissive normative order that sanctions the unbridled pursuit of self-advantage by military means, including preventive intervention and warfare.

India is also an up-and-coming power, enjoying an economy that has been growing for two decades at more than 6 percent a year. By mid-century it is expected to have 1.6 billion people with a larger, highly educated working-age population than China.[55] Like China, India's ascendancy is not assured. Budget deficits, widespread poverty, a problematic infrastructure, and other obstacles could hamper its growth. Still, most forecasts estimate that India's gross domestic product will surpass France's in 2020, Germany's a few years later, and Japan's shortly after 2030.[56] As Figure 7.3 depicts, India's percentage share of the world gross domestic product is expected to rank third in 2050, behind only the United States and China.

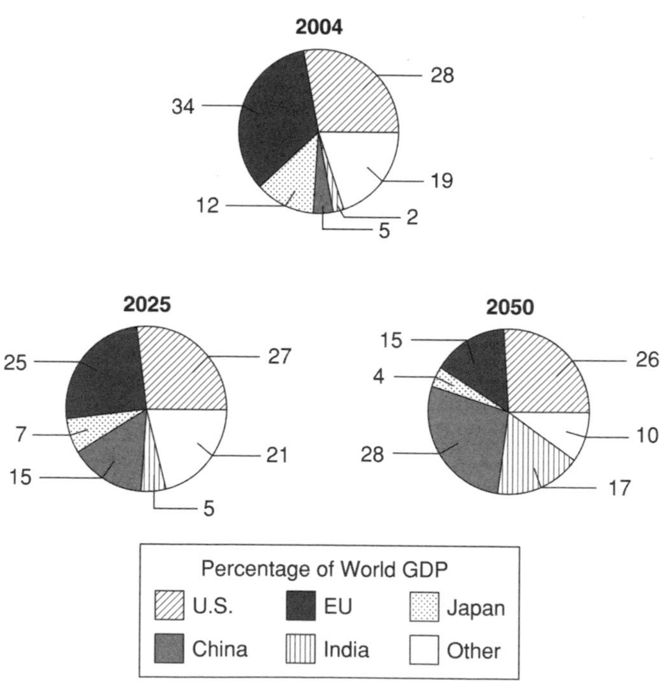

Figure 7.3 The Changing Global Economy *Source:* BusinessWeek *(August 22/28, 2005): 58;* World Bank, *World Development Indicators 2006: 198.*

With the rise of China and India over the next few decades, America's unipolar moment will eventually enter a long twilight. When their ascent is combined with the possibilities of a revitalized Japan and Russia, an enlarged, more well-integrated European Union,[57] and the political awakening of restless and resentful young people scattered throughout the world's poorer countries, "the international landscape of a few decades hence may resemble that of Easter Island: dominated by giants, and battered by tempestuous winds of change."[58] In absolute terms, the United States will continue to possess awesome capabilities; in relative terms, however, its lead over others will have diminished. The dilemma this creates for U.S. leaders is that "the United States has very little experience with a world that consists of many powers and which it can neither dominate nor from which it can simply withdraw in isolation."[59]

Managing Power Transitions

One of the principal tasks for U.S. policymakers after the war in Iraq will be to manage the coming global power shift from unipolarity to either bipolarity or, more likely, multipolarity. To succeed, America will have to reconcile itself to ascending powers, accepting their desire to have a voice in shaping the global future. Perhaps the foremost historical example of a state at the top of the power pyramid accommodating itself to the loss of its premier position was Great Britain at the end of the nineteenth century. It is an example worth considering today, as the United States faces challenges from new centers of international power. Let us review the record of British accommodation to its declining power relative to rivals and the lessons it suggests for the American Imperium today.

Coping with the Descent from Power: The British Experience

British security policy traditionally had two objectives: (1) to maintain maritime supremacy in order to defend the British Isles and protect overseas commercial interests and (2) to prevent any state from achieving control over Europe. To achieve the first objective, the British constructed a fleet that was the equal of the next two largest navies. To accomplish the second, British policymakers sought to maintain a balance of power on the Continent. "It has become almost an historical truism," Sir Eyre Crowe wrote in a 1907 memorandum on British foreign policy, "to identify England's secular policy with the maintenance of this balance by throwing her weight now in this scale and now in that, but ever on the side opposed to the political dictatorship of the strongest single State or group at a given time."[60]

By the close of the nineteenth century, however, Great Britain could not continue its policy of "splendid isolation." It was, in the words of Joseph Chamberlain, the colonial secretary, "a weary Titan." The country faced stiff industrial and commercial competition from powerful rivals whose economies were growing faster than her own: "Whereas in 1880 the United Kingdom still contained 22.9 percent of total world manufacturing output, that figure had shrunk to 13.6 percent by 1913; and while its share of world trade was 23.2 percent in 1880, it was only 14.1 percent in 1911–1913."[61]

Threats to British interests also loomed on every horizon as London began to find it difficult to afford an empire upon which the sun never set. Disputes had broken out with the United States over the border between Venezuela and British Guiana, with the Russians over Persia and the borderlands of India, with the French at Fashoda on the upper Nile, and with Germany over southern Africa. If China and the Ottoman Empire continued to disintegrate, additional conflicts were sure to arise. Great Britain was overextended and, as the costly Boer War (1899–1902) demonstrated, the British would either have to resuscitate their capacity to act unilaterally on the world stage or tailor their foreign policy ends to shrinking military and economic means.

One way to maintain Britain's capacity to influence global events was to forge a working relationship with a rising nation that otherwise might become a potent competitor. Although Lord Salisbury, the British prime minister, preferred to retain a "free hand" in foreign affairs and questioned the wisdom of linking Britain to partners whose strategic value remained in doubt, Colonial Secretary Chamberlain argued that Britain could no longer afford to go it alone. Slowly and warily the British began taking steps to end their isolation. Among the first and most important steps was a rapprochement with an ascending United States. Under the terms of the 1850 Clayton-Bulwer Treaty, Great Britain and the United States had pledged to exercise joint control over any isthmian canal linking the Atlantic and Pacific oceans through Central America. In what they saw as a major concession to Washington, the British agreed in the Hay-Pauncefote Treaty of 1900 to permit the United States to build and operate such a canal. A year later, in an effort to further improve relations between the two countries, they allowed the United States to fortify the canal. By appeasing the Americans, British policymakers hoped to dampen potential conflict with a rising power and therein bring overseas commitments into line with available capabilities.

Once Great Britain reconciled itself to America's new position in the global hierarchy, it was more comfortable taking additional steps away from its former posture of splendid isolation. In 1902 it signed a treaty of alliance with Japan that was intended to shore up the British position in East Asia and let the Royal Navy deal with challenges elsewhere. This was followed up by Anglo-French Entente of 1904, which granted freedom of action to France in Morocco and to Britain in Egypt, settled outstanding colonial differences in places as distant as Siam and New Hebrides, and resolved questions concerning fisheries off the coast of Newfoundland. Concerned with rising German naval expenditures and Berlin's heavy-handed behavior in the 1906 Algeciras conference on French claims in Morocco, the British next moved to reduce friction with Russia along the central Asian boundaries of their respective empires. The Russians were of the same mind, having recently been defeated by the Japanese at the battle of Mukden and again at Tsushima Strait. As a result of this convergence of interests, in the Anglo-Russian convention of 1907, Russia recognized a

British sphere of influence in the south and east of Persia, and in exchange the British recognized a Russian sphere in the north. Additional agreements were reached on Afghanistan and Tibet.

The British policy of coping with relative decline stands in stark contrast to the unsuccessful grand strategy of Spain during the ministry of Don Gaspar de Guzmán, known today as the Count-Duke Olivares. From 1621 until his fall from power 22 years later, Olivares chose "not to reassess and scale down Spain's traditional foreign policy objectives, but to reform and rationalize existing structures in the hope of making those objectives more attainable. In any clash between the claims of foreign policy and the availability of resources, the predisposition was to assume that the international emergency was too great to be shirked, and that somehow or other the resources would be found."[62] Conversely, when the British confronted a similar situation four centuries later, they made room for a rising America and reached a series of formal and informal arrangements with some of their adversaries to prevent foreign policy commitments from outrunning resources. Which path will the American Imperium follow?

The Contours of a Multipolar Future

Like Great Britain a century ago, the United States today faces vexing foreign policy problems on all horizons. At the same time that it is engaged in a war on global terrorism, Washington is trying to secure Afghanistan and Iraq, diffuse WMD threats in Iran and North Korea, rehabilitate its reputation throughout the Islamic world, repair relations with traditional allies in Europe and Latin America, and adjust to the growing power of China and India.

The rise of Asia's giants is especially important for two reasons. First, it presages a gradual, inexorable shift in the structure of the international system away from American unipolarity toward some variation of multipolarity. Second, because some forms of multipolarity are more war-prone than others,[63] it is imperative that the United States use the time it still has at the summit of world power to craft rules and institutions that will usher in a stable variant of multipolarity. The most critical task in this regard is preventing the division of a future multipolar world into separate blocs, one led by the United States and the other by China or some other great power. What America does in the waning years of its unipolar moment will set forces in motion that will shape the global future, for better or worse. If the great powers of tomorrow split into rival camps, there is little chance that competitors in one policy arena (e.g., military supremacy) will emerge as partners somewhere else (e.g., economic leadership), so as to reduce the competition. Rather, the gains made by one side will be seen as losses by the other, ultimately causing minor disagreements to grow into larger face-offs from which neither coalition is willing to retreat.

Since the international system of the mid-twenty-first century will probably include several extremely powerful states with global security interests, it is critical that they do not become bitter adversaries that draw others into their segregated blocs. To avoid such a polarized environment, it is important for them to belong to international institutions that provide mutually beneficial rewards, so potential competitors have incentives to collaborate and a stake in continued cooperation. The chance of a great-power war may seem remote today, but it is foolhardy to assume that it could not occur under different international conditions. Many of the world's established and rising powers face unprecedented scarcities in available water, energy, natural resources, and labor. Rapid changes in the distribution of wealth fostered by these scarcities comprise a tinderbox that could easily ignite. According to Mark Leonard, these vulnerabilities "may encourage 'defensive imperialism': powerful countries taking over states to prevent them serving as bases or breeding grounds for hostile states."[64] His scenario forecasts a destabilizing transfer of economic growth from north and west to the global south and east, and that this division will separate the world into four rival and potentially hostile poles "split along two axes: between democracies and autocracies, and between countries seeking a balance of power and those that want a world organized around international law and institutions."

Aside from the danger of armed conflict among these poles, the security threats of the future will still include terrorists with global reach, as well as myriad problems associated with climate change, environmental degradation, and cross-border drug trafficking and infectious diseases. None of these global problems can be resolved without substantial great-power cooperation; they all are truly transnational problems that necessitate global solutions.

The Possibilities and Perils Confronting America

As power in the international system becomes more diffused, what foreign policy should the United States adopt in order to prevent the emergence of a fractious, unstable form of multipolarity, one where the most powerful states become polarized in rival, antagonistic blocs? Three general courses of action exist: America can act unilaterally; it can develop specialized bilateral alliances; or it can engage in some form of broad, multilateral collaboration with many countries.

Of course, each option has many possible variations, and the foreign policies of most major powers contain a mix of acting single-handedly, joining with a partner, and cooperating globally. What matters is the relative emphasis on "going it alone" versus "going it with others"[65] and whether joint action is defined in inclusive or exclusive terms.

Unilateral policies, although attractive because they symbolize national autonomy and confident self-reliance, are unlikely to be viable in a multipolar future. Frustration with the conduct of the war in Iraq has led many people to call for a reduction in the scale of American commitments. However, a U.S. retreat from active participation in world affairs would jeopardize efforts to deal with the many threats to global security that require active American international engagement.

A continuation of the Bush administration's unilateralism would be equally harmful. Although the United States will hold unrivaled military might for some time, many of the international problems on the horizon cannot be solved by using military power. Moreover, as a result of Washington's unrestrained investment in its capacity to pursue an ambitious military strategy without serious attention to how the human and material costs will be met, concerned observers fear that several factors are eroding America's global stature. These include:

- *America's security goals do not mesh with the country's military resources.* As a result of the war in Iraq, the U.S. military's troop strength, equipment, and supplies have been stretched thin. As one commentator summarizes the situation, "an ever leaner, numerically smaller military is being asked to patrol an ever larger part of the world."[66] For much of American history, writes former Secretary of Commerce Peter Peterson, "going to war was like organizing a large federal jobs program, with most of the work done by inexpensive, quickly trained recruits. Today, it is more like a NASA moon launch, entailing a massive logistical tail supporting a professionally managed and swiftly deteriorating body of high-tech physical capital." Keeping just two divisions operating in Iraq for a week costs $1 billion, he points out. Maintaining them for a year would cost the entire gross domestic product of New Zealand.[67]
- *The cost of the war in Iraq is far greater than previously thought.* Although the Bush administration originally pegged the war's cost at roughly $70 billion, estimates from economists Joseph Stiglitz and Linda Bilmes place the real cost between $1 trillion and $2 trillion, when such factors as lifetime care of wounded soldiers and the economic value of the lost productive capacity of National Guard and Reserve troops are included in the calculations.[68]
- *The U.S. economic engine is idling while competitors are speeding.* The United States is suffering under a staggering federal debt burden. According to projections from the Congressional Budget Office, total federal spending adjusted for inflation will have increased by 30.5 percent during President Bush's tenure in office (with military spending rising by 48 percent since 2001). Meanwhile, America's current-account deficit widened by more than 20 percent in 2005 to reach a staggering $805 billion, or 6.4 percent of the gross domestic product.[69] By borrowing heavily from Asian creditors (especially China, Japan, and South Korea), the country is becoming increasingly dependent upon (and vulnerable to) foreign economic powers. By 2026, "the federal debt could equal the nation's annual economic growth, if nothing is done. At that point, the interest on the debt would begin to explode [and] U.S. bonds would achieve junk bond status. . . ." According to this estimate, "the U.S. government could possibly lose its AAA bond rating—a development

that would have major domestic and international implications."[70] Compounding the problem, the nation's trade deficit climbed to $725.8 billion in 2005, up 17.5 percent over the previous year. "No nation," writes Donald White, "has been able to continue to sustain preeminence indefinitely with a chronic trade deficit or as a debtor."[71]

- *America's educational system is beginning to lag behind many of its economic competitors.* The failure to invest wisely in education is propagating a "creativity crisis" that threatens to make the United States less competitive in the years ahead, especially in the natural sciences.[72] The United States awards more doctorates in the sciences than any other country, but it ranks 25th when the number of graduates is adjusted for population size. Similarly, although in absolute terms America spends more on science than anyone else, federal funding of research and development has declined to the point that six countries now spend more as a percentage of GDP than the United States. With fewer foreign nationals that have been educated in U.S. graduate schools seeking employment (and citizenship) in the United States, and with the retirement of the "baby boomers," America may face a shortage of highly skilled mathematicians, scientists, and engineers in the years ahead. As General Electric Chief Executive Jeffrey Immelt laments, in 2005 America "had more sports-exercise majors graduate than electrical engineering grads."[73]
- *Fears about terrorist attacks have spawned security policies that threaten to erode American civil liberties and international humanitarian law.*[74] At home, the USA Patriot Act has expanded the discretionary power of federal officials to conduct far-reaching surveillance operations on U.S. citizens, while a 2002 Executive Order has allowed the National Security Agency to eavesdrop without a warrant on international phone calls, e-mails, and other forms of electronic communication, even if one party to the communication was within the United States. Abroad, the Bush administration has labeled detainees held at the U.S. naval station at Guantánamo Bay "unlawful enemy combatants," a vague term that has led many legal scholars to question whether the United States is willing to abide by the 1949 Geneva Convention on Prisoners of War. When combined with the interrogation techniques used in Iraq's Abu Ghraib prison, the administration's equivocations about banning torture, and the use of rendition (transferring prisoners to other countries), critics charge that the methods used to fight the global war on terror have seriously eroded America's international reputation.

The United States, as columnist Charles Krauthammer asserts, may still be a marvel of creativity, innovation, and entrepreneurial spirit,[75] but its current domestic difficulties and the prohibitive costs of acting alone on the world stage will make a unilateralist foreign policy problematic for America in a multipolar future.

An alternative to unilateralism is joining with selected states in a series of special, ad hoc relationships. On the surface, this option also appears attractive. Yet in a world lacking the stark simplicities of the Cold War, differentiating friend from foe is exceedingly difficult, particularly when allies in the realm of military security may be trade competitors in a cutthroat global marketplace. As a result, special relationships can breed resentment that one side is enjoying most of the benefits while the other is shouldering most of the burdens. Instead of adding predictability to international affairs, a series of "coalitions of the willing" would foster a fear of encirclement among those who perceive themselves as targets of these combinations. Whether they entail informal cooperative understandings or formal treaties of alliance, all bilateral partnerships have a common drawback: they promote a politics of exclusion that can spur dangerously polarized forms of multipolarity, in which competitors align by forming countercoalitions.

Beyond forming specialized arrangements with an ad hoc coalition of the willing, the United States has the option of establishing broader associations. Two common variants of this option are concerts and collective security organizations. The former involve regularized consultation among those at the top of the global hierarchy; the latter, full participation by all states. A concert constructed to manage the international system jointly and prevent disputes from escalating to war offers the benefit of helping control the major-power rivalries that often spawn polarized blocs, though at the cost of ignoring the interests of those not belonging to the elite group. Alternatively, the all-inclusive nature of collective security allows every voice to be heard, but exacerbates the problems of providing a timely response to threatening situations. Moreover, under collective security schemes in the past, consensus building has usually proven both difficult and delayed, especially in identifying the culpable party, in choosing an appropriate response, and in implementing the selected course of action.

What may be needed to make multilateralism a viable option is a two-tiered, modular approach that combines elements of a great-power concert with elements of collective security. Under such an arrangement, the great powers at the center of policy deliberations would change as different kinds of problems arise, with some taking the lead on certain security issues and others on a different set of issues. Their proceedings would be anchored in a larger collective security framework, where small and medium powers would have a voice in pending matters if their interests were affected or if they possessed expertise in dealing with the issue in question. For this scheme to work, great and small powers alike would have to adopt a posture of mutual self-restraint, complying with international norms on an equal basis and expecting to benefit as a whole over the long run rather than on every issue all of the time.

Multilateral support from a concert-based collective security system may buttress the legitimacy of America's actions on the world stage, but at what cost? Because there are times when international institutions may be used by others to stall American action on a contentious issue, some people doubt that they hold much promise for enhancing America's national security. In the words of one advocate of a Pax Americana, international institutions are "a forum for the weak to unite to tie the U.S. Gulliver down through the process of soft balancing."[76] Indeed, the school of thought known as political realism takes as its point of departure the expectation that all lesser states will act in their national self-interest by seeking to counter the world's dominant state in order to preserve their autonomy and voice in determining international developments. Multilateral diplomacy, they conclude, provides an arena for them to constrain the powerful. So in this regard, the "Americaphobia" expressed in international institutions is not just a reaction to the Iraq war; it is also the reflection of a profound lack of trust in an imperious power that has the capacity to do great harm to those with whom it comes into conflict. That fear is not likely to recede, even when America's strength begins to decline relative to others, for, to realists, this is precisely the condition under which dominant states are the most dangerous.

Although it is difficult to verify a grand theory such as political realism, the failure of its basic axioms to correspond with state practice, especially under today's changing circumstances, would cast doubt on its adequacy. This, we contend, is the case with respect to the key assumptions of the realist image of world politics. Contrary to its claims of its most hard-line proponents who contend that ethical considerations in the formulation and conduct of foreign policy are dangerous, there is a significant body of empirical evidence that suggests American leaders in a multipolar world would be well served by departing from the path the Bush administration and its neoconservative advisers have taken since 9/11. The dangers of their enthusiastic acceptance of the unilateral use of military force for regime change are now readily apparent. The time is ripe to reconsider how restoring an emphasis on the ideals of the American diplomatic tradition can serve the country's long-term interests. To strike that balance, realism must find some common ground with the rules for international behavior embraced by the school of thought known as liberal idealism. That refashioning, as we shall see, would call for a more multilateral and less militaristic foreign policy—one fully engaged with international organizations, respectful of the advantages in upholding international law, attentive to strengthening America's reputation abroad, and mindful of the value in working with others to promote human rights and civil liberties by peaceful means.

Recovering America's Lost Liberal Heritage

America's founding fathers believed Europe's monarchies were untrustworthy and warned that participating in balance-of-power politics with authoritarian governments would result in a violation of America's ideals and an erosion of its democratic institutions. Refusing to accept a foreign policy guided by raw power politics, they advocated instead leading by moral example. The United States would not assume responsibility for the world, even in the name of freedom. It would not seek to impose its political system and way of life on others. It is this legacy—the idealist face of the American diplomatic tradition—that in the aftermath of 9/11 has been lost.

No idealist principle commands more attention or serves as a better example of a standard of ethical conduct than the tenet: "Do unto others as you would have them do unto you." The Golden Rule blends into one statement three elements of mutuality that render it a profound moral statement: a prescription (it instructs actors how they should act), impartial universality (it is a rule of behavior applicable to everyone), and reciprocity (it underscores the effects of one's actions on the subsequent behavior of others). This principle does not assign a separate code of conduct for the powerful. It speaks instead against the "might makes right" and "the end justifies the means" postulates underlying the belief that the preponderant power in a unipolar system is a law unto itself that can act without regard to the norms that apply to everyone else. Moreover, because every powerful global actor bears responsibility for the kind of international political culture that will emerge, it is imperative for the United States to try to shape that culture to its advantage, and that self-interest lies in behaving in a way that creates restrictive normative boundaries around great-power competition.

To hard-boiled realists, those who attempt to follow this moral code are doomed to be victimized. To base American security on the expectation that others will return equity for equity is an invitation to disaster. There is no substitute for power politics, such people assume, and it is naive to hope for one. Therefore the sword must be wielded to control adversaries.

But does the evidence on the pattern of interstate interactions back this argument? Or does the evidence support the idealism summarized by the Golden Rule? We submit that the predictions embodied in liberal idealism are borne out in actual fact in world politics; nations tend to treat other nations as they are treated, and this pattern in history provides ample justification for basing foreign policy on principled conduct, which is an important source of soft power.

Consider first the evidence derived from reinforcement theory developed by social psychologists and found in applications of social exchange and learning theories to international relations. The assumption central to these inquiries is that rewards and costs to each participant in a dyadic, two-party exchange will influence the kind of interaction that will commence, and experimental research has repeatedly found that: (1) an actor's behavior is a function of the characteristic mode of response of the target of action, (2) throughout a cycle of interaction, hostile behavior tends to elicit hostile responses, whereas cooperative behavior seldom does, and, most importantly for the question of integrating ascending powers within a rule-based order, (3) the repetition of positive actions toward another actor tends to make cooperative interactions more characteristic as the give and take of these collaborative exchanges increase over time.[77] States, in other words, do not act in a singularly characteristic (power-seeking, competitive) manner; instead, they emit behavior similar to that initiated by those with whom they are in frequent interaction and respond in a manner characteristic of the response of those with whom contact is repetitive. Liberal-idealist theories emphasize that actors are not intrinsically good or evil, but capable of acting in either fashion—and that some conditions will elicit the former, whereas others will elicit the latter. In this context, the liberal tradition counsels against the belief that evil may sometimes be done for the sake of a greater good because when that assumption is made the further opportunistic justification of evil follows.

Second, consider the overwhelming support for this finding that emerges from cross-national, comparative studies of foreign policy behavior. These studies show that for a variety of interstate relationships, the foreign policy acts a state directs at another are affected strongly by the prior acts of the target state.[78] Behavior tends to be reciprocated in these exchanges; cooperation breeds cooperation and hostility breeds hostility. Furthermore, the action-reaction pattern tends to be symmetrical: the volume and intensity of the cooperative or hostile actions of one side mirrors that of the other. At the risk of overgeneralizing, this body of research indicates that foreign policy behavior largely conforms to a tit-for-tat model of interstate interaction. States are selectively attentive to the actors in their environment, and they respond in kind to those with whom they are engaged in nonroutine, sequential action.

A third source of support for reciprocity can be found in research on the action-reaction dynamics of arms competition. To a remarkable degree, the Soviet Union and the United States responded to each other's strategic deployments in reciprocal terms during the Cold War. Initiatives taken by one party provoked similar countermeasures by the other, with each side perceiving its own actions as merely a defensive response to the other's initiatives. Intrigued by this pattern, the eminent social psychologist Charles E. Osgood argued that a nation seeking to live in a more peaceful environment should make modest conciliatory gestures, and then look for some similar conciliatory move by the beneficiary in return, which, if forthcoming, should be promptly rewarded.[79] This strategy was actually employed for a six-month period in 1963 by the Kennedy administration, and it appeared to have been working until an assassin's bullet brought the test to an abrupt end. Gestures made by the United States were at first suspected, eventually accepted, and then reciprocated by the Soviets, thereby easing tensions.[80] The lesson of this experience is that conflict between states may not be endemic, as political realists would contend; rather, a pattern of cooperation and trust may take root even between rival great powers.

Building trust is a slow process, however. Trust does not arise spontaneously in a cold, uncertain environment; it must be earned. States can gradually establish reputations for being trustworthy by making unconditional supportive gestures, by eschewing opportunities that a perfidious actor would have seized, and by consistently reciprocating acts of cooperation. According to what has been called the "augmentation principle," the greater the costs entailed by such behavior, the less a recipient will view it as the product of ulterior motives.[81]

The most constructive approach, we argue, is for the United States to build reciprocity-based trust among today's ascending world powers that may someday become America's peer-competitors in a multipolar system. By engaging rather than attempting to segregate those rising powers, and by integrating them within a restrictive normative order that appeals to universal interests, the United States can avoid hard-line policies that will eventually lead each side to square off against the other. This requires a respectful firm-but-conciliatory strategy that communicates amicable intentions, rewards cooperation, and punishes exploitative behavior. It contains four key attributes. First, it must begin with an overt cooperative action coupled with an invitation for the adversary to respond in kind. Except when a rival seeks total domination, a productive way to change negative perceptions "is to send them a message different from what they expect."[82] Acting inconsistently with ingrained enemy images and acknowledging the interests held by one's counterparts help break cycles of mistrust and mutual competition.

The second attribute to a firm-but-conciliatory strategy is clarity. All actions aimed at eliciting cooperation from an adversary should be simple, unambiguous, and verifiable. They should be announced publicly prior to their execution, explained as components within a deliberate series of moves aimed at reducing tensions, and completed on schedule even if the adversary does not immediately respond.

The third attribute is resolve. Conciliators should protect their interests and vigorously resist attempts by the other party to take advantage of concessions. Policies that combine rapid responses to an adversary's collaborative behavior, with slow replies to provocations, encourage exploitative behavior. The available evidence suggests that mutual cooperation is more easily resumed after punishing a provocation if the retaliation is slightly less than the infraction and is accompanied by a positive inducement.

The fourth attribute of a firm-but-conciliatory strategy is forbearance. Opportunistic noncooperation is neither overlooked nor excused; it is penalized, but not allowed to harden into a permanent obstacle to reconciliation. Reciprocity-based trust, in other words, is slowly built through a series of graduated, cumulative actions. Of course, trust cannot eradicate conflict. Rather, it prevents some disputes, curbs others before they escalate, and facilitates mutual problem solving when disagreements turn violent.

The challenge for an America facing many future perils abroad and looming problems at home is to conceive of, and act consistently upon, a principled strategy that is resolute in dealing with those who threaten the nation's security, firm in its promotion of U.S. interests, but accommodates itself to the gradual rise of new peer competitors. By basing foreign policy decisions on the precept that the only route to long-term peace and prosperity is to respond to others in the same way that Washington seeks others to respond to America, such a strategy would strive to enmesh ascending powers in a web of international accords and codes of conduct that smooths future power transitions and makes great-power cooperation more likely on common security problems, including nuclear proliferation and the threat of terrorists with global reach. Without an ethically inspired foreign policy that leads the way to a restrictive normative order that enjoys consensual support among the emerging great powers, a few decades from now the United States will likely find itself in a turbulent world that is hostile to its values and principles. As America stands at the apex of global power, it has more influence over the evolutionary direction of the future rules for international behavior than any other country. With great power comes great responsibility. Simply put, America has a unique opportunity to shape the future by leading an international effort to construct multinational institutions and norms that can provide a solid foundation for a peaceful and just world order.

The Prospect Ahead

The United States, asserts the February 2006 *Quadrennial Defense Review Report*, is engaged in a "long war." For the moment, the primary threats it faces come from shadowy international terrorist networks and hostile states like North Korea and Iran that seem determined to acquire nuclear arsenals. Nevertheless, envisioning this protracted war as an all-encompassing struggle that "will not end until every terrorist group of global reach has been found, stopped and defeated"[83] can easily distract the United States from adequately addressing the long-range, multifaceted challenges created by the rise of other potentially powerful rivals over the next 25 years.

A normative climate that accepts discretionary, preventive uses of force will only complicate efforts to manage this global power shift. In the aftermath of the 9/11 attacks, it was easy to sympathize with the old saw that an ounce of prevention was better than a pound of cure. Yet following a justifiable military move against the Taliban regime in Afghanistan that harbored Al Qaeda operatives involved in the 2001 attacks on New York and Washington with a preventive war against Iraq has tarnished America's image and eroded its legitimacy as a world leader. By acting in a rash unilateralist manner in seeking regime changes within states it sees as adversaries, the United States is fostering a permissive international normative order that will make it difficult to build a stable multipolar future. Decades ahead, when America's unipolar moment has faded and managing global affairs hinges on great-power compromise and consensus, "the United States will lament that it taught by example norms of self-interest rather than norms of reciprocity."[84]

To put this argument into a concluding policy prescription, the past history of world politics reveals that serious disputes accumulate within the cultures of mistrust spawned by permissive codes of interstate conduct. Ever suspicious about the intentions of others, national leaders of preponderant states are prone to overestimate their power, exaggerate the susceptibility of their opponents to preventive military action, and slip into a self-aggregating conflict spiral. Moreover, the very normative climate that they create to protect their position of primacy evokes behavior from others that can create a self-fulfilling prophecy of conflict. Without a modicum of trust, garbled intelligence reports can lead imperious leaders to embrace negative images of their rival's character, assume the worst about their intentions, and adopt brash, counterproductive foreign policies. *Hybris*, the ancients remind us, creates its own *nemesis*.

The lessons of history speak to leading by example. Global stability has been fostered in past unipolar periods when the preponderant state was willing to forego gains from actions that served its short-term parochial interests for the larger long-run benefits that accrued when the collective interests of the international community were promoted. To be sure, go-it-alone demonstrations of national will and military might can be a temptation; however, reality quickly sets in when costs, casualties, and international criticism soar. As expressed in what is called "hegemonic stability theory," a single preponderant state can advance world order, providing that it uses its clout to establish security and maintain rules that regulate behavior in key issue areas, from trade and monetary relations to humanitarian and environmental affairs.[85] For this to occur the leading state must be willing to communicate, consult, compromise, and coordinate its actions with others. It must follow a statecraft of self-restraint, practicing what it preaches and sacrificing for the common good rather than insisting that everything always go its way. In short, the leading state must be more than just a well-intentioned power; it must exercise influence prudently, working multilaterally to acquire international legitimacy for its actions.[86]

As a result of the preventive war that the United States has waged in Iraq as part of the Bush administration's global war on terrorism, a "trust gap" has opened between America and much of the international community. Following the Iraq war new security dilemmas are certain to arise.[87] To meet them the United States will need more than stubborn unilaterialism and overwhelming military might; it will need political suppleness and reliable diplomatic partners. Building partnerships requires a reputation for principled behavior. Not only are the offers made by a principled nation seen as more acceptable to wary nations and its agreements respected because they can be counted on, but forcible efforts to protect its interests are "recognized as such and are unlikely to be confused with more unlimited objectives that stir the antagonism or opposition of others."[88]

Perhaps the most important task for the United States during its unipolar moment will be to exercise principled leadership in building a normative consensus around the kinds of rules that will hold sway once global power is more widely dispersed within the international system. The rules of the game that the United States promotes when dealing with today's security challenges carry enormous implications for addressing the potentially far-more-difficult issues that are likely to arise as the tectonic plates of international power shift in the decades ahead. As the pioneering realist theoretician Hans J. Morgenthau argued, historically the preservation of peace has been facilitated by the creation of a transnational normative consensus, the main function of which was "to keep aspirations for power within socially tolerable bounds" by asserting that superior power "gives no right, either moral or legal, to do with that power all that it is physically capable of doing."[89] In the absence of leadership by the United States to construct a new consensus that disavows the precepts of a permissive code of international conduct, the future of the American Imperium seems destined to be truly imperiled.

It is time for America to reverse the recent directions in its foreign policy. It is time to embrace ideals for statecraft that will serve the country when it faces inevitable challenges to its preeminence on the world stage. At that point in time—and that time will surely come—the rules of the game that the United States preaches and practices today will have shaped the rules that influence international interactions when America no longer stands alone at the apex of world power. The issue is not whether the United States will have peer competitors by the middle of this century; it is whether this inevitable competition can be managed to avoid the accumulation of acute, polarizing crises that have characterized many pervious periods of multipolar rivalry.

Will the United States seize the opportunity to forge a stable and secure world order? Or will it fail to escape the perils that threaten to incarcerate its future?

Notes

1. Condoleezza Rice has predicted that it may take 30 to 40 years before we know whether the Bush policies were creative responses to 9/11 or disastrous ones. Cited in David J. Rothkopf, *Running the World: The Inside Story of the National Security Council and the Architects of American Power* (New York: PublicAffairs Press, 2004), p. 393.
2. Retrieved at http://www.whitehouse.gov/news/release/2003/11/20031106-2.html.
3. Speech by President George W. Bush on January 20, 2005, emphasis added, retrieved at http://www.whitehouse.gov/news/releases/2005/01/print/20050120.html.
4. Contrary to administration plans to use the existing bureaucracy to run the country under a replacement regime, Iraq's administrative structures dissolved when looters ransacked 17 of 23 government ministries and their staffs fled. With no contingency plan for this eventuality, the United States stumbled through several uncoordinated attempts to institute Iraqi self-governance. See Celeste J. Ward, *The Coalition Provisional Authority's Experience with Governance in Iraq*, Special Report 139 (Washington, DC: United States Institute of Peace, 2005).
5. The administration later conceded that building a representative, democratic government would take time. "Saddam Hussein devastated Iraq, wrecked its economy, ruined its infrastructure, and destroyed its human capital." It is unrealistic, the Bush team argued, "to expect a fully functioning democracy, able to defeat its enemies and peacefully reconcile generational grievances, to be in place less than three years after Saddam was finally removed from power." National Security Council, *National Strategy for Victory in Iraq* (Washington, DC: White House, 2005), p. 10.

6. Richard M. Nixon, *Beyond Peace* (New York: Random House, 1994), p. 38. Some presidents have been less enthusiastic in public about dictating democracy to others. For example, President Dwight D. Eisenhower asserted on April 16, 1953, that "Any nation's right to a form of government and economic system of its own choosing is inalienable. Any nation's attempt to dictate to other nations their form of government is indefensible." Cited in Gerhard von Glahn, *Law Among Nations* (New York: Macmillan, 1972), p. 174. On the history of American interventionism, see Ellen C. Collier, "Instances of Use of United States Armed Forces Abroad, 1797–1993," *Congressional Research Service Report for Congress* (October 7, 1993).
7. Four years later, Clinton signed the Iraq Liberation Act, which backed "efforts to remove the regime headed by Saddam Hussein . . . and to promote the emergence of a democratic government." For a discussion of the gathering support for reformist interventions and preventive uses of force prior to the Bush administration , see Thomas M. Nichols, "Anarchy and Order in a New Age of Prevention," *World Policy Journal* 22 (Fall 2005): 3–8. For an overview of the tenets of liberal international theory, including those postulating the pacifying consequences of democratization, see Mark W. Zacher and Richard A. Matthew, "Liberal International Relations Theory: Common Threads, Divergent Strands," in Charles W. Kegley, Jr., ed., *Controversies in International Relations Theory: Realism and the Neoliberal Challenge* (New York: St. Martin's, 1995), pp. 107–150.
8. John M. Collins, *Military Preparedness: Principles Compared with U.S. Practices* (Washington, DC: Congressional Research Service, 1994). Also see Warren Christopher, "A New Consensus of the Americas," *Dispatch* 5 (May 9, 1994): 3; and The White House, *A National Security Strategy of Engagement and Enlargement* (Washington, DC: U.S. Government Printing Office, 1994).
9. Cited in Kenneth Anderson et al., "Is There a Doctrine in the House? In Search of a Clinton Foreign Policy," *Harper's* 288 (January 1994): 64. See also Anthony Lake, "A Call to Enlarge Democracy's Reach," *The New York Times* (September 26, 1993): E3.
10. Warren Christopher, "America's Leadership, America's Opportunity," *Foreign Policy* 98 (Spring 1995): 14-15.
11. Morton H. Halperin, "Guaranteeing Democracy," *Foreign Policy* 91 (Summer 1993): 105.
12. David C. Hendrickson, "The Democratist Crusade," *World Policy Journal* 11 (Winter 1994–1995): 18–30; Tony Smith, *America's Mission: The United States and the Worldwide Struggle for Democracy in the Twentieth Century* (Princeton, NJ: Princeton University Press, 1994). This enthusiasm for democracy promotion derived from liberal theory and empirical evidence that supported the proposition that the diffusion of democratic governance throughout the world was a viable institutional remedy for war, because democratic states rarely if ever had waged war against other democracies. See Karen Rasler and William R. Thompson, *Puzzles of the Democratic Peace: Theory, Geopolitics and the Transformation of World Politics* (New York: Palgrave Macmillan, 2005).
13. For a statement of this position, see International Commission on Intervention and State Sovereignty, *The Responsibility to Protect* (Ottawa: International Development Research Centre, 2001), pp. 15–16.

14. James Crawford, *Democracy in International Law* (Cambridge, U.K.: Cambridge University Press, 1993), pp. 14, 20. Also see Thomas M. Franck, "The Emerging Democratic Entitlement," in Anthony D'Amato, ed., *International Law Anthology* (Cincinnati, OH: Anderson, 1994), pp. 367–373; Ian Vasquez, "Washington's Dubious Crusade for Hemispheric Democracy," *USA Today* 123 (January 1995): 56; Barry M. Blechman, "The Intervention Dilemma," *The Washington Quarterly* 18 (No. 1, 1995): 63; and George Soros, *The Bubble of American Supremacy* (New York: PublicAffairs, 2004), pp. 118–119.
15. For an argument against justifying military intervention by invoking a human right of popular sovereignty, see Jean L. Cohen, "Whose Sovereignty? Empire Versus International Law," *Ethics & International Affairs* 18 (No. 3, 2004): 1–24.
16. Charles W. Kegley, Jr. and Margaret G. Hermann, "A Glass Half Full," *Futures Research Quarterly* 13 (Spring 1997): 68.
17. Mark Peceny, "Two Paths to the Promotion of Democracy During U.S. Military Interventions," *International Studies Quarterly* 39 (No. 4, 1995): 377.
18. In interpreting the past record of American interventions, it is important to caution that U.S. action was undoubtedly only one among many possible causal factors that could have affected the rate and character of any political changes that unfolded. It is also necessary to be mindful that these interventions were different in scope and duration. Some—such as those in Korea, Vietnam, and the first Gulf War—involved many troops at substantial costs. Others—such as those in Lebanon (1958), Panama (1964), and Iran (1980)—were of short duration and entailed few casualties.
19. See James Meernik, "United States Military Intervention and the Promotion of Democracy," *Journal of Peace Research* 33 (No. 4, 1996): 400.
20. Charles W. Kegley, Jr., and Margaret G. Hermann, "The Political Psychology of Peace Through Democratization," *Cooperation and Conflict* 30 (March 1995): 15.
21. Stephen Van Evera, "American Intervention in the Third World: Less Would Be Better," in Charles W. Kegley, Jr., and Eugene R. Wittkopf, eds., *The Future of American Foreign Policy* (New York: St. Martin's Press, 1992), pp. 285–300. See also James Dibbins et al., *America's Role in Nation-Building: From Germany to Iraq* (Santa Monica, CA: RAND, 2003).
22. Minxin Pei, "Lessons of the Past," *Foreign Policy* 137 (July/August 2003): 52–54.
23. Tom Zeller, "Building Democracy Is Not a Science," *New York Times* (April 27, 2003): Section 4, 3.
24. Niall Ferguson, *Colossus: The Price of America's Empire* (New York: Penguin, 2004), p. 48.
25. Margaret G. Hermann and Charles W. Kegley, Jr., "The U.S. Use of Military Intervention to Promote Democracy: Evaluating the Record," *International Interactions* 24 (No. 2, 1998): 251. Also see David Rieff, *At the Point of a Gun: Democratic Dreams and Armed Intervention* (New York: Simon & Schuster, 2005), and Stephen Kinzer, *Overthrow: America's Century of Regime Change from Hawaii to Iraq* (New York: Henry Holt, 2006).
26. John M. Owen IV, "Democracy, Realistically," *The National Interest* 83 (Spring 2006): 37. Also see his *Liberal Peace, Liberal War* (Ithaca, NY: Cornell University Press, 1997), as well as Jack Snyder, "Empire: A Blunt Tool for Democratization," *Daedalus*

134 (Spring 2005): 60, and Edward D. Mansfield and Jack Snyder, *Electing to Fight* (Cambridge, MA: MIT Press, 2005).

27. David C. Hendrickson, "The Democratist Crusade," *World Policy Journal* (Winter 1994–1995): 18–19. Thomas Donnelly takes a different position, asserting that "were the founding generation alive today, it would advocate something like the Bush Doctrine." See his "What Is Within Our Powers? Preserving American Primacy in the Twenty-First Century," in James J. Hentz, ed., *The Obligations of Empire: United States' Grand Strategy for a New Century* (Lexington: University of Kentucky Press, 2004), p. 75.
28. Colin S. Gray, *The Sheriff: America's Defense of the New World Order* (Lexington: University Press of Kentucky, 2004), p. 90.
29. Thomas P. M. Barnett, *The Pentagon's New Map: War and Peace in the Twenty-First Century* (New York: Putnam, 2004), p. 177.
30. James P. Rubin, "Stumbling Into War," *Foreign Affairs* 82 (September/October 2003): 46–66. Another observer described the Bush administration's blotched diplomacy in the following terms: "Swaddled in abstract ideas, convinced of their own self-righteousness, incapable of self-criticism, indifferent to accountability, they turned a difficult undertaking into a needlessly deadly one." George Packer, *The Assassins' Gate: America in Iraq* (New York: Farrar, Straus and Giroux, 2005), p. 448.
31. Stephen M. Walt, *Taming American Power: The Global Response to U.S. Primacy* (New York: Norton, 2005), p. 130. Walt defines soft balancing against the United States as "the conscious coordination of diplomatic action in order to obtain outcomes contrary to U.S. preferences—outcomes that could not be gained if the balancers did not give each other some degree of mutual support" (p. 126, emphasis removed).
32. Joshua Micah Marshall, "Power Rangers," *The New Yorker* (February 2, 2004): 87.
33. Michael Hirsh, *At War With Ourselves: Why America Is Squandering Its Chance to Build a Better World* (New York: Oxford University Press, 2003), pp. 190, 203.
34. Edward Rhodes. "The Imperial Logic of Bush's Liberal Agenda," *Survival* 45 (Spring 2003): 143.
35. *Public Papers of the Presidents of the United States: Harry S Truman, 1945* (Washington, DC: U.S. Government Printing Office, 1961), p. 141. In a similar vein, Edmund Burke lamented that Great Britain's primacy in the nineteenth century would create anxieties elsewhere: "I dread our own power and our own ambition; I dread being too much dreaded. . . . We might say that we shall not abuse this astonishing and hitherto unheard of power. But every other nation will think we shall abuse it." Edmund Burke, "Remarks on the Policies of the Allies with Respect to France," in *Works of Edmund Burke*, Vol. 4 (Boston: Little, Brown, 1901), p. 157.
36. Robert Kagan, "America's Crisis of Legitimacy," *Foreign Affairs* 83 (March/April 2004): 81. Also see Robert F. Ellsworth and Dimitri K. Simes, "Realism's Shining Morality," *The National Interest* 78 (Winter 2004/05): 9. Examples of guidelines for the preventive use of military force include Ivo Daalder and James Steinberg, "The Future of Preemption,"*The American Interest* 1 (Winter 2005): 30–39; Whitley Kaufman, "What's Wrong with Preventive War?" *Ethics & International Affairs* 19 (No. 3, 2005): 38; Michael Ignatieff, *The Lesser Evil: Political Ethics in an Age of Terror* (Princeton, NJ: Princeton University Press, 2004), pp. 162–167; Allen

Buchanan and Robert O. Keohane, "Governing the Preventive Use of Force," *Ethics & International Affairs* 18 (No. 1, 2004): 1–22; and Lee Feinstein and Anne-Marie Slaughter, "A Duty to Prevent," *Foreign Affairs* 83 (January/February 2004): 136–150. Earlier arguments for preventive warfare are discussed in Richard Tuck, *The Rights of War and Peace* (New York: Oxford University Press, 1999), pp. 18–31.

37. Jim Garrison, *America as Empire: Global Leader or Rogue Power?* (San Francisco, CA: Berrett-Koehler, 2004), p. 186.

38. A. F. K. Organski, *World Politics* (New York: Alfred A. Knopf, 1958), pp. 326–333. Power refers to the capacity to control the behavior of others. National power is relational because it pertains to the ability of a state exercising power to make a target continue some course of action, change what it is doing, or refrain from acting. It is also situationally specific because the state wielding power may be able to reduce the probability of something it does not want to happen and increase the probability of a preferred outcome on some issues, but not on others. The more powerful the state, the wider the domain of targets and the greater the scope of issues that it can control. Scholars disagree on how to measure national power. Lacking a standard unit of account, they typically mix some combination of geographic, demographic, economic, and other tangible factors with intangible factors like leadership, morale, and cultural attraction. Like chefs at a chili cookoff, they all seem to have their own list of ingredients. Although their recipes differ, the results are remarkably similar: power is generally equated with those national capabilities that increase the range and potency of rewards and punishments at a state's disposal.

39. Daniel S. Geller, "Power and International Conflict," in John A. Vasquez, ed., *What Do We Know About War?* (Lanham, MD: Rowman & Littlefield, 2000), p. 268.

40. See the following works by Charles F. Doran: "Confronting the Principles of the Power Cycle: Changing Systems Structure, Expectations, and War," in Manus I. Midlarsky, ed., *Handbook of War Studies II* (Ann Arbor: University of Michigan Press, 2000), pp. 332–368; "Power Cycle Theory of Systems Structure and Stability: Commonalities and Complementarities," in Manus I. Midlarsky, ed., *Handbook of War Studies* (New York: Unwin Hyman, 1989), pp. 83–110; "Power Cycle Theory and the Contemporary State System," in William R. Thompson, ed., *Contending Approaches to World System Analysis* (Beverly Hills, CA: Sage, 1983), pp. 165–182; and, with Wes Parsons, "War and the Cycle of Relative Power," *American Political Science Review* 74 (December 1980): 947–965.

41. A. F. K. Organski and Jacek Kugler, *The War Ledger* (Chicago: University of Chicago Press, 1980), pp. 19–28.

42. James F. Hoge, Jr., "A Global Power Shift in the Making: Is the United States Ready?" *Foreign Affairs* 83 (July/August 2004): 2.

43. Excerpted from the 1992 *Defense Planning Guidance*, a document prepared to direct the preparation of the U.S. defense budget. *New York Times* (March 8, 1992): 14.

44. John Lewis Gaddis, "Grand Strategy in the Second Term," *Foreign Affairs* 84 (January/February 2005): 9. As Ken Menkhaus adds, the problem with looking at everything through a single lens is that it distorts our view of the political dynamics in other countries. "Local political realities are not always assessed in their own right, but instead are interpreted through, and reduced to, the logic of the war on

terrorism." See his "Somalia: In the Crosshairs of the War on Terrorism," *Current History* 100 (May 2002): 212.

45. For a discussion of this question, see Richard Haass, "What to Do About China," *U.S. News & World Report* (June 20, 2005): 52.

46. Ted C. Fishman, *China, Inc.* (New York: Scribner, 2005); Zheng Bijian, "China's 'Peaceful Rise' to Great-Power Status," *Foreign Affairs* 84 (September/October 2005): 18; Fareed Zakaria, "Does the Future Belong to China?" *Newsweek* (May 9, 2005): 28; Geoffrey Colvin, "America Isn't Ready," *Fortune* (August 1, 2005): 72; *The Economist* (December 17, 2005): 58. Many economists have argued that China's GDP has been understated due to inaccurate measures of its privately run services. According to findings reported in the country's January 2004 economic census, its GDP may be 16.8 percent larger than previously assumed. *The Economist* (December 24, 2005): 53; *The Economist* (March 25, 2006): 12.

47. U.S. National Intelligence Council, *Mapping the Global Future* (Washington, DC: Government Printing Office, 2004), p. 32. If national economies are compared using purchasing-power parity rates rather than market exchange rates, China is projected to overtake the United States in 2017. *The World in 2006* (London: The Economist, 2005), p. 62.

48. Zheng Bijian, "China's Peaceful Rise," p. 19. For an analysis of China's relative strengths and weaknesses, see Steve Chan, "Is There a Power Transition between the U.S. and China? The Different Faces of National Power," *Asian Survey* 45 (September/October 2005): 687–701.

49. Robert Harvey, *Global Disorder* (New York: Carroll & Graf, 2003), p. 143.

50. David M. Lampton, "Paradigm Lost: The Demise of 'Weak China,'" *The National Interest* 81 (Fall 2005): 75. Concerns about discontent in rural China, where approximately 70 percent of the population resides, have led Chinese Prime Minister Wen Jiabao to call for the building of a "new socialist countryside." According to government statistics, there were 87,000 public-order disturbances in rural China during 2005, an increase of 770 percent from a decade earlier. *Time* (March 13, 2006): 28.

51. Ronald L. Tammen et al. *Power Transitions: Strategies for the 21st Century* (New York: Chatham House, 2000), p. 179.

52. U.S. Department of Defense, *The Military Power of the People's Republic of China* (Washington, DC: Annual Report to Congress, 2005), pp. 13–14.

53. *The Wall Street Journal* (July 15, 2005): A8. His comments echoed similar statements made a decade earlier by Lt. General Xiong Guangkai, then deputy chief of staff of the People's Liberation Army. For a more elaborate discussion of this theme, see Qiao Liang and Wang Xiangsui, *Unrestricted Warfare* (Beijing: PLA Literature and Arts Publishing House, 1999).

54. Robert S. Ross, "Assessing the China Threat," *The National Interest* 81 (Fall 2005): 84–85.

55. Diana Farrell, "India Outsmarts China," *Foreign Policy* 152 (January/February 2006): 30–31.

56. National Intelligence Council, *Mapping the Global Future*, p. 32.

57. See Rockwell A. Sehnabel, with Francis X. Rocca, *The Next Superpower: The Rise of Europe and Its Challenge to the United States* (Lanham, MD: Rowman & Littlefield, 2006).
58. Coral Bell, "The Twilight of the Unipolar World," *The American Interest* 1 (Winter 2005): 21. On the political awakening of the Global South, see Zbigniew Brzezinski, "The Dilemma of the Last Sovereign," *The American Interest* 1 (Autumn 2005): 37–46.
59. Henry A. Kissinger, "World Must Tune to Post-Cold War Era," *China Daily* (January 18, 1993): 1. Although the United States may have little experience in this regard, Thomas P. M. Barnett argues that there is no viable alternative but to work with China (and conceivable other ascending powers) to craft a peaceful twenty-first–century world. See his *Blueprint for Action: A Future Worth Creating* (New York: Putnam, 2005), pp. 141, 156, 162.
60. Eyre Crowe, "The Containment of Germany," in Evan Luard, ed., *Basic Texts in International Relations* (New York: St. Martin's Press, 1992), p. 473.
61. Paul M. Kennedy, *The Rise and Fall of the Great Powers* (New York: Random House, 1987), p. 228.
62. J. H. Elliott, "Managing Decline: Olivares and the Grand Strategy of Imperial Spain," in Paul Kennedy, ed., *Grand Strategies in War and Peace* (New Haven, CT: Yale University Press, 1991), p. 96. For a comparative empirical assessment of the British, Spanish, and other preeminent powers' willingness to absorb the costs of leadership to promote liberal global norms and trade liberalization in order to maintain their premier position, see Mark R. Brawley, *Liberal Leadership: Great Powers and Their Challengers in Peace and War* (Ithaca, NY: Cornell University Press, 1993).
63. For evidence supporting this point, see Charles W. Kegley, Jr., and Gregory A. Raymond, "From Détente to Entente: Prospects for Establishing a Multipolarity of Peace," in Manus I. Midlarsky, John A. Vasquez, and Peter V. Gladkov, eds., *From Rivalry to Cooperation: Russian and American Perspectives on the Post-Cold War Era* (New York: HarperCollins, 1994), pp. 105–110.
64. Mark Leonard, "The Geopolitics of 2026," *The World of 2026* (London: *Economist*, 2006), p. 24.
65. The tension between "going it alone" and "going it with others" is addressed in David M. Malone and Yuen Foong Khong, eds., *Unilateralism and U.S. Foreign Policy* (Boulder, CO: Lynne Rienner, 2003), and in Stewart Patrick and Shepard Farman, eds., *Multilateralism and U.S. Foreign Policy: Ambivalent Engagement* (Boulder, CO: Lynne Rienner, 2002).
66. James Fallows, "The Hollow Army," *The Atlantic Online*, retrieved at http://www.theatlantic.com/issues/2004/03/fallows.htm.
67. Peter G. Peterson, "Riding for a Fall," *Foreign Affairs* 83 (September/October 2004): 112. The financial burden of the war in Iraq has been exacerbated by the Bush administration's lack of fiscal discipline. "We do not choose between guns and butter," complains one prominent editorial writer, "we have guns and butter *and* tax cuts." Mortimer B. Zuckerman, "Guns, Butter, and Hubris," *U.S. News & World Report* (February 2, 2004): 60. Instead of the $5.6 trillion surplus once estimated for the first decade of this century, the level of federal debt reached $9 trillion in April 2006, with foreign investors owning more than half of U.S. governing bonds.

68. *The Guardian*, retrieved at http://www.guardian.co.uk/Iraq/Story/0,2763,1681119,00.html.

69. *Time* (January 30, 2006): 35; *The Economist* (March 18, 2006): 9; Daniel Gross, "Globalization Offered Two Ways," *New York Times* (March 12, 2006): Week in Review, 3.

70. William Neikert, "Bush Budget Does Little for Deficit," *The State* (Columbia, SC), February 7, 2006: p. A6.

71. Donald W. White, "Mapping Decline: The History of American Power," *Harvard International Review* 27 (Fall 2005): 64.

72. Richard Florida, *The Flight of the Creative Class: The New Global Competition for Talent* (New York: HarperBusiness, 2005); Thomas Friedman, *The World Is Flat* (New York: Farrar, Straus and Giroux, 2005).

73. *Time* (February 13, 2006): 24; *U.S. News & World Report* (March 27, 2006): 50.

74. See especially Arthur M. Schlesinger, Jr., *War and the American Presidency* (New York: Norton, 2005), pp. 45–82. For a comparison to an earlier period in modern American history, see Haynes Johnson, *The Age of Anxiety: McCarthyism to Terrorism* (Orlando, FL: Harcourt, 2005), p. 529.

75. Charles Krauthammer, "Don't Believe the Hype. We're Still No. 1," *Time* (February 13, 2006): 41.

76. Deepak Lal, *In Praise of Empires: Globalization and Order* (New York: Palgrave Macmillan, 2004), p. 78. On the differences between realism and liberalism and their many variants, see Charles W. Kegley, Jr., ed., *Controversies in International Relations Theory: Realism and the Neoliberal Challenge* (New York: St. Martin's, 1995). On "soft balancing," see Robert J. Art, "Striking the Balance," *International Security* 30 (Winter 2005–2006): 177–196; Christopher Layne, *The Peace of Illusions: American Grand Strategy from 1940 to the Present* (Ithaca, NY: Cornell University Press, 2006); Seth G. Jones, *The Rise of Europe: Great Power Politics and Security* (New York: Cambridge University Press, 2006); T. V. Paul, "Soft Balancing in the Age of U.S. Primacy," *International Security* 30 (Summer 2005): 46–71. For analyses of why the bargaining and balancing tactics of America's great-power allies and rivals have been timid thus far, see Keir A. Lieber and Gerald Alexander, "Waiting for Balancing: Why the World Is Not Pushing Back," *International Security* 30 (Summer 2005): 109–139; and Stephen G. Brooks and William C. Wohlforth, "Hard Times for Soft Balancing," *International Security* 30 (Summer 2005): 72–108.

77. See Martin Patchen, "When Does Reciprocity in the Actions of Nations Occur?" *International Negotiation* 3 (No. 2, 1998): 171–196; and Robert Axelrod, *The Evolution of Cooperation* (New York: Basic Books, 1984). Also see Karthik Pancthanathan and Robert Boyd, "Indirect Reciprocity Can Stabilize Co-Operation Without the Second-Order Free Rider Problem," *Nature* 432 (November 2004): 499–502; Robert Cialdini, *Influence: Science and Practice*, 4th ed. (Boston: Allyn and Bacon, 2001). Long before the conduct of scientific studies of reciprocity, moral philosophers understood its value. Consider, for example, the following passage from Chapter 23, Book 15 of *The Analects* of Confucius: "Tsze-kung asked, saying, 'Is there one word which may serve as a rule of practice for one's life?' The Master said, 'Is not reciprocity such a word? What do you not want done to yourself, do not do to others.'"

78. For example, see Russell J. Leng, *Interstate Crisis Behavior, 18*[illegible] *ous Reciprocity* (Cambridge: Cambridge University Press, 199[illegible] and John R. Freeman, *Three-Way Street: Strategic Reciprocity* [illegible] (Chicago: University of Chicago Press, 1990); Gregory A. Ray[illegible] tween the Superpowers: Reciprocity and Conformity in [illegible] *Review of Canadian Studies* 17 (Summer 198[illegible]), [illegible]; William [illegible] procity in United States [illegible] Relations, Multiple Symmetry or [illegible] *American Journal of Political Science* 30 (No. 2, 1986): 421–[illegible]; William [illegible] and David Rapkin, "[illegible], Inertia, and Reciprocity: Coping with [illegible]," in Charles W. Kegley, Jr., and Pat McGowan, eds., *Foreign Polic*[illegible] (Beverly Hills, CA: Sage, 1981): 241–265; Neil Richardson, Charles [illegible] and Ann Agnew, "Symmetry and Reciprocity as Characteristics of Dy[illegible] Policy Behavior," *Social Science Quarterly* 62 (March 1981): 128–[illegible], and [illegible] Phillips and Robert C. [illegible], "Dynamic Foreign Policy Interactions: Reci[illegible] Uncertainty in Foreign Policy," *Sage International Yearbook of Foreign Polic*[illegible] Vol. [illegible] (Beverly Hills, CA: Sage, 197[illegible]): 227–266.

79. Charles E. Osgood, *An Alternative to War or Surrender* (Urbana: Univer[illegible] Illinois Press, 1962). Osgood used the acronym GRIT (graduated and reci[illegible] initiatives in tension reduction) to describe his strategy.

80. Amitai Etzioni, "The Kennedy Experiment," *Western Political Quarterly* 20 (1[illegible] 361–380. For evidence from laboratory studies, see Svenn Lindskold, P. Walters, H. Koutsourais, "Cooperators, Competitors, and Responses to GRIT," *Journal of Conflict Resolution* 27 (March 1983): 521–532; Svenn Lindskold, "Trust Development, the GRIT Proposal, and the Effects of Conciliatory Acts on Conflict and Cooperation," *Psychological Bulletin* 85 (July 1978): [illegible]; and M. Pilisuk and P. Skolnick, "Inducing Trust: A Test of the Osgood Proposal," *Journal of Personality and Social Psychology* 20 (Nov. 1, 1968): [illegible].

81. Harold Kelly, "The Process of Causal Attribution," *American Psychologist* 28 (No[illegible] 1, 1973): 107–128.

82. Roger Fisher and William Ury, *Getting to Yes* (Boston: Houghton Mifflin, 1981), p. 21.

83. Address by President George W. Bush to a joint session of Congress, reprinted in *The New York Times* (September 21, 2001), [illegible]

84. Charles A. Kupchan, *The End of the American Era: U.S. Foreign Policy and the Geopolitics of the Twenty-First Century* (New York: Alfred A. Knopf, 2002), [illegible]

85. The need captured by hegemonic stability theory for a benevolent hegemon to lead in setting standards for the conduct of other countries and to entice them to abide by this code of conduct was first given expression by Charles P. Kindleberger, *The World in Depression, 1929–1939* (Berkeley: University of California Press, 1973). Also see Robert O. Keohane, *After Hegemony: Cooperation and Discord in the World Political Economy* (Princeton, NJ: Princeton University Press, 1984).

86. Francis Fukuyama, *America at the Crossroads* (New Haven, CT: Yale University Press, 2006), pp. 190, 193.

87. For surveys of global trends unfolding in world politics and the security issues likely to become salient in the years ahead, see Charles W. Kegley, Jr. and Gregory A. Raymond, *The Global Future* (Belmont, CA: Wadsworth, 2005); Charles W. Kegley, Jr., *World Politics: Trend and Transformation*, 11th ed. (Belmont, CA: Wadsworth,

terrorism." See his "Somalia: In the Crosshairs of the War on Terrorism," *Current History* 100 (May 2002): 212.

45. For a discussion of this question, see Richard Haass, "What to Do About China," *U.S. News & World Report* (June 20, 2005): 52.

46. Ted C. Fishman, *China, Inc.* (New York: Scribner, 2005); Zheng Bijian, "China's 'Peaceful Rise' to Great-Power Status," *Foreign Affairs* 84 (September/October 2005): 18; Fareed Zakaria, "Does the Future Belong to China?" *Newsweek* (May 9, 2005): 28; Geoffrey Colvin, "America Isn't Ready," *Fortune* (August 1, 2005): 72; *The Economist* (December 17, 2005): 58. Many economists have argued that China's GDP has been understated due to inaccurate measures of its privately run services. According to findings reported in the country's January 2004 economic census, its GDP may be 16.8 percent larger than previously assumed. *The Economist* (December 24, 2005): 53; *The Economist* (March 25, 2006): 12.

47. U.S. National Intelligence Council, *Mapping the Global Future* (Washington, DC: Government Printing Office, 2004), p. 32. If national economies are compared using purchasing-power parity rates rather than market exchange rates, China is projected to overtake the United States in 2017. *The World in 2006* (London: The Economist, 2005), p. 62.

48. Zheng Bijian, "China's Peaceful Rise," p. 19. For an analysis of China's relative strengths and weaknesses, see Steve Chan, "Is There a Power Transition between the U.S. and China? The Different Faces of National Power," *Asian Survey* 45 (September/October 2005): 687–701.

49. Robert Harvey, *Global Disorder* (New York: Carroll & Graf, 2003), p. 143.

50. David M. Lampton, "Paradigm Lost: The Demise of 'Weak China,'" *The National Interest* 81 (Fall 2005): 75. Concerns about discontent in rural China, where approximately 70 percent of the population resides, have led Chinese Prime Minister Wen Jiabao to call for the building of a "new socialist countryside." According to government statistics, there were 87,000 public-order disturbances in rural China during 2005, an increase of 770 percent from a decade earlier. *Time* (March 13, 2006): 28.

51. Ronald L. Tammen et al. *Power Transitions: Strategies for the 21st Century* (New York: Chatham House, 2000), p. 179.

52. U.S. Department of Defense, *The Military Power of the People's Republic of China* (Washington, DC: Annual Report to Congress, 2005), pp. 13–14.

53. *The Wall Street Journal* (July 15, 2005): A8. His comments echoed similar statements made a decade earlier by Lt. General Xiong Guangkai, then deputy chief of staff of the People's Liberation Army. For a more elaborate discussion of this theme, see Qiao Liang and Wang Xiangsui, *Unrestricted Warfare* (Beijing: PLA Literature and Arts Publishing House, 1999).

54. Robert S. Ross, "Assessing the China Threat," *The National Interest* 81 (Fall 2005): 84–85.

55. Diana Farrell, "India Outsmarts China," *Foreign Policy* 152 (January/February 2006): 30–31.

56. National Intelligence Council, *Mapping the Global Future*, p. 32.

57. See Rockwell A. Sehnabel, with Francis X. Rocca, *The Next Superpower: The Rise of Europe and Its Challenge to the United States* (Lanham, MD: Rowman & Littlefield, 2006).
58. Coral Bell, "The Twilight of the Unipolar World," *The American Interest* 1 (Winter 2005): 21. On the political awakening of the Global South, see Zbigniew Brzezinski, "The Dilemma of the Last Sovereign," *The American Interest* 1 (Autumn 2005): 37–46.
59. Henry A. Kissinger, "World Must Tune to Post-Cold War Era," *China Daily* (January 18, 1993): 1. Although the United States may have little experience in this regard, Thomas P. M. Barnett argues that there is no viable alternative but to work with China (and conceivable other ascending powers) to craft a peaceful twenty-first–century world. See his *Blueprint for Action: A Future Worth Creating* (New York: Putnam, 2005), pp. 141, 156, 162.
60. Eyre Crowe, "The Containment of Germany," in Evan Luard, ed., *Basic Texts in International Relations* (New York: St. Martin's Press, 1992), p. 473.
61. Paul M. Kennedy, *The Rise and Fall of the Great Powers* (New York: Random House, 1987), p. 228.
62. J. H. Elliott, "Managing Decline: Olivares and the Grand Strategy of Imperial Spain," in Paul Kennedy, ed., *Grand Strategies in War and Peace* (New Haven, CT: Yale University Press, 1991), p. 96. For a comparative empirical assessment of the British, Spanish, and other preeminent powers' willingness to absorb the costs of leadership to promote liberal global norms and trade liberalization in order to maintain their premier position, see Mark R. Brawley, *Liberal Leadership: Great Powers and Their Challengers in Peace and War* (Ithaca, NY: Cornell University Press, 1993).
63. For evidence supporting this point, see Charles W. Kegley, Jr., and Gregory A. Raymond, "From Détente to Entente: Prospects for Establishing a Multipolarity of Peace," in Manus I. Midlarsky, John A. Vasquez, and Peter V. Gladkov, eds., *From Rivalry to Cooperation: Russian and American Perspectives on the Post-Cold War Era* (New York: HarperCollins, 1994), pp. 105–110.
64. Mark Leonard, "The Geopolitics of 2026," *The World of 2026* (London: *Economist*, 2006), p. 24.
65. The tension between "going it alone" and "going it with others" is addressed in David M. Malone and Yuen Foong Khong, eds., *Unilateralism and U.S. Foreign Policy* (Boulder, CO: Lynne Rienner, 2003), and in Stewart Patrick and Shepard Farman, eds., *Multilateralism and U.S. Foreign Policy: Ambivalent Engagement* (Boulder, CO: Lynne Rienner, 2002).
66. James Fallows, "The Hollow Army," *The Atlantic Online*, retrieved at http://www.theatlantic.com/issues/2004/03/fallows.htm.
67. Peter G. Peterson, "Riding for a Fall," *Foreign Affairs* 83 (September/October 2004): 112. The financial burden of the war in Iraq has been exacerbated by the Bush administration's lack of fiscal discipline. "We do not choose between guns and butter," complains one prominent editorial writer, "we have guns and butter *and* tax cuts." Mortimer B. Zuckerman, "Guns, Butter, and Hubris," *U.S. News & World Report* (February 2, 2004): 60. Instead of the $5.6 trillion surplus once estimated for the first decade of this century, the level of federal debt reached $9 trillion in April 2006, with foreign investors owning more than half of U.S. governing bonds.

68. *The Guardian*, retrieved at http://www.guardian.co.uk/Iraq/Story/0,2763,1681119,00 .html.

69. *Time* (January 30, 2006): 35; *The Economist* (March 18, 2006): 9; Daniel Gross, "Globalization Offered Two Ways," *New York Times* (March 12, 2006): Week in Review, 3.

70. William Neikert, "Bush Budget Does Little for Deficit," *The State* (Columbia, SC), February 7, 2006: p. A6.

71. Donald W. White, "Mapping Decline: The History of American Power," *Harvard International Review* 27 (Fall 2005): 64.

72. Richard Florida, *The Flight of the Creative Class: The New Global Competition for Talent* (New York: HarperBusiness, 2005); Thomas Friedman, *The World Is Flat* (New York: Farrar, Straus and Giroux, 2005).

73. *Time* (February 13, 2006): 24; *U.S. News & World Report* (March 27, 2006): 50.

74. See especially Arthur M. Schlesinger, Jr., *War and the American Presidency* (New York: Norton, 2005), pp. 45–82. For a comparison to an earlier period in modern American history, see Haynes Johnson, *The Age of Anxiety: McCarthyism to Terrorism* (Orlando, FL: Harcourt, 2005), p. 529.

75. Charles Krauthammer, "Don't Believe the Hype. We're Still No. 1," *Time* (February 13, 2006): 41.

76. Deepak Lal, *In Praise of Empires: Globalization and Order* (New York: Palgrave Macmillan, 2004), p. 78. On the differences between realism and liberalism and their many variants, see Charles W. Kegley, Jr., ed., *Controversies in International Relations Theory: Realism and the Neoliberal Challenge* (New York: St. Martin's, 1995). On "soft balancing," see Robert J. Art, "Striking the Balance," *International Security* 30 (Winter 2005–2006): 177–196; Christopher Layne, *The Peace of Illusions: American Grand Strategy from 1940 to the Present* (Ithaca, NY: Cornell University Press, 2006); Seth G. Jones, *The Rise of Europe: Great Power Politics and Security* (New York: Cambridge University Press, 2006); T. V. Paul, "Soft Balancing in the Age of U.S. Primacy," *International Security* 30 (Summer 2005): 46–71. For analyses of why the bargaining and balancing tactics of America's great-power allies and rivals have been timid thus far, see Keir A. Lieber and Gerald Alexander, "Waiting for Balancing: Why the World Is Not Pushing Back," *International Security* 30 (Summer 2005): 109–139; and Stephen G. Brooks and William C. Wohlforth, "Hard Times for Soft Balancing," *International Security* 30 (Summer 2005): 72–108.

77. See Martin Patchen, "When Does Reciprocity in the Actions of Nations Occur?" *International Negotiation* 3 (No. 2, 1998): 171–196; and Robert Axelrod, *The Evolution of Cooperation* (New York: Basic Books, 1984). Also see Karthik Pancthanathan and Robert Boyd, "Indirect Reciprocity Can Stabilize Co-Operation Without the Second-Order Free Rider Problem," *Nature* 432 (November 2004): 499–502; Robert Cialdini, *Influence: Science and Practice*, 4th ed. (Boston: Allyn and Bacon, 2001). Long before the conduct of scientific studies of reciprocity, moral philosophers understood its value. Consider, for example, the following passage from Chapter 23, Book 15 of *The Analects* of Confucius: "Tsze-kung asked, saying, 'Is there one word which may serve as a rule of practice for one's life?' The Master said, 'Is not reciprocity such a word? What do you not want done to yourself, do not do to others.'"

78. For example, see Russell J. Leng, *Interstate Crisis Behavior, 1816–1980: Realism Versus Reciprocity* (Cambridge: Cambridge University Press, 1993); Joshua Goldstein and John R. Freeman, *Three-Way Street: Strategic Reciprocity and World Politics* (Chicago: University of Chicago Press, 1990); Gregory A. Raymond, "Canada Between the Superpowers: Reciprocity and Conformity in Foreign Policy," *American Review of Canadian Studies* 17 (Summer 1987): 221–236; William J. Dixon, "Reciprocity in United States-Soviet Relations: Multiple Symmetry or Issue Linkage?" *American Journal of Political Science* 30 (No. 2, 1986): 421–445; William R. Thompson and David Rapkin, "Conflict, Inertia, and Reciprocity: Coping with the Western Bloc," in Charles W. Kegley, Jr., and Pat McGowan, eds., *Foreign Policy: USA/USSR* (Beverly Hills, CA: Sage, 1982): 241–265; Neil Richardson, Charles W. Kegley, Jr., and Ann Agnew, "Symmetry and Reciprocity as Characteristics of Dyadic Foreign Policy Behavior," *Social Science Quarterly* 62 (March 1981): 128–138; and Warren R. Phillips and Robert C. Crain, "Dynamic Foreign Policy Interactions: Reciprocity and Uncertainty in Foreign Policy," *Sage International Yearbook of Foreign Policy Studies*, Vol. 2 (Beverly Hills, CA: Sage, 1974): 227–266.
79. Charles E. Osgood, *An Alternative to War or Surrender* (Urbana: University of Illinois Press, 1962). Osgood used the acronym GRIT (graduated and reciprocated initiatives in tension reduction) to describe his strategy.
80. Amitai Etzioni, "The Kennedy Experiment," *Western Political Quarterly* 20 (1967): 361–380. For evidence from laboratory studies, see Svenn Lindskold, P. Walters, and H. Koutsourais, "Cooperators, Competitors, and Responses to GRIT," *Journal of Conflict Resolution* 27 (No. 3, 1983): 521–532; Svenn Lindskold, "Trust Development, the GRIT Proposal, and the Effects of Conciliatory Acts on Conflict and Cooperation," *Psychological Bulletin* 85 (July 1978): 772–793; and M. Pilisuk and P. Skolnick, "Inducing Trust: A Test of the Osgood Proposal," *Journal of Personality and Social Psychology* 20 (No. 1, 1968): 122–133.
81. Harold Kelly, "The Process of Causal Attribution," *American Psychologist* 28 (No. 1, 1973): 107–128.
82. Roger Fisher and William Ury, *Getting to Yes* (Boston: Houghton Mifflin, 1981), p. 21.
83. Address by President George W. Bush to a joint session of Congress, reprinted in *The New York Times* (September 21, 2001): B4
84. Charles A. Kupchan, *The End of the American Era: U.S. Foreign Policy and the Geopolitics of the Twenty-First Century* (New York: Alfred A. Knopf, 2002), p. 295.
85. The need captured by hegemonic stability theory for a benevolent hegemon to lead in setting standards for the conduct of other countries and to entice them to abide by this code of conduct was first given expression by Charles P. Kindleberger, *The World in Depression, 1929–1939* (Berkeley: University of California Press, 1973). Also see Robert O. Keohane, *After Hegemony: Cooperation and Discord in the World Political Economy* (Princeton, NJ: Princeton University Press, 1984).
86. Francis Fukuyama, *America at the Crossroads* (New Haven, CT: Yale University Press, 2006), pp. 190, 193.
87. For surveys of global trends unfolding in world politics and the security issues likely to become salient in the years ahead, see Charles W. Kegley, Jr. and Gregory A. Raymond, *The Global Future* (Belmont, CA: Wadsworth, 2005); Charles W. Kegley, Jr., *World Politics: Trend and Transformation*, 11th ed. (Belmont, CA: Wadsworth,

2007); Dan Caldwell and Robert J. Williams, *Seeking Security in an Insecure World* (Lanham, MD: Rowman and Littlefield, 2006); and Jeffrey W. Legro, *Rethinking the World: Great Power Strategies and International Order* (Ithaca, NY: Cornell University Press, 2005).

88. Morton A. Kaplan and Nicholas deB. Katzenbach, *The Political Foundations of International Law* (New York: John Wiley & Sons, 1961), p. 344.

89. Hans J. Morgenthau, *Politics Among Nations*, 6th ed. (New York: Alfred A. Knopf, 1985), pp. 239, 243–244.

INDEX

Note: Page references followed by *f* and *t* refer to figures and tables respectively; those followed by *n* refer to notes.